YOGASŪTRA
OF
PATAÑJALI

YOGASŪTRA OF PATAÑJALI

With the Commentary of Vyāsa

Translated from Sanskrit into English with Copious Notes

BANGALI BABA

MOTILAL BANARSIDASS PUBLISHERS
PRIVATE LIMITED • DELHI

First Edition: Delhi, 1976
Reprint: Delhi, 1979, 1982, 1990, 1996, 1999, 2002, 2005

ISBN: 81-208-0154-7 (Cloth)
ISBN: 81-208-0155-5 (Paper)

MOTILAL BANARSIDASS
41 U.A. Bungalow Road, Jawahar Nagar, Delhi 110 007
8 Mahalaxmi Chamber, 22 Bhulabhai Desai Road, Mumbai 400 026
236, 9th Main III Block, Jayanagar, Bangalore 560 011
120 Royapettah High Road, Mylapore, Chennai 600 004
Sanas Plaza, 1302 Baji Rao Road, Pune 411 002
8 Camac Street, Kolkata 700 017
Ashok Rajpath, Patna 800 004
Chowk, Varanasi 221 001

Printed in India
BY JAINENDRA PRAKASH JAIN AT SHRI JAINENDRA PRESS,
A-45 NARAINA, PHASE-I, NEW DELHI 110 028
AND PUBLISHED BY NARENDRA PRAKASH JAIN FOR
MOTILAL BANARSIDASS PUBLISHERS PRIVATE LIMITED,
BUNGALOW ROAD, DELHI 110 007

PREFACE

The Indian system of Philosophy is the store-house which has supplied spiritual food, through the ages, to all the nations of the world. Other teachings, whatever they be, are but the sauces and the spices, useful so long as this philosophy supplies the spiritual inspiration.

The Indian Philosophical system comprises six Darśanas viz. Nyāya, Vaiṣeśika, Sāṁkhya, Yoga, Mīmāṁsā, Vedānta. Every one of these systems claims to lead the aspirant to the goal of Final Emancipation.

A number of modern philosophers hold that these six texts are separate philosophies, independent of one another. Again, there are other philosophers who think that the six philosophical texts are not contradictory but contributory to one another. As a matter of fact, both these schools have no basis for their assertions. The six philosophical texts are neither self-contradictory nor independent of one another. Rather they are the six successive steps of one and the same ladder. The science of yoga alone can put an end to the above confusion and controversy. It alone can show that the steps of philosophical ladder are harmoniously linked to one another. It alone can teach the systematic process on following which the aspirant can achieve realization of the existing Reality.

The Yoga Sūtra of Patañjali is divided into four Chapters. It comprises aphorisms on the system of yoga. The aphorisms relate to the subject of Spiritual Absorption (*Samādhi*), Means of Practice (*Sādhanā*), Accomplishments (*Vibhūti*) and Emancipation (*Kaivalya*). To expound further: Chapter I explains the grades of spiritual Action for the restraint of the exhibitive operations of the mind. Until that is done no yogic achievement is possible. Ch. II deals with the process of Material Action which can attenuate the gross impurities that have entered into the mind. Ch. III pertains to the Dissolutionary change of the worldly life by means of *saṁyama*. Ch. IV explains the working of threefold action : the present action, the stored-up action and the regulated fruitive action. It teaches how the individual soul, released from the bond of actions realizes the Reality of the Supreme Being wherein the individual souls merge as rivers do into the ocean. The entire system of Yoga, in all its categories, is nowhere better treated than in this book.

CONTENTS

CHAPTER 1

अथ योगानुशासनम् ॥ १ ॥

Now it is the final teaching of Yoga—1

यस्त्यक्त्वा रूपमाद्यं प्रभवति जगतोऽनेकधानुग्रहाय
प्रक्षीणक्लेशराशिर्विषमविषधरोऽनेकवक्त्रः सुभोगी ।
सर्वज्ञानप्रसूतिर्भुजगपरिकरः प्रीतये यस्य नित्यं
देवोऽहीशः स वोऽव्यात्सितविमलतनुर्योगदो योगयुक्तः ॥१॥

अथ योगानुशासनम् । अथेत्ययमधिकारार्थः । योगानुशासनं शास्त्रमधिकृतं वेदितव्यम् । योगः समाधिः । स च सार्वभौमश्चित्तस्य धर्मः । क्षिप्तं मूढं विक्षिप्तमेकाग्रं निरुद्धमिति चित्तभूमयः ।

The term[1] "now" has been used in the sense of achievement. "The final[2] teaching of Yoga" should be understood to mean that "the first portion of the Science of Yoga has been achieved". The Yoga is Spiritual Absorption (*Samādhi*). It is the characteristic of the mind, pervading all its planes[3]. (1) Raving (kṣipta), (2) Forgetful (*Mūḍha*)[4], (3) Oscillating (*Vikṣipta*)[5], (4) One-pointed (*Ekāgra*) and (5) Restrained (*Niruddha*)—these (five) are the mental planes.

तत्र विक्षिप्ते चेतसि विक्षेपोपसर्जनीभूतः समाधिर्न योगपक्षे वर्तते । यस्त्वेकाग्रे चेतसि सद्भूतमर्थं प्रद्योतयति क्षिणोति च क्लेशान्कर्मबन्धनानि श्लथयति निरोधमभिमुखं करोति स संप्रज्ञातो योग इत्याख्यायते । स च वितर्कानुगतो विचारानुगत आनन्दानुगतोऽस्मितानुगत इत्युपरिष्टान्निवेदयिष्यामः । सर्ववृत्तिनिरोधे त्वसंप्रज्ञातः समाधिः ॥१॥

There in the oscillating mind[6] contemplation, being subordinate to special engagement, does not stand on the side of Yoga. On the other hand, that (contemplation),—which being in the one-pointed mind, illuminates the existing reality, destroys the afflictions, loosens the bondage of actions and brings forth the Restraint,—is called the Cognitive-Spiritual-Absorption. Moreover, it is followed by Supposition (*Vitarka*), Clear Vision (*Vicāra*), Joy (*Ānanda*) and

---

1. The term *Yoga* signifies the whole Course of Action beginning from its Starting Limit of Material Action upto the Finishing End of Spiritual Absorption. The Dharma-Sūtra precedes the Yoga-Sūtra. Hence the term 'Now' has been used in the Aphorism with a view to showing the standard of qualification for having recourse to Spiritual Action, i.e. the fulfilment of Enjoyment makes a man qualified for the grade of Emancipation. In other words, the execution of the duties prescribed by the Dharma-Sūtra brings about necessary perfections to the mind tending towards Spiritual Absorption.

2. By this, it is clear that Patañjali is not the author of Yoga. Yoga has descended from the Lord of Creation; Patañjali simply elucidates it in a systematic process.

3. This denotes the kingly nature of Yoga; it can go through all the planes of the mind. The king can go all over his kingdom, but an ordinary man cannot enter into the palace. Similarly the one-pointed mind can travel through all the three lower planes.

4 The mental state in sleep or in swoon, etc., where there is want of cognition, is the second plane.

5. Vikṣipta means specially engaged, i.e., the serving mind; it works between two ends,—either failure or success, as in the case of Mathematician or a Scientist, his mind is not one-pointed This is called the Oscillating mind.

6. By this, it should be understood that the preceding two have been included in the third.

Egoism (*Asmitā*). We shall explain all this further on; but the Ultra-Cognitive-Spiritual-Absorption appears on the cessation of all operations.

योगश्चित्तवृत्तिनिरोधः ॥ २ ॥

(The final end of) Yoga is the restraint of mental operations—2

तस्य लक्षणाभिधित्सयेदं सूत्रं प्रववृते। योगश्चित्तवृत्तिनिरोधः। सर्वशब्दाग्रहणात्संप्रज्ञातोऽपि योग इत्याख्यायते। चित्तं हि प्रख्याप्रवृत्तिस्थितिशीलत्वात् त्रिगुणम्। प्रख्यारूपं हि चित्तसत्त्वं रजस्तमोभ्यां संसृष्टमैश्वर्यविषयप्रियं भवति। तदेव तमसाऽनुविद्धमधर्माज्ञानावैराग्यानैश्वर्योपगं भवति। तदेव प्रक्षीणमोहावरणं सर्वतः प्रद्योतमानमनुविद्धं रजोमात्रया धर्मज्ञानवैराग्यैश्वर्योपगं भवति। तदेव रजोलेशमलापेतं स्वरूपप्रतिष्ठं सत्त्वपुरुषान्यताख्यातिमात्रं धर्ममेघध्यानोपगं भवति। तत्परं प्रसंख्यानमित्याचक्षते ध्यायिनः।

This aphorism starts with the object of giving a definition of Yoga:—Yoga is the restraint of mental operations. By not taking the word "all", the Cognitive—Spiritual-Absorption also is called Yoga[1]. The mind is, in fact, possessed of the three Energies; because it has the qualities of illumination, activity and inertia. The mental essence (intellect), which is indeed of the form of illumination, being commingled with the active and the inert Energies (*Rajas* and *Tamas*) becomes fond of power and sense-objects (1). The same simply being intermixed with the inert Energy (*Tamas*) comes to the state of the want of its merit, *absence of its* knowledge, *absence of its* non-attachment and power (2). The same with the veil of ignorance destroyed and illuminated from all sides, being intermixed with the mere Active Energy (*Rajas*),—follows its own merit, knowledge, non-attachment and power (3). The same, being free from the least impurity of the Active-Energy (*Rajas*), becomes self-established and being the only revelation of the distinction between the Essence (intellect) and the Puruṣa, approaches the state of meditation known as the Cloud of Virtue (*Dharma-Megha*) (4). The contemplatives call it the payment of the Last Debt (*Parama Prasaṅkhyāna*)[2].

चितिशक्तिरपरिणामिन्यप्रतिसंक्रमा दर्शितविषया शुद्धा चानन्ता च सत्त्वगुणात्मिका चेयमतो विपरीता विवेकख्यातिरिति। अतस्तस्यां विरक्तं चित्तं तामपि ख्यातिं निरुणद्धि। तदवस्थं चित्तं संस्कारोपगं भवति स निर्बीजः समाधिः। न तत्र किंचित्संप्रज्ञायत इत्यसंप्रज्ञातः। द्विविधः स योगश्चित्तवृत्तिनिरोध इति ॥ २ ॥

"The Con-Science-Power (*Puruṣa*)[3] is unchanging, unmoving, having the sphere of objects presented to it, pure and infinite; and the Essence-power (*Buddhi*) is made up of the Energies and so it is opposite to THAT ("the *Puruṣa*"),—this cognition of distinction is the "Intellective Revelation" (*Viveka-khyāti*). After this the mind, being displeased with that (state), restrains even this Revelation. In this situation the mind becomes joined with the last habitual potency (*Saṁskāra*). This is the Seed-less Spiritual-Absorption (5).* "The Ultra-Cognitive" means "nothing is cognized there". This Yoga, the restraint of mental operations, is two-fold.

---

1. If the term "all" were put before "mental operations", then the Cognitive-Spiritual-Absorption would not have got its stand on the side of Yoga; because in this Spiritual-Absorption, the mind gives up its exhibitive operations and acts upon the suppressive functions (*Y.S.* III 9-12).

2. This is the finishing limit of Action known as the state of *Sādhanacatuṣṭaya-sampanna* (accomplished with the four sorts of practices) of Lord Śaṅkara and is otherwise called the Material Freedom (*kārya-vimukti*). *Dhīra, Brahma-bhūta, Sthita-prajña, Brāhmī-sthiti, Sāṅkhya*, are only its different synonyms used in the *Bhagavad Gītā*.

3. Cit=Pure Con-Science: *Citiḥ*=Con-Science; *Caitanya*=Consciousness; *Cetana*=Conscious; these terms will be technically used here.

* These are the five respective planes as have been described in the preceding aphorism. In the description of the second plane of the mind, we are to note that in this case, the mind approaches the state of inactivity which has no connection with the acquirement of virtue, vice etc., because these are obtained with the help of the Active Energy only. The last plane of the mind is known as *Brahma-nirvāṇa*, Final Emancipation, Supreme Goal, Immortality, etc. of the *Gītā*. This is the subject of the Brahma-Sūtra termed "Spiritual Freedom" (*citta-vimuktiḥ*). It is self-manifested and is not dependent upon any action.

तदा द्रष्टुः स्वरूपेऽवस्थानम् ॥ ३ ॥

Then the staying of the Perceiver in his real Self—3

तदवस्थे चेतसि विषयाभावाद् बुद्धिबोधात्मा पुरुषः किंस्वभाव इति ? तदा द्रष्टुः स्वरूपेऽवस्थानम् । स्वरूपप्रतिष्ठा तदानीं चितिशक्तिर्यथा कैवल्ये । व्युत्थानचित्ते तु सति तथापि भवन्ति न तथा ॥ ३ ॥

In that state of the mind and in the absence of all objects, what will be the character of the Puruṣa who is the very self of the intellectual perception? Then the staying of the Perceiver[1] is in his real Self. At that time the Con-Science-Power is self-established as in Absoluteness. In the exhibitive mind however, though it (the Con-Science-Power) is similarly established, yet it does not appear as such.

वृत्तिसारूप्यमितरत्र ॥ ४ ॥

Conformity to the operations elsewhere—4

कथं तर्हि ? दर्शितविषयत्वाद् वृत्तिसारूप्यमितरत्र । व्युत्थाने याश्चित्तवृत्तयस्तदविशिष्टवृत्तिः पुरुषः । तथा च सूत्रम् । एकमेव दर्शनं ख्यातिरेव दर्शनमिति । चित्तमयस्कान्तमणिकल्पं संनिधिमात्रोपकारि दृश्यत्वेन स्वं भवति पुरुषस्य स्वामिनः । तस्माच्चित्तवृत्तिबोधे पुरुषस्यानादिः सम्बन्धो हेतुः ॥ ४ ॥

How then? On account of the fact of objects being presented to Him, conformity to the operations takes place elsewhere. Whatever be the operations of the mind in its exhibitive habit, the Puruṣa becomes possessed of (those) states which are inseparable from those (functions). Further there is a similar aphorism:—Observation is but one; Revelation alone is the Observation. The mind like a loadstone, by direct proximity, becomes the helping mate of the Puruṣa, the Lord, on account of its perceptibility. Therefore the beginningless relation of the Puruṣa with the mind becomes the cause of his perception of the mental operations.

वृत्तयः पञ्चतय्यः क्लिष्टाक्लिष्टाः ॥ ५ ॥

The operations are fivefold, painful and not-painful—5

ताः पुनर्निरोद्धव्या बहुत्वे सति, चित्तस्य वृत्तयः पञ्चतय्यः क्लिष्टाक्लिष्टाः । क्लेशहेतुकाः कर्माशयप्रचये क्षेत्रीभूताः क्लिष्टाः । ख्यातिविषया गुणाधिकारविरोधिन्योऽक्लिष्टाः । क्लिष्टप्रवाहपतिता अप्यक्लिष्टाः । क्लिष्टच्छिद्रेष्वप्यक्लिष्टा भवन्ति । अक्लिष्टच्छिद्रेषु क्लिष्टा इति । तथाजातीयकाः संस्कारा वृत्तिभिरेव क्रियन्ते । संस्कारैश्च वृत्तय इति । एवं वृत्तिसंस्कारचक्रमनिशमावर्तते । तदेवंभूतं चित्तमवसिताधिकारमात्मकल्पेन व्यवतिष्ठते प्रलयं वा गच्छतीति ॥ ५ ॥

They, the (exhibitive) operations of the mind should, however, be restrained on account of their manifoldness. The operations of the mind are five-fold, painful and not-painful. The painful are those that are the causes of afflictions in the form of breeding ground for the growth of the vehicle-of-actions. The not-painful are those that have the sphere of revelation and are adverse to the functions of the Energies. The not-painful remain the same though fallen into the flow of the painful and though present within the intervals of the painful[2]. The painful also remain painful even though present within the intervals of the not-painful[3]. The habitual potencies (*Saṁskāra*) of the respective classes are generated by the operations alone. Further the operations are generated by the habitual potencies. Thus the wheel of operations and habitual potencies is revolving without any stoppage. Such a mind, being free from its Duties, stands by itself[4] and goes to cessation[5].

---

1. *Dṛk*=Pure perceptivity; *Dṛśiḥ*=Perceptivity; *Dṛṣṭi*=Simple Perception; *Draṣṭā*=Perceiver; *Darśana*=Perceiving Instrument; *Dṛśya*=Perceivable or Perceptible. The terms will be technically used in this Science.
2. The austerities and study, etc., though painful at the time of performance, become not-painful in the long run.
3. The sensual enjoyments, though not-painful in the beginning, become painful at the end.
4. This happens in the case of the Cognitive-Spiritual-Absorption.
5. This refers to the Ultra-Cognitive-Spiritual-Absorption.

प्रमाणविपर्ययविकल्पनिद्रास्मृतयः ॥ ६ ॥

Real cognition, Perversive cognition, Fiction, Sleep and Memory (are the operations)—6

प्रत्यक्षानुमानागमाः प्रमाणानि ॥ ७ ॥

Perception, Inferenee and Verbal Cognition are the real cognitions—7

ताः क्लिष्टाश्चाक्लिष्टाश्च पञ्चधा वृत्तयः प्रमाणविपर्ययविकल्पनिद्रास्मृतयः । प्रत्यक्षानुमानागमाः प्रमाणानि ।

Those painful and not-painful five-fold operations are Real cognition, Perversive cognition, Fiction, Sleep and Memory. Perception, Inference and Verbal Cognition are the Real Cognitions.

इन्द्रियप्रणालिकया चित्तस्य बाह्यवस्तूपरागात्तद्विषया सामान्यविशेषात्मनोऽर्थस्य विशेषावधारणप्रधाना वृत्तिः प्रत्यक्षं प्रमाणम् । फलमविशिष्टः पौरुषेयश्चित्तवृत्तिबोधः । बुद्धेः प्रतिसंवेदी पुरुष इत्युपरिष्टादुपपादयिष्यामः ।

Perception is the mental operation about the external objects, it takes up the colour of those things through the channel of the senses and is the determinative chief of the specific character of the object endowed with generic and specific nature. The result is the inseparable knowledge of the mental operations with reference to the Puruṣa. We shall establish later on that the Puruṣa is the reflective perceiver of the intellect.

अनुमेयस्य तुल्यजातीयेष्वनुवृत्तो भिन्नजातीयेभ्यो व्यावृत्तः संबन्धो यस्तद्विषया सामान्यावधारणप्रधाना वृत्तिरनुमानम् । यथा देशान्तरप्राप्तेर्गतिमच्चन्द्रतारकं चैत्रवत् । विन्ध्यश्चाप्राप्तेरगतिः ।

Inference is the mental operation regarding the sphere of relation which shows the connection with the same class and the disconnection from the different class of the inferrable object, and is the determinative chief of generic nature. As for example—on account of the changing of places, the moon and the stars are inferred to have motion like Caitra (some person); the Vindhya (mountain) is inferred to be motionless owing to the absence of its movement.

आप्तेन दृष्टोऽनुमितो वार्थः परत्र स्वबोधसङ्क्रान्तये शब्देनोपदिश्यते शब्दात्तदर्थविषया वृत्तिः श्रोतुरागमः । यस्याश्रद्धेयार्थो वक्ता न दृष्टानुमितार्थः स आगमः प्लवते । मूलवक्तरि तु दृष्टानुमितार्थे निर्विप्लवः स्यात् ॥ ६-७ ॥

The object, seen or inferred by a competent man, is prescribed by words for transferring his knowledge to another. The mental operation concerning the object derived from the word, is the verbal cognition to the hearer. The verbal cognition,—with reference to the object which is neither seen nor inferred by the speaker, the meaning of whose words is not worthy of regard,—remains unsteady. But in the case of the Original Speaker[1] it (the verbal cognition) is undoubtedly steady with reference to the object whether perceived or inferred.

विपर्ययो मिथ्याज्ञानमतद्रूपप्रतिष्ठम् ॥ ८ ॥

Perversive Cognition is the false knowledge established in a show not its own—8

विपर्ययो मिथ्याज्ञानमतद्रूपप्रतिष्ठम् । स कस्मान्न प्रमाणं यतः प्रमाणेन बाध्यते । भूतार्थविषयत्वात्प्रमाणस्य । तत्र प्रमाणेन बाधनमप्रमाणस्य दृष्टम् । तद्यथा द्विचन्द्रदर्शनं सद्विषयेणैकचन्द्रदर्शनेन बाध्यत इति । सेयं पञ्चपर्वा भवत्यविद्या । अविद्याऽस्मितारागद्वेषाभिनिवेशाः क्लेशा इति । एत एव स्वसंज्ञाभिस्तमो मोहो महामोहस्तामिस्रोऽन्धतामिस्र इति । एते चित्तमलप्रसङ्गेनाभिधास्यन्ते ॥ ८ ॥

Perversive Cognition is the false knowledge established in a show not its own. Why is it not the real cognition? Because it is destroyed by the real cognition, as the real cognition has the sphere of reality of an existing object. The cessation of perversive-cognition by the strength of real cognition, is seen. As for example—the seeing of double moon is removed by the sight of one moon which is the real fact. It is this Non-Science (*Avidyā*) which is possessed of five steps:—Non-Science, Egoism (*Asmitā*), Attraction (*Rāga*), Aver-

1. The Original Speaker is Īśvara. By this, the author strengthens the authority of the Vedic Scriptures. Hereby we are authorised to refute the contradictory theories of our modern teachers.

sion (*Dveṣa*) and Clinging-to-life (*Abhiniveśa*) which are termed *afflictions*. The following are their individual names:- Dark (*Tamaḥ*), Ignorance (*Moha*), Extreme ignorance (*Mahā-moha*), Stupidity (*Tāmisra*), Blind stupidity (*Andha-tāmisra*). These will be described in the context of mental impurities.[1]

शब्दज्ञानानुपाती वस्तुशून्यो विकल्पः ॥ ९ ॥

Fiction, following the literal idea, is devoid of substance—9

शब्दज्ञानानुपाती वस्तुशून्यो विकल्पः। स न प्रमाणोपारोही। न विपर्ययोपारोही। वस्तुशून्यत्वेऽपि शब्दज्ञानमाहात्म्यनिबन्धनो व्यवहारो दृश्यते। तद्यथा चैतन्यं पुरुषस्य स्वरूपमिति। यदा चितिरेव पुरुषस्तदा किमत्र केन व्यपदिश्यते? भवति च व्यपदेशे वृत्तिः। यथा चैत्रस्य गौरिति। तथा प्रतिषिद्धवस्तुधर्मो निष्क्रियः पुरुषः। तिष्ठति बाणः स्थास्यति स्थित इति गतिनिवृत्तौ धात्वर्थमात्रं गम्यते। तथाऽनुत्पत्तिधर्मा पुरुष इति। उत्पत्तिधर्मस्याभावमात्रमवगम्यते, न पुरुषान्वयी धर्मः। तस्माद्विकल्पितः स धर्मस्तेन चास्ति व्यवहार इति ॥ ९ ॥

Fiction, following the literal idea, is devoid of substance. Neither does it stand on the real cognition, nor on the perversive cognition[2]. Although it is devoid of the substance, yet its use depending upon the strength of the literal idea is seen. As for example—Puruṣa has the "nature of consciousness", when Con-Science (*Citiḥ*), itself is the Puruṣa, then what is here signified by whom? there must be some connection in signification[3] as Caitra has cow. Similarly "Puruṣa is inactive" means "He has the characteristic denied to the Substance"[4]. If it is said "Bāṇa (a person) is, will be and was,"—the meaning of the root alone goes to "the cessation of motion"[5]. Similarly in the phrase "Puruṣa has the characteristic of the negation of birth",—the absence of the characteristic of being born alone is to be understood[6]. There is no characteristic keeping connection with the Puruṣa. Therefore, this characteristic is imposed and thereby the use exists.

अभावप्रत्ययालम्बना वृत्तिर्निद्रा ॥ १० ॥

Sleep is the 'mental' operation having for its grasp the cognition of absence—10

अभावप्रत्ययालम्बना वृत्तिर्निद्रा। सा च संप्रबोधे प्रत्यवमर्शात्प्रत्ययविशेषः। कथं? सुखमहमस्वाप्सम्। प्रसन्नं मे मनः प्रज्ञां मे विशारदीकरोति। दुःखमहमस्वाप्सं स्त्यानं मे मनो भ्रमत्यनवस्थितम्। गाढं मूढोऽहमस्वाप्सम्, गुरूणि मे गात्राणि, क्लान्तं

---

1. In the sphere of this cognition, there is some existing substance; but by not knowing the true nature of that substance, this perversive-cognition takes it for an object of similar show having the opposite nature. The logics of "rope and snake", 'oyster-shell and silver' etc., should be understood here.

2. The real cognition acts upon the real nature of an existing object; the perversive-cognition also acts upon the existing object but by its opposite nature of a similar show. Here in the case of this Fiction, there is no substance or no existing object: simply depending upon words, it creates something anew by fabrication only. The logics of "the castle in the air" (*khapuṣpa*), "the horns of a hare" (*Śaśa-sṛṅga*), "the son of a barren female" (vandhyā-putra) should be understood here.

3. The connection exists between two things, but the Puruṣa is absolute; this connection, therefore, relating to him is fabricated.

4. Puruṣa has no quality, this negation of the quality which belongs to the Objective-Matter (*Pradhāna*) is attributed to Him.

5. Puruṣa has no movement; but still the tense pertaining to the change of time, is attributed to him.

6. Though Puruṣa has no positive characteristic, yet He is attributed with the negative one.

Our present confused notions of Jñāna (ज्ञान) and Bhakti are the eminent instances for our better understanding of the nature of "fiction".

There are some people who take it for granted that Jñāna (knowledge) and Bhakti (devotion) are two separate existing things—one is male and the other is female; these two are of opposite sex, hence they are diametrically opposed to each other. But it is a known fact that Jñānam is not masculine but is neuter.

However, we do not find in English any single term equivalent to Bhakti. "Devotion" is not at all its proper synonym. "Knowledge" comes from the root "to know" (Jñā—to work mentally). *Bhakti* comes from the root *Bhaj*,—to serve mentally. Hence, the derivative meaning of "Bhakti" is "mental action"; and *Jñāna* also signifies the same meaning. This is the dreadful nature of this Fiction that shows their mutual opposite character (*Y.S.* IV-10).

मे चित्तम्, अलसं मुषितमिव तिष्ठतीति। स खल्वयं प्रबुद्धस्य प्रत्यवमर्शो न स्यादसति प्रत्ययानुभवे। तदाश्रिताः स्मृतयश्च तद्विषया न स्युः। तस्मात्प्रत्ययविशेषो निद्रा। सा च समाधावितरप्रत्ययवन्निरोद्धव्येति ॥ १० ॥

Sleep is the mental operation[1] having the cognition of absence for its grasp. Further, on awakening, this specific sort of cognition comes from studious thought such as—I had a refreshing sleep, my mind is cheerful, it makes my intelligence clear[2]; I slept painfully; my mind is sluggish, it wanders unsteady[3]; I had a deep dark and dense sleep, my limbs are heavy, my *mind* is tired, it rests idle as if senseless.[4] Had there been no experience of such cognition, indeed this recollection of an awakened (person) would not have taken place, there would have been no remembrances regarding those (thoughts) dependent upon those (cognitions). Therefore sleep is a particular form of cognition; further it must be restrained like all other (exhibitive) notions for Spiritual-Absorption.[5]

अनुभूतविषयासंप्रमोषः स्मृतिः ॥११॥

Memory is the absence of loss (i.e. retention) of the experienced objects—11

अनुभूतविषयासंप्रमोषः स्मृतिः। किं प्रत्ययस्य चित्तं स्मरति, आहोस्विद्विषयस्येति ? ग्राह्योपरक्तः प्रत्ययो ग्राह्यग्रहणोभयाकारनिर्भासस्तज्जातीयकं संस्कारमारभते। स संस्कारः स्वव्यञ्जकाञ्जनस्तदाकारामेव ग्राह्यग्रहणोभयात्मिकां स्मृतिं जनयति। तत्र ग्रहणाकारपूर्वा बुद्धिः। ग्राह्याकारपूर्वा स्मृतिः। सा च द्वयी भावितस्मर्तव्या चाभावितस्मर्तव्या च। स्वप्ने भावितस्मर्तव्या। जाग्रत्समये त्वभावितस्मर्तव्येति। सर्वाश्चैताः स्मृतयः प्रमाणविपर्ययविकल्पनिद्रास्मृतीनामनुभवात्प्रभवन्ति। सर्वाश्चैता वृत्तयः सुखदुःखमोहात्मिकाः। सुखदुःखमोहाश्च क्लेशेषु व्याख्येयाः। सुखानुशयी रागः। दुःखानुशयी द्वेषः। मोहः पुनरविद्येति। एताः सर्वा वृत्तयो निरोद्धव्याः। आसां निरोधे संप्रज्ञातो वा समाधिर्भवत्यसंप्रज्ञातो वेति ॥ ११ ॥

Memory is the absence of loss (i. e., retention) of the experienced objects. Does the mind remember cognition or the object?[6] The cognition, being coloured by the receivable object, appears in the form of both the receivable object and the receiving instrument and begins the formation of habitual potency of the same class. This habitual potency, being possessed of the colour of its own manifestative cause, produces simply the memory of the same form and nature of both the receivable objects and the receiving instrument. There, intelligence is that in

1. Here the author specially mentions the term "operation" in this aphorism. By this, it should be understood that there must be some hidden significance in it and that it is nothing but "a particular kind of cognition". In other words, we are to note that "Sleep" is not at all a state in which the mind can be free from all its exhibitive operations.

2. Harmonious or *Sāttvika* Sleep.

3. Disturbed or *Rājasa* Sleep.

4. Inert or *Tāmasa* Sleep.

5. We can remember only those things which have been experienced previously and can never remember any thing not experienced before. Hence if we judge carefully about sleep we can easily find out two aspects of our consciousness in the sleeping state. From one point of view, I become unconscious and from the other I remain conscious of my own unconsciousness. Had it not been so, how could I remember my unconsciousness? Thus the one is the lower self, and the other is the Higher. The lower self is subject to the conscious state (*jāgrata*), the sub-conscious state (*svapna*) and the unconscious state (*suṣupti*), i.e., the waking, dreaming and sleeping conditions, On the other hand the Higher Self always remains in the Super-conscious state (*turīya*) which is called the unchanging position (*kūṭastha*). The theory of this science is to make this lower self or citta free from his subjection to the functions of the three Energies which are the cause of his affliction, action and fruition. So the commentator says that this sleep is a peculiar sort of mental operation which is not realised by many of us. They believe that Absoluteness consists in the inactivity of the mind as in the sleeping state. In fact, this sleep must be restrained like other exhibitive operations for Spiritual-Absorption. The state which our lower self will attain on being freed from this subjection, will be the subject of the Brahma Sūtra.

6. In the Vedānta philosophy Consciousness is classified in four divisions :—*Pramā*=Con-Science (Pure Subjective Consciousness); *Pramātā*=Cognitive Consciousness or the Perceiver (the Lower Subjective Manifestation); *Pramāṇa*=the instrumental or the cognitional consciousness (lower self or Citta); *Prameya*=cognizable consciousness (the gross mind). Here the instrumental and the gross phenomena are the material aspects of Consciousness; and the other two are the Spiritual aspects.

which the receiving instrument precedes the object[1]; and the memory (remembrance) is that in which the receivable object[2] precedes the receiving instrument. Further it (the memory) is two-fold,—the Produced memorablia (*Bhāvita-smartavyā*) and the Un-produced-memorablia (*Abhāvita-smartavyā*). In dream, comes the produced memorablia and in waking,—the unproduced — memorablia[3]. All these memories (the remembrances) rise from the experience of real cognition, perversive-cognition, fiction, sleep and memory. And all these mental operations are of the nature of pleasure, pain and ignorance. Further pleasure, pain and ignorance should be described in connection with the *afflictions*. Attachment follows the experience of pleasure. Aversion follows the experience of pain. Ignorance however is Non-science. All these mental operations must be restrained. On their restraint, comes either the Cognitive-Spiritual-Absorption or the Ultra-Cognitive-Spiritual-Absorption.

अभ्यासवैराग्याभ्यां तन्निरोधः ॥ १२॥

Their restraint comes from Practice and Non-attachment—12

अथासां निरोधे क उपाय इति? अभ्यासवैराग्याभ्यां तन्निरोधः। चित्तनदी नामोभयतोवाहिनी या वहति कल्याणाय वहति पापाय च। या तु कैवल्यप्राग्भारा विवेकविषयनिम्ना सा कल्याणवहा। संसारप्राग्भारा अविवेकविषयनिम्ना पापवहा। तत्र वैराग्येण विषयस्रोतः खिलीक्रियते। विवेकदर्शनाभ्यासेन विवेकस्रोत उद्घाटयत इत्युभयाधीनश्चित्तवृत्ति निरोधः ॥ १२ ॥

Now what is the means of restraining them? Their restraint comes from Practice and Non-attachment. In fact the stream of mind flows both ways either towards beatitude or towards evil. That however, which has the load of Absoluteness in front and is inclined towards the sphere of Intellective Distinguishing Power[4], is the flow of beatitude; and that which has the load of rebirth in front and is inclined towards the sphere of Ignorance, is the flow of evil. There the flow towards sense-objects is closed by non-attachment. And the current of Intellective Distinguishing Power is opened up by the practice of the Intellective Revelation; thus the restraint of mental operations is dependent upon both.

तत्र स्थितौ यत्नोऽभ्यासः ॥ १३ ॥

There the practice is the effort for steadiness—13

तत्र स्थितौ यत्नोऽभ्यासः। चित्तस्यावृत्तिकस्य प्रशान्तवाहिता स्थितिस्तदर्थः प्रयत्नो वीर्यमुत्साहस्तत्संपिपादयिषया तत्साधनानुष्ठानमभ्यासः॥१३॥

Steadiness (in restraint) is the peaceful flowing of the mind freed from the (exhibitive) operations[5]. Effort is the vigour and inclination for that aim[6]. Practice is the course of proceeding with the means for the purpose of attaining that (aim).[7]

स तु दीर्घकालनैरन्तर्यसत्कारासेवितो दृढभूमिः ॥ १४ ॥

That (restraint) however, being served for a long time without stoppage and with earnestness, becomes firmly established—14

---

1. Intelligence is the Productive-faculty (*Abhijñā-pratyakṣa*).
2. Memory is the Reproductive-faculty (*Pratyabhijñā-pratykṣa*) of the Vedānta-Darśana.
3. Produced memorablia is the *Prātibhāsika-Sattā* (the visionary phenomenon or the creation of the mind); and the unproduced-memorablia is the *Vyāvahārika-Sattā* (the worldly phenomenon or the creation of God). The Vedānta-Darśana does not take notice of this Unproduced-memorablia; because the Pure Subjective State has been dealt with in it. We should always bear in mind that the stepping ground of the Vedānta-Darśana is the full achievement of the four practices (the *Sādhana-chatuṣṭaya*) known as the standard of qualification for seeking after Brahma.

   The aim of this Yoga-Sūtra is to teach the process and the characters of the suppressive habit after gradual destruction of the exhibitive ones; so this science begins with the unproduced memorablia.
4. The term 'Practice' here refers to the complete performance of the Prescribed Duties in accordance with the division of Caste and Life-order, because this is the only means of acquiring real Non-attachment towards worldly objects. There is no single term in English to express the meaning of *Viveka*. *Viveka* is the Intellective Power to distinguish the Spirit from the Matter and it gets its stand on the Subjective Manifestation of the Cognitive-Spiritual-Absorption.
5. The object or the aim.
6. The effort for its achievement.
7. The means of attaining that aim.

स तु दीर्घकालनैरन्तर्यसत्कारासेवितो दृढभूमि: । दीर्घकालासेवितो निरन्तरासेवित: सत्कारासेवित: तपसा ब्रह्मचर्येण विद्यया श्रद्धया च संपादित:सत्कारवान्दृढभूमिर्भवति । व्युत्थानसंस्कारेण द्रागित्येवानभिभूतविषय इत्यर्थ: ।। १४ ।।

That restraint however, being served for a long time without stoppage and with earnestness, becomes firmly established. "Served for long time", "served without stoppage", "served with earnestness" mean that Restraint, being accomplished with penance, with continence, with the knowledge of the systematic course and with vehement aspiration (*śraddhā*), gets welcome and firmly established. It means that it (restraint) is the subject which cannot be conquerred quickly by the exhibitive habitual potency.[1]

दृष्टानुश्रविकविषयवितृष्णस्य वशीकारसंज्ञा वैराग्यम् ।। १५ ।।

Non-attchment is the controlling-consciousness of a person who has no craving for visible and Scriptural enjoyment—15

दृष्टानुश्रविकविषयवितृष्णस्य वशीकारसंज्ञा वैराग्यम् । स्त्रियोऽन्नपानमैश्वर्यमिति दृष्टविषये विरक्तस्य स्वर्गवैदेह्यप्रकृतिलयत्वप्राप्तावानुश्रविकविषये वितृष्णस्य दिव्यादिव्यविषयसंप्रयोगेऽपि चित्तस्य विषयदोषदर्शिन: प्रसंख्यानबलादनाभोगात्मिका हेयोपादेयशून्या वशीकारसंज्ञा वैराग्यम् ।। १५ ।।

Non-attachment is the controlling consciousness of a person who has no craving for visible and Scriptural enjoyments. Of a person who is displeased with the visible enjoyments such as women, food, drinks and powers, and who is free from the desire for the Scriptural enjoyments viz: the attainment of the states of heaven, Videha and Prakṛtilaya and whose mind, even in the contact with divine and worldly objects finds defects in them by the strength of the Intellective Power of Meditation,—the controlling consciousness being of the nature of non-enjoyment and being devoid of attraction and aversion, is Non-attachment.[2]

तत्परं पुरुषख्यातेर्गुणवैतृष्ण्यम् ।। १६ ।।

That (non-attachment) is the highest when there comes in the desirelessness for the qualities derived from the revelation of the Puruṣa—16

तत्परं पुरुषख्यातेर्गुणवैतृष्ण्यम् । दृष्टानुश्रविकविषयदोषदर्शी विरक्त: । पुरुषदर्शनाभ्यासात्तच्छुद्धिप्रविवेकाप्यायितबुद्धिर्गुणेभ्यो व्यक्ताव्यक्तधर्मभ्यो विरक्त इति ।

He who finds defects in visible and audible objects, is called "non-attached". He whose intellect is absorbed in the full reflection of the Puruṣa's purity caused by the practice of the revelation of the Puruṣa, is termed non-attached with the qualities of manifested[3] and unmanifested[4] nature.

तदद्वयं वैराग्यम् । तत्र यदुत्तरं तज्ज्ञानप्रसादमात्रं यस्योदये सति योगी प्रत्युदितख्यातिरेवं मन्यते- प्राप्तं प्रापणीयम् । क्षीणा: क्षेतव्या: क्लेशा: । छिन्न: श्लिष्टपर्वभवसंक्रमो यस्याविच्छेदाज्जनित्वा म्रियते मृत्वा च जायत इति ।

Thus this non-attachement is two-fold. There that which is the latter, is but the pure luminosity of Spiritual Knowledge, on the rise of which, the Yogi shining with the rise of this Revelation thinks thus,—(Now) the obtainable has been obtained, the destroyable afflictions have been destroyed, the strong chain of revolving birth has been broken, and if it is not torn asunder, the creatures being born die, and being dead are born again.

ज्ञानस्यैव परा काष्ठा वैराग्यम् । एतस्यैव हि नान्तरीयकं कैवल्यमिति ।। १६ ।।

---

1. By this, our commentator gives special stress on practice. It is obvious that this practice is not at all an easy-going-path. The restraint of mental operations requires so many qualifications for its achievement and cannot be attained simply by the knowledge of books.

2. By this, it is apparent that Non-attached Yogi is always displeased with and free from desire for the enjoyable objects alone but not envious of the enjoyers of those objects; and secondly he does not enjoy luxury on the lame excuse of desirelessness as many people do.

3. Manifested qualities are those that are related to the body.

4. Unmanifested are those that are connected with the intellective sphere (*Y.S.* III-50).

Non-attachment is indeed the highest state of Knowledge; because Absoluteness follows immediately after this.[1]

वितर्कविचारानन्दास्मितारूपानुगमात्संप्रज्ञातः ॥ १७ ॥

The Spiritual-absorption is Cognitive owing to the accompaniment of the appearance of Supposition, Clear Vision, Rapture and Egoism—17

अथोपायद्वयेन निरुद्धचित्तवृत्तेः कथमुच्यते संप्रज्ञातः समाधिरिति? वितर्कविचारानन्दास्मितारूपानुगमात्संप्रज्ञातः । वितर्कः चित्तस्यालम्बने स्थूल आभोगः । सूक्ष्मो विचारः । आनन्दो ह्लादः । एकात्मिका संविदस्मिता । तत्र प्रथमश्चतुष्टयानुगतः समाधिः सवितर्कः, द्वितीयो वितर्कविकलः सविचारः, तृतीयो विचारविकलः सानन्दः, चतुर्थस्तद्विकलोऽस्मितामात्र इति । सर्व एते सालम्बनाः समाधयः ॥ १७ ॥

Now why is the Spiritual-Absorption called Cognitive in regard to a Yogi possessed of the mental operations restrained by this two-fold means? The Spiritual-Absorption is cognitive because of the accompaniment of the apperance of Supposition, Clear Vision, Rapture and Egoism. Supposition (*Vitarka*) means the gross expanse for mental grasp, the subtle is Clear Vision (*Vicāra*), Rapture (*Ānanda*) is gladness; the cognition of unified nature is Egoism (*Asmitā*). There the first Spiritual-Absorption, being followed by all the four (appearances) is termed "Suppositional" (*Savitarka*)[2] ; the second, being deprived of Supposition, is accompanied with Clear Vision (*Savicāra*) ; the third, being deprived of investigation, is rapturous (*Ānanda*) and the fourth, going beyond that (rapture), is Pure Egoism (*Asmitā-mātra*). All these Spiritual-Absorptions are possessed of some support.

विरामप्रत्ययाभ्यासपूर्वः संस्कारशेषोऽन्यः ॥ १८ ॥

The other, being preceded by the practice of the cessational cognition has the end of the habitual potencies —18

अथासंप्रज्ञातः समाधिः किमुपायः किंस्वभावो वेति ? विरामप्रत्ययाभ्यासपूर्वः संस्कारशेषोऽन्यः । सर्ववृत्तिप्रत्यस्तमये संस्कारशेषो निरोधश्चित्तस्य समाधिरसंप्रज्ञातः । तस्य परं वैराग्यमुपायः । सालम्बनो ह्यभ्यासः तत्साधनाय न कल्पत इति विरामप्रत्ययो निर्वस्तुक आलम्बनीक्रियते । स चार्थशून्यः । तदभ्यासपूर्वकं हि चित्तं निरालम्बनमभावप्राप्तमिव भवतीत्येष निर्बीजः समाधिरसंप्रज्ञातः ॥ १८ ॥

Now what is the means of attaining the Ultra Cognitive-Spiritual-Absorption and what is its nature ? The other, being preceded by the practice of the cessational cognition, has the end of the habitual potencies. On the cessation of all operations, the restraint of the mind which has the end of the habitual potencies, is the Ultra-Cognitive Spiritual-Absorption. The Highest Non-

---

1. By this, it is clear that wherever there is knowledge, there must be non-attachment; again wherever there is non-attachment, there must be neutrality and non-enjoyment of luxury (as has been described in the preceding aphorism). If these qualities are wanting in a person who thinks himself to be wise, he must be an object of pity however great may be his style and status.

2. By this, it should be understood that from the first Suppositional appearance alone, i.e. only from the gross expanse the other three Absorbent faculties will appear one after another. As for example, when a person appears in full dress, we cannot see the exact shape and form of his body. Finally, we can see his full structure only after removing his clothes one after another. Similarly in the case of Spiritual Absorption, the gross form for mental grasp is essentially necessary. Then after gradually penetrating through it by means of the systematic process, the other Absorbent Cognitions will be manifested one after another.

The Suppositional appearance and the manifestation of Clear Vision, i.e., the gross and the subtle appearances combined correspond to the Elemental manifestation (*Adhibhūta* of the *Gītā*; the rapturous appearance is the instrumental or the Divine manifestation (*Adhidaiva*, i.e., *karaṇa-grāhya*) and the appearance of unified nature is the subjective (*Adhiyajña Ahaṁ-grāhya*) of the *Gītā*. Hence *Vitarka*, *Vicāra*, *Ānanda* and *Asmitā*, i.e., the Gross, Subtle, Instrumental and the Subjective manifestations are the four successive Absorbent Cognitions known as the *Sthūla*, *Sūkṣma*, *Karaṇa-grāhya* and *Ahaṁ-grāhya* respectively. Further, the Subjective (*Ahaṁgrāhya*) appearance will be divided into two aspects—the Receiver *Puruṣa* (the Cognitive or the Unchanging Consciousness) and the *Mukta Puruṣa* (the Pure Consciousness or Con-Science). Further Īśvara is the Special *Puruṣa* as He is far beyond the sphere of Action. All this should be ascertained from the Terminology chart at the end of this book.

attachment[1] is the means of attaining it, because the practice, depending on some support, is not able to bring about its accomplishment, i.e., the cessational cognition which is apparently not substantial is made its support. It is devoid of interests; because the mind, being attended with that practice, becomes supportless as if it has ceased to exist.[2] This is the Seedless Ultra-Cognitive-Spiritual-Absorption.

भवप्रत्ययो विदेहप्रकृतिलयानाम् ॥ १९ ॥

Dependence upon Objective Existence is for the Videhas and the Prakṛtilayas—19.

स खल्वयं द्विविधः—उपायप्रत्ययो भवप्रत्ययश्च । तत्रोपायप्रत्ययो योगिनां भवति। भवप्रत्ययो विदेहप्रकृतिलयानाम् । विदेहानां देवानां भवप्रत्ययः । ते हि स्वसंस्कारमात्रोपयोगेन चित्तेन कैवल्यपदमिवानुभवन्तः स्वसंस्कारविपाकं तथाजातीयकमतिवाहयन्ति। तथा प्रकृतिलयाः साधिकारे चेतसि प्रकृतिलीने कैवल्यपदमिवानुभवन्ति, यावन्न पुनरावर्ततेऽधिकारवशाच्चित्तमिति ॥ १९ ॥

This (Ultra-Cognitive-Spiritual-Absorption) is, in fact, of two descriptions:—Dependence upon the Systematic process and Dependence upon Objective Existence. There, the dependence on Systematic process is the way of the Yogis; and the dependence upon Objective Existence belongs to the Videhas and the Prakṛtilayas. Dependence upon Objective Existence belongs to the Videhas, the gods[3]; because they,—while experiencing a state similar to Absoluteness by the help of the mind which is attended with its own habitual potencies alone,—spend their own potential fruition suitable to that (Absolute) state. Similarly the Prakṛtilayas[4] experience a state similar to Absoluteness by the help of the duty-bound mind merged into the Intensive Cause (Prakṛti), until the mind comes back through the influence of its duties.

श्रद्धावीर्यस्मृतिसमाधिप्रज्ञापूर्वक इतरेषाम् ॥२०॥

This is preceded by Faith, Courage, Retentive Power, Spiritual Absorption and Intellective Vision in the case of others—20.

श्रद्धावीर्यस्मृतिसमाधिप्रज्ञापूर्वक इतरेषाम् । उपायप्रत्ययो योगिनां भवति। श्रद्धा चेतसः संप्रसादः। सा हि जननीव कल्याणी योगिनं पाति तस्य हि श्रद्दधानस्य विवेकार्थिनो वीर्यमुपजायते । समुपजातवीर्यस्य स्मृतिरुपतिष्ठते। स्मृत्युपस्थाने च चित्तमनाकुलं समाधीयते । समाहितचित्तस्य प्रज्ञाविवेक उपावर्तते ।

येन यथार्थं वस्तु जानाति । तदभ्यासात्तत्द्विषयाच्च वैराग्यादसंप्रज्ञातः समाधिर्भवति ॥ २० ॥

This (Ultra Cognitive-Spiritual-Absorption) being dependent upon the systematic process happens to the Yogis. Faith[5] means the vehement aspiration of

1. This is the Supreme Self of the Subjective Manifestation, the *Mukta Puruṣa* or Con-Science which is the Subject of the Vedānta-Darśana; it cannot be achieved by any action; simply the Highest Non-Attachment, i.e., the cessation of all actions is the means to this end.

2. Here the Commentator makes this subject over to the Vedānta Darśana.

3. The Videhas are those that, after performing the Scriptural Virtuous Actions such as *Trināciketa Agni*, *Agni-hotra*, etc., as have been prescribed in the Vedas, attain the state of freedom similar to absoluteness (the *Muṇḍakopaniṣad*, Chapter II Part 1). They are not to return to human life but they will become the Presiding Officers in the future creation. As for instance, King Suratha will be the Eighth Manu after the reign of the Vaivasvata Manu.

4. The Prakṛtilayas are those that simply believe in the objective principles known as the elementary truths and pass out of their bodies only by the strength of breath-control (*prāṇāyāma*) without purifying their mind by the systematic process of Yoga. They think that the mind is the sole principle and there is nothing beyond it. According to them, it is the mind alone which brings on the pairs of opposites such as pleasure and pain. So they try to do away with the mind by virtue of its laxity as in hibernation. Hence they are to come back to rebirth by the force of the Exciting Cause of the duties of relativity. That the duties are nothing more or less than Experience and Emancipation will be described later.

5. Many of us think that Bhakti and Faith are equal in meaning. But if we carefully examine these two terms, we can find a great gulf between them. The term "Bhakti" has already been proved to signify "mental action" whereas Faith is the "mental tendency". The same tendency takes different names according to the difference of the spheres of its function. In other words, it takes the names of faith (*śraddhā*), love (*prema*), affection (*sneha*), desire (*kāma*) anger (*krodha*), avarice (*lobha*), conceit (*mada*), ignorance (*moha*) and envy (*mātsarya*) according to the spheres of its operation such as—high aim, equal standard, low level, sense-object, repulsion, attachment, vanity, I-ness and My-ness and jealousy at another's prosperity respectively.

the mind. It indeed sustains the Yogi like a benevolent mother. Courage, in fact, is born in that Faithful aspirant seeking after the Intellective Distinguishing Power. Retentive Power comes to the fully courageous; further, on the acquisition of the Retentive Power the mind being freed from disturbance, becomes Spiritually Absorbed. The Intellective Vision, by which the yogi understands the Substance in reality, comes to the Spiritually Absorbed mind. By the practice of these (Faith, etc.) and from the non-attachment towards the respective objects thereof, comes the Ultra-Cognitive-Spiritual-Absorption.

तीव्रसंवेगानामासन्नः ॥ २१ ॥

It is nearest to the extremely courageous Yogis.—21

ते खलु नव योगिनो भवन्ति । मृदुमध्याधिमात्रोपाया भवन्ति । तद्यथा—मृदूपायो मध्योपायोऽधिमात्रोपाय इति । तत्र मृदूपायस्त्रिविध: । मृदुसंवेगो मध्यसंवेगस्तीव्रसंवेग इति । तथा मध्योपायस्तथाऽधिमात्रोपाय इति । तत्राधिमात्रोपायानां तीव्रसंवेगानामासन्न: समाधिलाभ: समाधिफलं च भवतीति ॥ २१ ॥

The Yogis are, indeed, of nine classes; they are given to the practice of mild, middle and intense methods, i.e., they have mild manner, middle manner and intense manner. There the mild method is threefold such as — mild courage, middle courage and intense courage. Similar is the middle method and also the intense method. There the achievement of Spiritual Absorption and the fruit thereof become nearest to the extremely courageous who are practising by the intense method.[1]

मृदुमध्याधिमात्रत्वात्ततोऽपि विशेषः ॥ २२ ॥

There is also a further distinction according to the degree of mild, middling and intense.—22

मृदुमध्याधिमात्रत्वात्ततोऽपि विशेष: । मृदुतीव्रो मध्यतीव्रोऽधिमात्रतीव्र इति । ततोऽपि विशेष: । तद्विशेषान्मृदुतीव्रसंवेगस्यासन्न:, ततो मध्यतीव्रसंवेगस्याधिमात्रोपायस्यासन्नतर:, तस्मादधिमात्रतीव्रसंवेगस्याधिमात्रोपायस्यासन्नतम: समाधिलाभ: समाधिफलञ्चेति ॥ २२ ॥

Mildly intense, middlingly intense and intensely intense. In accordance with this comparison, the attainment of Spiritual Absorption and the fruit thereof become nearest to the mildly intense courageous, more nearest to the middlingly intense courageous and most nearest to the intensely intense courageous given to practice through the most intense method.

ईश्वरप्रणिधानाद् वा ॥ २३ ॥

Or from profound meditation upon Īśvara.—23

किमेतस्मादेवासन्नतर: समाधिर्भवति? अथास्य लाभे भवत्यन्योऽपि कश्चिदुपायो न वेति ईश्वरप्रणिधानाद्वा । प्रणिधानाद्भक्तिविशेषादावर्जित ईश्वरस्तमनुगृह्णात्यभिध्यानमात्रेण । तदभिध्यानमात्रादपि योगिन आसन्नतर: समाधिलाभ: समाधिफलं च भवतीति ॥ २३ ॥

Is it the only means by which the Spiritual Absorption becomes speediest? Or, is there any other means for its attainment or not? Or from profound meditation upon Īśvara[2]. Īśvara, being drawn by Profound Meditation which is a particular

---

1. The term 'achievement', showing action, refers to the Cognitive-Spiritual-Absorption which is dependent upon Action, and the term 'fruit' signifies the Ultra-Cognitive-Spiritual-Absorption beyond the sphere of Action.

2. This alternative means of restraining the mental operations is only possible for the yogis of an advanced stage, who have acquired Non-attachment towards worldly objects in a very early age due to the ready fruit of their white Actions done in their provious life, as we find in the case of Jaḍa Bharata, Dhruva, etc. As for example: A weak man stands by need of some external support in the form of a stick for walking; but a strong man can walk by himself without any external help. In the former case, although the stick is needful, yet it by itself does not carry the man. He himself has to walk. Hence the act of walking is the same for both of them. Similarly the preceding means is for those that are fully confident of their own powers and do not want any external help besides themselves; they take the parts of their own body as the objects for the practice of their mental concentration and meditation.

This aphorism is for them that are fully confident of Divine Powers. They take the different forms of Īśvara as the object of their mental concentration and meditation. Further these forms have been prescribed in the Vedic Scriptures in accordance with the special manifestations of his powers. Though they are of different tastes, yet the nature of the application to the method is the same for all. All this will be explained later.

kind of Spiritual Action, favours him as a result of his deep meditation alone. Simply from that deep meditation, the attainment of Spiritual Absorption and the fruit thereof become also speediest for the Yogi.

क्लेशकर्मविपाकाशयैरपरामृष्टः पुरुषविशेष ईश्वरः ॥ २४ ॥

Īśvara is the Special Puruṣa unaffected by the vehicles (कर्माशय) of affliction, action and fruition—24.

अथ प्रधानपुरुषव्यतिरिक्तः कोऽयमीश्वरो नामेति ? क्लेशकर्मविपाकाशयैरपरामृष्टः पुरुषविशेष ईश्वरः । अविद्यादयः क्लेशाः । कुशलाऽकुशलानि कर्माणि । तत्फलं विपाकः तदनुगुणा वासना आशयास्ते च मनसि वर्तमानाः पुरुषे व्यपदिश्यन्ते । स हि तत्फलस्य भोक्तेति । यथा जयः पराजयो वा योद्धृषु वर्तमानः स्वामिनि व्यपदिश्यते । यो ह्यनेन भोगेनापरामृष्टः स पुरुषविशेष ईश्वरः ।

Now who is, indeed, this Īśvara besides the Pradhāna (the Active Principal Material Cause) and the Puruṣa (the Inactive Efficient cause)? Īśvara is the Special Puruṣa[1] unaffected by the vehicles of affliction, action and fruition. The Non-Science and the rest are the afflictions, the actions are the productive of virtue and vice, and their consequence is the fruition. The habitual residua (वासना) having the qualifications (of the former three), are the vehicles. Further they, being present in the mind, are ascribed to the Puruṣa; because he is the enjoyer of their fruit. As for example—victory or defeat belonging to the soldiers is ascribed to their lord. He who is in fact unaffected by this enjoyment, is the Special Puruṣa,—Īśvara.

कैवल्यं प्राप्तास्तर्हि सन्ति च बहवः केवलिनः । ते हि त्रीणि बन्धनानि छित्त्वा कैवल्यं प्राप्ताः, ईश्वरस्य च तत्संबन्धो न भूतो न भावी । यथा मुक्तस्य पूर्वा बन्धकोटिः प्रज्ञायते नैवमीश्वरस्य । यथा वा प्रकृतिलीनस्योत्तरा बन्धकोटिः संभाव्यते नैवमीश्वरस्य । स तु सदैव मुक्तः सदैवेश्वर इति ।

Then, there are the numerous absolute entities who have attained Absoluteness, because they have attained the absolute state after cutting those three bonds. However Īśvara neither had, nor will have any connection with those bonds. As the distinction of the previous bondage of the liberated is understood so there is nothing of that sort in regard to Īśvara. Or as the certainty of future bondage of the Prakṛtilaya is supposed so there is nothing of that kind relating to Īśvara. On the other hand, Īśvara is ever free, ever the Lord[2].

योऽसौ प्रकृष्टसत्त्वोपादानादीश्वरस्य शाश्वतिक उत्कर्षः स किं सनिमित्त आहोस्विन्निर्निमित्त इति? तस्य शास्त्रं निमित्तम् । शास्त्रं पुनः किं निमित्तम् ? प्रकृष्टसत्त्वनिमित्तम् । एतयोः शास्त्रोत्कर्षयोरीश्वरसत्त्वे वर्तमानयोरनादिः संबन्धः । एतस्मादेतद्भवति सदैवेश्वरः सदैव मुक्त इति ।

Now has the Eternal Excellence of Īśvara due to His acceptance of the Supreme Essence (of intelligence), any function or has it no function at all? Its function is to manifest the Scriptures. What, again, is the function of the Scriptures? The function is to show the Supreme Essence (of intelligence)[3]. There is a beginningless relation between the Scriptures and the Supreme Excellence which have their existence in the Essence of

---

1. This aphorism refers to *Satyam* (the Supreme Truth) of the Vedānta. We should not be confused by the apparent similarity of the words. There can be no confusion if we carefully look into the meaning of the definitions of those words in the different texts. Īśvara of this Yoga-Sūtra is the same as Brahma of the Vedānta-Darśana; and the Active Īśvara of the Vedānta-Darśana known as the Single Soul has been defined in this text as the *Pūrva Siddha* (the First Perfect Entity, vide *Y.S.* chapter III—44 and IV—4).

2. By this it is clear that the modern religious prophets can never be Īśvara; they may be liberated or great in power; but they are all seen to be affected by afflictions, etc.

3. Each science begins with some hypothesis. As for example—Geometry begins with the 'point' What is its definition ? The 'point' has simply position, but no dimension. If we argue here from the beginning that wherever there is position, there must be some dimension; so this definition is defective. Then is there any Geometrician who can prove the Geometrical truths without the help of the said definition of the point ? Similarly our Spiritual Science or the Vedic Scriptures also begin with some hypothesis. And this hypothesis in the case of each text is nothing but Faith—the vehement aspiration after the respective truth by obeying the laws and process in the regular course. Accordingly our Author has described, in the aphorism 20, the gradual steps for realising the truth dealt with in this Science.

Īśvara[1]. From this, it is evident that He is ever free, ever the Lord.

तच्च तस्यैश्वर्यं साम्यातिशयविनिर्मुक्तम् । न तावदैश्वर्यान्तरेण तदतिशय्यते । यदेवातिशयि स्यात्तदेव तत्स्यात् । तस्माद्यत्र काष्ठाप्राप्तिरैश्वर्यस्य स ईश्वर इति । न च तत्समानमैश्वर्यमस्ति । कस्माद्? द्वयोस्तुल्ययोरेकस्मिन्युगपत्कामितेऽर्थे नवमिदमस्तु पुराणमिदमस्त्वित्येकस्य सिद्धावितरस्य प्राकाम्यविघातादूनत्वं प्रसक्तम् । द्वयोश्च तुल्ययोर्युगपत्कामितार्थप्राप्तिर्नास्ति, अर्थस्य विरुद्धत्वात् ।

Further His divinity is without any equal or excess. This is not excelled by any other divinity. Whatever is the highest, is His Divinity. For this reason, where there is the highest attainment of Divinity, that is Īśvara. Again there is no other divinity equal to that (of Him). Why? Because if a single object be simultaneously desired by two equal powers contending "let it be new", "let it be old", then on the success of one the deficiency of the other is inferred owing to the non-fulfilment of his irresistible will. Further there can be no simultaneous attainment of the desired object by both the equal powers on account of the contradiction of their purposes.

तस्माद्यस्य साम्यातिशयैर्विनिर्मुक्तमैश्वर्यं स एवेश्वरः । स च पुरुषविशेष इति ॥ २४ ॥

Hence He alone, whose Divinity is free from other equal or superior power, is Īśvara, and He is the Special Puruṣa.[2]

तत्र निरतिशयं सर्वज्ञबीजम् ॥ २५ ॥*

There the omniscient-seed is unsurpassed—25.

किं च? तत्र निरतिशयं सर्वज्ञबीजम् । यदिदमतीतानागतप्रत्युत्पन्नप्रत्येकसमुच्चयातीन्द्रियग्रहणमल्पं बह्विति सर्वज्ञबीजमेतद्विवर्द्धमानं यत्र निरतिशयं स सर्वज्ञः । अस्ति काष्ठाप्राप्तिः सर्वज्ञबीजस्य सातिशयत्वात्परिमाणवदिति । यत्र काष्ठाप्राप्तिर्ज्ञानस्य स सर्वज्ञः स च पुरुषविशेष इति । सामान्यमात्रोपसंहारे च कृतोपक्षयमनुमानं न विशेषप्रतिपत्तौ समर्थमिति । तस्य संज्ञादिविशेषप्रतिपत्तिरागमतः पर्यन्वेष्या । तस्यात्मानुग्रहाभावेपि भूतानुग्रहः प्रयोजनम्, ज्ञानधर्मोपदेशेन कल्पप्रलयमहाप्रलयेषु संसारिणः पुरुषानुद्धरिष्यामीति । तथा चोक्तम् । आदिविद्वान्निर्माणचित्तमधिष्ठाय कारुण्याद्भगवान्परमर्षिरासुरये जिज्ञासमानाय तन्त्रं प्रोवाचेति ॥ २५ ॥

What more? There (in Him) the omniscient-seed is unsurpassed. The smaller or larger super-sensuous perception of the single or of the collective regarding the past, the future and the present, is the omniscient-seed[3]. He in whom this being expanded becomes unsurpassed, is the omniscient. The omniscient-seed has its highest culmination due to its greatest expansion as in the case of dimension[4]. (Again) He in Whom there is the highest culmination of knowledge, is the Omniscient and He is the Special Puruṣa. Further Inference is of service only for establishing general ideas; it is not able to establish the specific nature of a thing. The particular knowledge of His name, etc., is to be investigated from the Vedas[5]. Although He has no interest of His own, yet He has the necessity of conferring benefit upon the creatures—"I shall libe-

---

1. Īśvara is absolute, simply His Essence known as His Power is correlated with the Vedas: which are the highest authority. As for example, our bodily strength may be increased by proper physical exercise, or may be decreased by illness; but we remain the same in existence. Similar is the case with Īśvara. By disobeying the laws of the Vedas and by not performing the Vedic rites, we cannot realise the special manifestation of His power; and that becomes the cause of degradation of the world (*B.G.* XV-1). The world may increase or decrease, i.e., the Vedic authority may be in force or not, but He remains the same.

2. People may ask if Īśvara is Omnipotent, can He create another Īśvara equal to Him? In reply to this question we can say that a person can be the whole and sole proprietor of his property only when he has neither any co-sharer nor any higher holder of that thing.

*. This aphorism denotes the *Jñānam* (Pure Con-science) of the Vedānta.

3. This defines the seed.

4. It denotes the possession of the seed of omniscience relating to Īśvara.

5. It has been explained in the preceding aphorism that the Power of Īśvara has different manifestations according to their distinctive functions and so also takes different names such as Brahmā (with attribute), Viṣṇu, Devī; they are the gods known as the presiding officers of the created universe. The words "particular knowledge of His names" signify that each god has his distinctive power and function. So we are instructed to find them out from the Vedas, i. e., we can fulfil all our interests whether worldly prosperity or liberation by propitiating those respective deities only by the obedience to the Vedic laws and nothing else.

rate the worldly Puruṣas by the instruction of knowledge and virtue throughout the creations (*kalpas*), the periodical dissolutions (*pralaya*) and great dissolutions (*mahā-pralaya*) of the world." So it has been said— The first wise Being, the all-powerful, the Great Sage, assumed a created mind and out of compassion taught the Science to the questioning Āsuri[1].

स एष पूर्वेषामपि गुरुः कालेनानवच्छेदात्
॥ २६ ॥*

He is also the Preceptor of all the ancient teachers on account of His not being limited by time—26.

स एष पूर्वेषामपि गुरुः कालेनानवच्छेदात् । पूर्वे हि गुरवः कालेनावच्छिद्यन्ते यत्रावच्छेदार्थेन कालो नोपावर्तते स एषः पूर्वेषामपि गुरुः । यथास्य सर्गस्यादौ प्रकर्षगत्या सिद्धस्तथातिक्रान्तसर्गादिष्वपि प्रत्येतव्यः ॥ २६ ॥

All the ancient teachers are, indeed, limited by time[2]. It is He whom time cannot reach as an object of limitation. As the fact that He is the Preceptor even of all the ancient teachers is established by the Highest Authority (the *Vedas*) in the beginning of this creation, so the same fact must be understood in regard to the past creations also[3].

तस्य वाचकः प्रणवः ॥ २७ ॥**

The Praṇava (the one syllabic word) is Connotative of Him—27.

तस्य वाचकः प्रणवः । वाच्य ईश्वरः प्रणवस्य । किमस्य संकेतकृतं वाच्यवाचकत्वमथ प्रदीपप्रकाशवदवस्थितमिति? स्थितोऽस्य वाच्यस्य वाचकेन सह संबन्धः । संकेतस्त्वीश्वरस्य स्थितमेवार्थमभिनयति । यथावस्थितः पितापुत्रयोः संबन्धः संकेतेनावद्योत्यते अयमस्य पिता, अयमस्य पुत्र इति । सर्गान्तरेष्वपि वाच्यवाचकशक्त्यपेक्षस्तथैव संकेतः क्रियते ॥ २७ ॥

Īśvara is Connoted by the (Connotative) Praṇava (*Aum*). Now is the relation between the connoted and the connotative conventional or inherent like the lamp and the light? The relation of the connoted (*Īśvara*) is inherent in the connotative (*Aum*). The convention again, exhibits only the inherent truth of Īśvara[4]. As the inherent relation between the father and the son is expressed by the convention alone,—this is the father, this is the son; in different creations also the similar convention alone, depending upon the power of the connoted and the connotative, is applied.

तज्जपस्तदर्थभावनम् ॥ २८ ॥

Its repetition and the development of its truth—28.

संप्रतिपत्तिनित्यतया नित्यः शब्दार्थसंबन्ध इत्यागमिनः प्रतिजानते । विज्ञातवाच्यवाचकत्वस्य योगिनः तज्जपस्तदर्थभावनम् । प्रणवस्य जपः प्रणवाभिधेयस्य चेश्वरस्य भावनम् । तदस्य योगिनः प्रणवं जपतः प्रणवार्थं च भावयतश्चित्तमेकाग्रं संपद्यते । तथा चोक्तम्—

स्वाध्यायाद्योगमासीत योगात्स्वाध्यायमामनेत् ।
स्वाध्याययोगसंपत्त्या परमात्मा प्रकाशते ॥
इति ॥ २८ ॥

As the Perfect Knowledge is eternal, the Vedic teachers assert that the relation between word and its meaning is eternal. In the case of the Yogi to whom the relation between the Connoted and the Connotative is known, its repetition and

1. We are to note the significance of the expression "questioning Āsuri". It denotes that the Spiritual Science is a hidden treasure; it should not be divulged to the vulgar people by means of lectures from a public platform. It should be communicated to those only who are really willing to know. Further, "He assumed a created mind" signifies that knowledge is not always in manifested condition in Him.

* This aphorism denotes *Anantam* (Eternity) of the Vedānta.

2. It denotes the unchangeability of the Divinity of Īśvara even in spite of the changes of Creators in different creations.

3. The relation is inherent with reference to the Absolute (*Nirguṇa*) aspect of Īśvara, i.e., without any relation to the manifestation of the Self-expressive Principle (or Power).

* This aphorism denotes "Brahma" of the Vedānta.

4. It is conventional with reference to the relative, (*Saguṇa*) aspect. i.e., keeping relation with the phenomenal creation. As for example, the son exists in the father with reference to the primitive state of the former; but when he is born, no body can know the relation between them without convention. Hence the *Praṇava* (the one syllabic word) keeps both the relations and does not change even by the changes of creations.

the gradual development of its Truth, i.e., the repetition of Praṇava (*Aum*) and the Revelation of Īśvara connoted by Praṇava, are sure to follow[1]. The mind of the Yogi, who repeats the Praṇava and reveals its truth, is made one-pointed. So it has been said:—By study, Yoga is developed; by Yoga the study is confirmed; and the Highest- Self is revealed by the combined power of the study and Yoga[2].

ततः प्रत्यक्चेतनाधिगमोऽप्यन्तरायाभावश्च ॥ २९ ॥

Therefrom the attainment of the inner soul and also the absence of impediments—29.

किं चास्य भवति? ततः प्रत्यक्चेतनाधिगमोऽप्यन्तरायाभावश्च। ये तावदन्तराया व्याधिप्रभृतयस्ते तावदीश्वरप्रणिधानान्न भवन्ति स्वरूपदर्शनमप्यस्य भवति यथैवेश्वरः पुरुषः शुद्धः प्रसन्नः केवलोऽनुपसर्गस्तथायमपि बुद्धेः प्रतिसंवेदी यः पुरुषस्तमधिगच्छति ॥ २९ ॥

What more happens to him? Therefrom, the attainment of the inner soul and also the absence of impediments. Whatever impediments there may be such as disease etc., cease to exist from the profound meditation upon Īśvara and he gets also the sight of his own Real Self. Just as Īśvara is the Puruṣa pure, absolute and devoid of attributes, so also the Yogi understands his inner Puruṣa who is the reflective perceiver of the intellect[3].

व्याधिस्त्यानसंशयप्रमादालस्याविरतिभ्रान्तिदर्शनालब्धभूमिकत्वानवस्थितत्वानि चित्तविक्षेपास्तेऽन्तरायाः ॥ ३० ॥

Disease, Debility, Doubt, Inadvertence, Sloth, Sensuality, Wrong Understanding, Non-attainment of the plane and Instability,—these mental distractions are the impediments—30.

अथ केऽन्तराया ये चित्तस्य विक्षेपाः? पुनस्ते कियन्तो वेति? व्याधिस्त्यानसंशयप्रमादालस्याविरतिभ्रान्तिदर्शनालब्धभूमिकत्वानवस्थितत्वानि चित्तविक्षेपास्तेऽन्तरायाः। नवान्तरायाश्चित्तस्य विक्षेपाः। सहैते चित्तवृत्तिभिर्भवन्ति। एतेषामभावे न भवन्ति। पूर्वोक्ताश्चित्तवृत्तयः। तत्र व्याधिर्धातुरसकरणवैषम्यम्। स्त्यानमकर्मण्यता चित्तस्य। संशय उभयकोटिस्पृग्विज्ञानं स्यादिदमेवं नैवं स्यादिति। प्रमादः समाधिसाधनानामभावनम्। आलस्यं कायस्य चित्तस्य च गुरुत्वादप्रवृत्तिः। अविरतिश्चित्तस्य विषयसंप्रयोगात्मा गर्द्धः। भ्रान्तिदर्शनं विपर्ययज्ञानम्। अलब्धभूमिकत्वं समाधिभूमेरलाभः। अनवस्थितत्वं यल्लब्धायां भूमौ चित्तस्याप्रतिष्ठा। समाधिप्रतिलम्भे हि सति तदवस्थितं स्यादिति। एते चित्तविक्षेपा नव योगमला योगप्रतिपक्षा योगान्तराया इत्यभिधीयन्ते ॥ ३० ॥

Now what are the impediments that are the distractions of the mind? Or again how many are they? Disease, debility, doubt, inadvertence, sloth, sensuality, wrong understanding, non-attainment of the plane and instability,—these mental distractions are the impediments. These nine impediments are the mental distractions. They arise with the mental operations. In the absence of these (mental operations), they (the impediments) cannot arise. The mental operations have

1. The significance of this aphorism is identical with that of the Seventeenth aphorism in this chapter. It means that the simple utterance of Mantras by a so-called devotee with a rosary in hand cannot reveal the genuine nature of Truth to him; but a good deal of learning of the science is required for success in this matter, because this 'repetition' is possible for him only who knows the relation between the Connoted and the Connotative. The Praṇava has four steps :—(1) The Waking state (*Jāgrat*) means the gross and the subtle appearances (*sthūla* and *sūkṣma*); (2) the dreaming state (*svapna*) signifies the instrumental phenomenon (*karaṇa grāhya*) (3) the sleeping state (*suṣupti*) denotes the subjective phenomenon (*Ahaṁgrāhya*); and (4) the fourth is the highest subjective or the Eternal state (*turīyātīta*). Hence it is proved that the process of the revelation of the Truth signified by Praṇava is the gross, the subtle, the instrumental and the subjective appearances successively as have been described in the aphorism 17 (vide the *Praśnopaniṣad* question—5).

2. By this it is obvious that Yoga cannot be effected without the help of study; so here the term "repetition" refers to study alone which signifies the systematic Vedic culture together with the process of advancement in the ladder of Spiritualism. Hence it is evident that to think over and over again upon the Laws of the Scriptures and to work in accordance with those laws are the only means of attaining the Supreme Goal.

3. The Yogi who proceeds in the path of Emancipation by means of the external support, gets the same result as that achieved by a Yogi who depends upon his own power for his success; or to be more explicit, they both have the revelation of the Inner Soul.

been previously described. There, disease is the inequality of the humours, the constituent fluid and the sense organs. Debility is the inertness of the mind. Doubt is the knowledge touching both ends whether it may be thus, or may not be thus. Inadvertence is the want of investigation about the means of Spiritual-Absorption. Sloth is the absence of exertion of the mind and body on account of heaviness. Sensuality is the greediness of the mind for sense-enjoyments. Wrong understanding is the perversive knowledge. Non-attainment of the plane is the failure to attain the state of Spiritual-Absorption. Instability is that which is unfixity of the mind on the attained plane; because it becomes confirmed only on the acquisition of the (Subjective manifestation of the) Spiritual Absorption. These mental distractions are called the nine impurities of Yoga, the enemies of Yoga, the impediments of Yoga.

दुःखदौर्मनस्याङ्गमेजयत्वश्वासप्रश्वासा विक्षेपसहभुवः ॥ ३१ ॥

Pain, dejection, unsteadiness of limbs, inspiration and expiration are the companions of the distractions—31.

दुःखदौर्मनस्याङ्गमेजयत्वश्वासप्रश्वासा विक्षेपसहभुवः । दुःखमाध्यात्मिकमाधिभौतिकमाधिदैविकं च । येनाभिहताः प्राणिनस्तदुपघाताय प्रयतन्ते तद्दुःखम् । दौर्मनस्यमिच्छाविघाताच्चेतसः क्षोभः । यदङ्गान्येजयति कम्पयति तदङ्गमेजयत्वम् । प्राणो यद् बाह्यं वायुमाचामति स श्वासः । यत्कौष्ठ्यं वायुं निःसारयति स प्रश्वासः । एते विक्षेपसहभुवः, विक्षिप्तचित्तस्यैते भवन्ति । समाहितचित्तस्यैते न भवन्ति ॥ ३१ ॥

The suffering,—pertaining to body and mind, caused by the created beings, or inflicted by the supernatural powers,—being injured by which living beings try to do away with it, is pain. Dejection is the disturbance of the mind owing to the non-fulfilment of desire. That which shakes, i.e., moves the limbs, is the unsteadiness thereof. The breath which draws in the external air, is inspiration and that which throws out the internal air, is expiration. These are the companions of the distractions. They arise in the distracted mind. They do not arise in the case of him who is Spiritually Absorbed.[1]

तत्प्रतिषेधार्थमेकतत्त्वाभ्यासः ॥ ३२ ॥

For their Prevention, the practice of one truth—32

अथैते विक्षेपाः समाधिप्रतिपक्षास्ताभ्यामेवाभ्यासवैराग्याभ्यां निरोद्धव्याः । तत्राभ्यासस्य विषयमुपसंहरन्निदमाह — तत्प्रतिषेधार्थमेकतत्त्वाभ्यासः । विक्षेपप्रतिषेधार्थमेकतत्त्वावलम्बनं चित्तमभ्यसेत् । यस्य तु प्रत्यर्थनियतं प्रत्ययमात्रं क्षणिकं च चित्तं तस्य सर्वमेव चित्तमेकाग्रं, नास्त्येव विक्षिप्तम् । यदि पुनरिदं सर्वतः प्रत्याहृत्यैकस्मिन्नर्थे समाधीयते तदा भवत्येकाग्रमित्यतो न प्रत्यर्थनियतम् ।

Now these distractions, the opponents of Spiritual-Absorption are to be restrained simply by these two means,—practice and non-attachment. There he (the author), in concluding the subject of practice, says—for their prevention, the practice of one truth. For the prevention of the distractions, let (the Yogi) habituate his mind to be dependent upon one truth. However, in the case of him who asserts that the mind is fixed to every object and is a mere conception and momentary, then all his mind is one-pointed only, there would be no distracted mind at all. If on the other

1. Many of us have a wrong idea about the spiritual Absorption. They think it to be breath-control only and nothing else. In fact, breath-control may be a preliminary help for the concentration of the mind but it is not by itself the Spiritual Absorption (*YS* II 49-52). We may not judge of the mental state of a man but can easily interpret his bodily signs. It is clear from this commentary that he who has control over his mind, must have steady limbs, i.e., the steady posture, and must have his breath confined within the nostrils for all time (vide *B.G.* V—27).

By the standard of this commentary, let us judge the bodily signs of the modern Yogis or of the wise who are advertised to be the liberated souls by the help of innumerable disciples and various press-notes. Can a single sign even be found in them that are given to the enjoyments of luxury on a pose of renunciation? Many people think Yoga to be something different from Jñāna (knowledge) and they assume the airs of a Jñāni (wise). But the fact is that there can be no separate manifestation of Jñāna without Yoga.

hand, it being drawn away from all sides, is concentrated on one object, then it becomes one-pointed; hence it (the mind) is not fixed to every object.

योऽपि सदृशप्रत्ययप्रवाहेन चित्तमेकाग्रं मन्यते तस्यैकाग्रता यदि प्रवाहचित्तस्य धर्मस्तदेकं नास्ति प्रवाहचित्तं क्षणिकत्वात् । अथ प्रवाहांशस्यैव प्रत्ययस्य धर्मः स सर्वः सदृशप्रत्ययप्रवाही वा विसदृशप्रत्ययप्रवाही वा प्रत्यर्थनियतत्वादेकाग्र एवेति विक्षिप्तचित्तानुपपत्तिः । तस्मादेकमनेकार्थमवस्थितं चित्तमिति ।

Again in the case of him who thinks the mind to be one-pointed by a similar flow of ideas[1],—if his one-pointedness be the characteristic of the flowing mind, that cannot be one owing to the momentariness of the flowing mind. If again it be the characteristic of the notion which is a portion of the flow, then all that whether flowing on similar notion or flowing on dissimilar notion will be always one-pointed on account of the fixity of the mind in every object; so there is no room for a distracted mind. Therefore the mind is one, possessed of many objects and constant.

यदि च चित्तेनैकेनानन्विताः स्वभावभिन्नाः प्रत्यया जायेरन्नथ कथमन्यप्रत्ययदृष्टस्यान्यः स्मर्ता भवेत् ? अन्यप्रत्ययोपचितस्य च कर्माशयस्यान्यः प्रत्युपभोक्ता भवेत् ? कथंचित्समाधीयमानमप्येतद् गोमयपायसीयन्यायमाक्षिपति । किं च, स्वात्मानुभवापह्नवश्चित्तस्यान्यत्वे प्राप्नोति । कथं यदहमद्राक्षं तत्स्पृशामि यच्चास्प्राक्षं तत्पश्याम्यहमितिप्रत्ययः सर्वस्य प्रत्ययस्य भेदे सति प्रत्ययिन्यभेदेनोपस्थितः? एकप्रत्ययिविषयोऽयमभेदात्मा अहमिति प्रत्ययः । कथमत्यन्तभिन्नेषु चित्तेषु वर्तमानं सामान्यमेकं प्रत्ययिनमाश्रयेत् ? स्वानुभवग्राह्यश्चायमभेदात्मा अहमितिप्रत्ययः । न च प्रत्यक्षस्य माहात्म्यं प्रमाणान्तरेणाभिभूयते । प्रमाणान्तरं च प्रत्यक्षबलेनैव व्यवहारं लभते । तस्मादेकमनेकार्थमवस्थितं च चित्तम् ॥ ३२ ॥

If however the cognitions, unconnected with one mind and separate by nature, are born, how then can one be the rememberer of the cognition experienced by another ? How can one be the consequent enjoyer of the vehicle of action accumulated by another cognition ? If anyhow it be solved, it illustrates the logic of "Cow-dung and milk".[2] Moreover, on the variousness of the mind, the negation of one's own self-experience comes in. On the variousness of such cognitions as—what I saw, I touch; what I touched, I see—how can the cognition "I" remain identical in the cogniser ? The cognition "I" which is of identical nature, is the sphere of a single cogniser. In the case of the entirely different minds, how can it (the cognition) exist in one common constant cogniser ? Further this cognition "I" which is of the identical nature, is to be grasped by one's own perception. Moreover, the power of perception can never be defeated by any other means of real cognition. Other means of real cognition, however, get their functions by the strength of perception alone. Therefore the mind is one, possessed of many objects and constant.

मैत्रीकरुणामुदितोपेक्षाणां सुखदुःखपुण्यापुण्यविषयाणां भावनातश्चित्तप्रसादनम् ॥ ३३ ॥

The transparency of the mind comes from the development of friendship, compassion, joy and neutrality regarding the spheres of pleasure, pain, virtue and vice respectively—33

यस्य चित्तस्यावस्थितस्येदं शास्त्रेण परिकर्म निर्दिश्यते तत्कथम् ? मैत्रीकरुणामुदितोपेक्षाणां सुखदुःखपुण्यापुण्यविषयाणां भावनातश्चित्तप्रसादनम् । तत्र सर्वप्राणिषु सुखसंभोगापन्नेषु मैत्रीं भावयेत्, दुःखितेषु करुणाम्, पुण्यात्मकेषु मुदिताम्,

1. This is also the opinion of many so-called philosophers who consider that to think over the meaning of the Mahāvākyas alone, viz. *Aham Brahmāsmi* (I am Brahma) etc. is the one-pointedness of the mind. From the commentary it is clear that they have no correct ideas about the subject-matter of the Vedānta Darśana. Moreover, the mental firmness and pleasure which they enjoy, are but born of the inert-Energy (*tāmasika*, vide the *Gītā* Chapter XVIII verses 35, 39).

2. By this the commentator refutes the manifoldness of the mind, i.e., the theory of momentary conception. He illustrates by the fallacy of logic that "milk is derived from the cow", "the cow-dung also is derived from the cow ; therefore the cow-dung is equal to milk." Such will be the fate of those that try to solve the theory of momentary conception by manifoldness of the mind.

अपुण्यशीलेषूपेक्षाम्। एवमस्य भावयतः शुक्लो धर्म उपजायते। ततश्च चित्तं प्रसीदति। प्रसन्नमेकाग्रं स्थितिपदं लभते ॥ ३३ ॥

How is this embellishment of the constantmind prescribed by this Science? The transparency of the mind comes from the development of friendship, compassion, joy and neutrality regarding the spheres of pleasure, pain, virtue and vice respectively. There, the Yogi should cultivate (the feeling of) friendship towards all living beings engaged in the enjoyment of pleasure,—compassion towards the sufferers,—joy towards the virtuous and neutrality towards the vicious. Thus the white characteristic comes to the Yogi who is given to such culture. Further, the mind becomes transparent therefrom; the transparent mind becomes one-pointed and thence attains the position of steadiness.[1]

प्रच्छर्दनविधारणाभ्यां वा प्राणस्य ॥ ३४ ॥

Or from the expulsion or retention of breath—34

प्रच्छर्दनविधारणाभ्यां वा प्राणस्य। कौष्ठ्यस्य वायोर्नासिकापुटाभ्यां प्रयत्नविशेषाद्वमनं प्रच्छर्दनं विधारणं प्राणायामस्ताभ्यां वा मनसः स्थितिं संपादयेत् ॥ ३४ ॥

The expulsion is to throw out the air of the lungs through the nostrils by special effort. Retention is the breath-control (*prāṇāyāma*). The Yogi should achieve the steadiness of the mind by these as an optional measure.[2]

विषयवती वा प्रवृत्तिरुत्पन्ना मनसः स्थितिनिबन्धिनी* ॥ ३५ ॥

And the sense-objective manifestation being produced becomes the cause of steadiness of the mind—35

विषयवती वा प्रवृत्तिरुत्पन्ना मनसः स्थितिनिबन्धिनी। नासिकाग्रे धारयतोऽस्य या दिव्यगन्धसंवित्सा गन्धप्रवृत्तिः। जिह्वाग्रे रससंवित्। तालुनि रूपसंवित्। जिह्वामध्ये स्पर्शसंवित्। जिह्वामूले शब्दसंविदित्येताः प्रवृत्तय उत्पन्नाश्चित्तं स्थितौ निबध्नन्ति, संशयं विधमन्ति, समाधिप्रज्ञायां च द्वारीभवन्तीति।

एतेन चन्द्रादित्यग्रहमणिप्रदीपरश्म्यादिषु प्रवृत्तिरुत्पन्ना विषयवत्येव वेदितव्या।

यद्यपि हि तत्तच्छास्त्रानुमानाचार्योपदेशैरवगतमर्थतत्त्वं सद्भूतमेव भवति, एतेषां यथाभूतार्थप्रतिपादनसामर्थ्यात्तथापि यावदेकदेशोऽपि कश्चिन्न स्वकरणसंवेद्यो भवति तावत्सर्वं परोक्षमिवापवर्गादिषु सूक्ष्मेष्वर्थेषु न दृढां बुद्धिमुत्पादयति। तस्माच्छास्त्रानुमानाचार्योपदेशोपोद्बलनार्थमेवावश्यं कश्चिदर्थविशेषः प्रत्यक्षीकर्तव्यः। तत्र तदुपदिष्टार्थैकदेशप्रत्यक्षत्वे सति सर्वं सूक्ष्मविषयमपि आ अपवर्गाच्छ्रद्धीयते। एतदर्थमेवेदं चित्तपरिकर्म निर्दिश्यते। अनियतासु वृत्तिषु तद्विषयायां वशीकारसंज्ञायामुपजातायां समर्थं स्यात्तस्य तस्यार्थस्य प्रत्यक्षीकरणायेति। तथा च सति श्रद्धावीर्यस्मृतिसमाधयोऽस्याप्रतिबन्धेन भविष्यन्तीति ॥ ३५ ॥

The faculty of the supernatural smell, which comes to the Yogi who concentrates his mind upon the fore-part of the nose, is the smell manifestation. The faculty of taste on the fore-part of the tongue,—the faculty of colour upon the palate,—the faculty of touch in the middle of the tongue and the faculty of sound at the root of the tongue,—these manifestations being produced fasten the mind to steadiness, destroy doubts and become the portals of Spiritual-Absorbent Cognition.

By this, the manifestation in the lights of the moon, the sun, the planet, the

1. Without cultivating these helping qualities, nobody can acquire knowledge. Mere knowledge of books and apparent self-surrender to God (*Śaraṇāgati*) cannot save a man from the cycle of rebirth.

2. This aphorism has no separate significance from that of the process described in the second chapter; because there the commentator quotes this aphorism in support of aphorism 53. Hence it is certain that this breath-control (*prāṇāyāma*) itself is not the goal known as the Spiritual-Absorption, but is an alternative method of mental purification for obtaining the said four good qualities such as Friendship, etc.

* The teaching of this aphorism should not be regarded as an alternative means for the purification of the mind, because the aphorism has not been put in the fifth case-ending like other aphorisms signifying alternative means. Hence this teaching is compulsory for all.

jewel, the lamp, etc., is to be understood as sense objective.[1]

Although the respective realities of things learnt through the instruction of Science, inference and teachers,—are in fact really existent on account of their powers of establishing the respective truths, yet so long as even a single portion does not become cognizable by one's own sense, all that remains as if vague; they cannot produce firm belief in the subtle objects such as Emancipation, etc. Therefore in order to confirm the instruction of the Science, inference and teacher,[2] at least some distinguishing quality of the Substance must be experienced. There through the experiment of some portion of the Substance taught by them, the subtle portion including Emancipation is also paid full attention to.[3] For this reason the mental embellishment has been prescribed. When the conscious power of full control over the unrestrained (mental) operations with regard to its sphere of functions is produced, then the mind is able to positively observe those respective truths. Such being the case, faith, courage, retentive power, Spiritual-Absorption and Intellective-Vision come to him without any obstacle.

विशोका वा ज्योतिष्मती ॥ ३६ ॥

And, the appearance of the painless and effulgent state—36

विशोका वा ज्योतिष्मती । प्रवृत्तिरुत्पन्ना मनसः स्थितिनिबन्धिन्यनुवर्तते । हृदयपुण्डरीके धारयतो या बुद्धिसंविद् बुद्धिसत्त्वं हि भास्वरमाकाशकल्पं तत्र स्थितिवैशारद्यात्प्रवृत्तिः सूर्येन्दुग्रहमणिप्रभारूपाकारेण विकल्पते । तथास्मितायां समापन्नं चित्तं निस्तरङ्ग-महोदधिकल्पं शान्तमनन्तमस्मितामात्रं भवति । यत्रेदमुक्तम्—'तमणुमात्रमात्मानमनुविद्यास्मीति एवं तावत्संप्रतिजानीत इति ।'

एषा द्वयी विशोका विषयवती अस्मितामात्रा च प्रवृत्तिर्ज्योतिष्मतीत्युच्यते यया योगिनश्चित्तं स्थितिपदं लभत इति ॥ ३६ ॥

(The preceding aphorism)—"the sense-objective manifestation being produced becomes the cause of the steadiness of the mind", being read with (this aphorism) "And the appearance of the painless and effulgent state", completes the sense. The intellectual understanding[4] of the Yogi who concentrates upon the lotus of the heart, is indeed the Intellective Essence luminous like the sky. Due to the mind being well established there (in that Essence), the manifestation is supposed to be in the form of the light of the sun, the moon, the planets and the jewels. In the same way, the mind being transformed into Egoism becomes purely Egoistic, calm and infinite like the waveless ocean. There (in this connection) it has been said:—The Yogi recognizing

1. Here the commentator is speaking of the Yoga-light which first comes to the Yogi when he penetrates through the gross mental-grasp. There is nothing in this phenomenal world, which can be compared to that light. It appears in the shape of enjoyable manifestation within the reach of his mental grasp. In this case, the Yogi acquires his Intellective Vision, that is to say, his third eye becomes open, which enables him to take this light.

2. A gunner can hit his aim only through the adoption of these three points—the back-sight, the fore-sight and the target being in the same line. Similarly the union of these three—the Science, one's own mind and the instruction of the teacher—is the cause of proper success. Further the term "Science" being placed in the first place, refers to the Vedic Scriptures and signifies their Highest Authority. The want of this culture is the cause of our present degradation. Neither the selfish teachers, whose only aim is to gratify their own senses, teach the full science systematically, nor do the sluggish students who wish to procure God by their foul money and want to know the Spiritual Science in sum and substance, i.e., the Rāmāyaṇa in one verse, the Gītā in five verses,—apply proper effort for the purpose; nor is there any Science which is not corrupted by the sectarians by the misinterpretation of the texts and by the representation of their partial views. How can we hope for solid success?

3. The commentator has already explained the Spiritual Absorption to be of two descriptions. The first portion of it termed the "Cognitive Spiritual Absorption" must be enjoyed as the sense-objective manifestation. This is the distinguishing feature, i.e., the material portion of the Existing Reality which is known as the Substance. And the subtle portion of the Spiritual-Absorption is Ultra-Cognitive and is called the Spiritual Freedom which is the subject of the Vedānta Darśana.

4. The gross mental grasp, the subtle, the instrumental and the subjective manifestations as have been described in I 17.

that simple atomic Self[1] thus fully understands the manifestation as "I am all".

This two-fold manifestation,—the painless sense-objective and the purely Egoistic, is called the effulgent (state) by which the Yogi's mind attains the position of steadiness.

वीतरागविषयं वा चित्तम् ॥ ३७ ॥

And the mind becomes possessed of the sphere of complete disappearance of attachment—37

वीतरागविषयं वा चित्तम् । वीतरागचित्तालम्बनोपरक्तं वा योगिनश्चित्तं स्थितिपदं लभत इति ॥ ३७ ॥

And the Yogi's mind being coloured by the grasp of the thought of complete disappearance of attachment, attains the position of steadiness.[2]

स्वप्ननिद्राज्ञानालम्बनं वा* ॥ ३८ ॥

And the grasp of the knowledge of dream and of sleep—38

स्वप्ननिद्राज्ञानालम्बनं वा । स्वप्नज्ञानालम्बनं वा निद्राज्ञानालम्बनं वा तदाकारं योगिनश्चित्तं स्थितिपदं लभत इति ॥ ३८ ॥

The Yogi's mind having the grasp of the knowledge of dream and having the grasp of the knowledge of sleep, becomes possessed of those forms and attains the position of steadiness.

यथाभिमतध्यानाद्वा ॥ ३९ ॥

Or from meditation upon one's own choice—39

यथाभिमतध्यानाद्वा । यदेवाभिमतं तदेव ध्यायेत् । तत्र लब्धस्थितिकमन्यत्रापि स्थितिपदं लभत इति ॥३९ ॥

The Yogi should meditate upon whatever may be his choice. The mind, attaining steadiness there, attains the position of steadiness in other places also.

परमाणुपरममहत्त्वान्तोऽस्य वशीकारः ॥४०॥

The control over the extremity of the smallest minuteness and of the highest expansiveness comes to him.—40.

परमाणुपरममहत्त्वान्तोऽस्य वशीकारः । सूक्ष्मे निविशमानस्य परात्परमाण्वन्तं स्थितिपदं लभत इति । स्थूले निविशमानस्य परममहत्त्वान्तं स्थितिपदं चित्तस्य । एवं तामुभयीं कोटिमनुधावतो

---

1. There are some who think that the Nyāya-Śāstra (logic) is contradictory to the Vedānta Darśana on account of their differences in their theories. According to the theory of the Nyāya the Atom (*aṇu*) is Eternal (*Nitya*); but the theory of the Vedānta holds that Bhūma (*Brahma*) is Eternal (*Nitya*). An intelligent science-student can easily understand the process and its truth how the atomic gaseous form of water is all-pervading and most powerful of all its states whether solid or liquid and how the light of Ultra-X-Rays holds power greater than any other light. It is well known that the more subtle a thing is, the more powerful and expansive it becomes.

2. There is no term in the commentary to signify that the Yogi should concentrate his mind on, or should fix it to, something. On the other hand, we find that the mind becomes automatically transformed into and coloured by this kind of support. Further, the term "mind" has not been used in the fifth case-ending. Hence it is obvious that this aphorism does not signify an alternative means but is in the context of the mental embellishment termed "the sense-objective manifestation". An ordinary person identifies himself with his external body from toe to head. But when the Yogī reaches the third and the fourth steps of the Spiritual-Absorbent-Cognition known as the instrumental and the subjective manifestations, he sees his existence quite separate from his body. In other words, he always sees himself fully unattached to the body. This is called the thought of complete disappearance of attachment.

*This aphorism also has not been used in the fifth case-ending, so it does not keep any connection with alternative means. On the other hand, this has been put in the first case; so it is clear that the term "mind" should be drawn from the preceding aphorism. The commentary also denotes the same idea. It has already been established in the tenth aphorism that sleep is a particular kind of cognition of the exhibitive mental operations and it must be restrained like all other operations.

An ordinary man enjoys these three states,—the waking, the dreaming and the sleeping successively. But the Yogī enjoys these states in waking condition alone. In other words, the dreaming and the sleeping states become the object of his direct perception; he crosses over these states one after another. These are the same instrumental and subjective manifestations of the Spiritual-Absorbent-Cognition; so the Yogī becomes the seer of all the states and gradually reaches the superconscious state, the Ultra-Cognitive-Spiritual-Absorption. The same four divisions of the Cognitive-Spiritual-Absorption have been described and will also be described later on in different contexts by different names and by different modes.

योऽस्याप्रतीघातः स परो वशीकारस्तद्वशीकारात्परिपूर्णं योगिनश्चित्तं न पुनरभ्यासकृतं परिकर्मापेक्षत इति ॥ ४० ॥

The (Yogi's) mind, entering into the subtle, attains the position of steadiness into the last extremity of the minutest of minutes. When entering into the gross, the position of steadiness into the last extremity of the highest expansiveness comes to his mind. Thus this irresistible power following both these extremities, is the highest control. The Yogi's mind entirely full of that control, does not depend any more upon other embellishments produced by practice.

क्षीणवृत्तेरभिजातस्येव मणेर्ग्रहीतृग्रहणग्राह्येषु तत्स्थतदञ्जनतासमापत्तिः ॥ ४१ ॥

The transformation of the mind whose (exhibitive) operations have been destroyed, assumes like a high class crystal, the colour of that on which it rests in relation to the receiver, the receiving instrument and the receivable object.—41.

अथ लब्धस्थितिकस्य चेतसः किंस्वरूपा किंविषया वा समापत्तिरिति ? तदुच्यते क्षीणवृत्तेरभिजातस्येव मणेर्ग्रहीतृग्रहणग्राह्येषु तत्स्थतदञ्जनतासमापत्तिः । क्षीणवृत्तेरिति प्रत्यस्तमितप्रत्ययस्येत्यर्थः । अभिजातस्येव मणेरिति दृष्टान्तोपादानम् । यथा स्फटिक उपाश्रयभेदात्तत्तद्रूपोपरक्त उपाश्रयरूपाकारेण निर्भासते तथा ग्राह्यालम्बनोपरक्तं चित्तं ग्राह्यसमापन्नं ग्राह्यस्वरूपाकारेण निर्भासते । तथा भूतसूक्ष्मोपरक्तं भूतसूक्ष्मसमापन्नं भूतसूक्ष्मस्वरूपाभासं भवति ।

What is the character and what is the sphere of the operative transformation of the mind which has obtained rest ? That is now being described. The transformation of the mind whose operations have been destroyed, assumes like a high class crystal the colour of that on which it rests in relation to the receiver, the receiving instrument and the receivable object. "The mind, whose operations have been destroyed" means "the mind whose (exhibitive) cognitions have been subjugated". "Like a high class crystal" is the acceptation of an example. As a high class crystal due to its contiguity to various objects, being coloured by that respective hue, shines in the form of that proximate support; so also the mind coloured by the receivable support, being transformed into that, shines with the form of the manifestation of the receivable object.[1] Similarly coloured by the subtle element, it being transformed into that, gets manifested in the form of the manifestation of the subtle element (b).

तथा स्थूलालम्बनोपरक्तं स्थूलरूपसमापन्नं स्थूलरूपाभासं भवति । तथा विश्वभेदोपरक्तं विश्वभेदसमापन्नं विश्वरूपाभासं भवति ।

Similarly coloured by the gross element it being transformed into that, gets manifested in the form of the manifestation of the gross element (a). Similarly coloured by the universal difference, it being transformed into that, gets manifested into the manifestation of the universal form (c).

तथा ग्रहणेष्वपीन्द्रियेष्वपि द्रष्टव्यम् । ग्रहणालम्बनोपरक्तं ग्रहणसमापन्नं ग्रहणस्वरूपाकारेण निर्भासते । तथा ग्रहीतृपुरुषालम्बनोपरक्तं ग्रहीतृपुरुषसमापन्नं ग्रहीतृपुरुषस्वरूपाकारेण निर्भासते । तथा मुक्तपुरुषालम्बनोपरक्तं मुक्तपुरुषसमापन्नं मुक्तपुरुषस्वरूपाकारेण निर्भासत इति । तदेवमभिजातमणिकल्पस्य चेतसो ग्रहीतृग्रहणग्राह्येषु पुरुषेन्द्रियभूतेषु या तत्स्थतदञ्जनता तेषु स्थितस्य तदाकारापत्तिः सा समापत्तिरित्युच्यते ॥ ४१ ॥

Similarly it should be observed in the case of receiving instrument, i.e., the senses (d); coloured by the receiving instrument, it being transformed into that shines in the form of manifestation of the receiving senses. Similarly coloured by the support of the Receiver Puruṣa, it

1. Here the "receivable object" is to be understood as the Substance with all its successive steps of the changes which have been explained in II. 19, III. 13. Further, the marks bearing (a), (b), (d) and (e) denote the four successive steps of the Cognitive Spiritual Absorption in the form of the Gross, the Subtle, the Instrumental and the Subjective manifestations respectively. The mark "(c)" signifies the conscious and unconscious objects in the Specific Step of the Energies. And the mark (f) refers to the Ultra-Cognitive Spiritual Absorption.

being transformed into that, shines in the form of the manifestation of the Receiver Puruṣa (e). Similarly coloured by the support of the Free Puruṣa, it being transformed into that, shines in the form of the manifestation of the Free Puruṣa (f). Thus that transformation,—which is the colouring of the mind similar to a high class crystal, by that (support) on which it rests and becomes established in that in relation to the receiver, the receiving instrument and the receivable object, i.e., the Puruṣa, the senses and the elements,—is called the operative transformation (of the mind).

तत्र शब्दार्थज्ञानविकल्पैः सङ्कीर्णा सवितर्का समापत्तिः ॥ ४२ ॥

There the suppositional thought-transformation is mixed up with the option of word, object and idea—42

तत्र शब्दार्थज्ञानविकल्पैः संकीर्णा सवितर्का समापत्तिः । तद्यथा गौरिति शब्दो गौरित्यर्थो गौरिति ज्ञानमित्यविभागेन विभक्तानामपि ग्रहणं दृष्टम् । विभज्यमानाश्चान्ये शब्दधर्मा अन्येऽर्थधर्मा अन्ये विज्ञानधर्मा इत्येषां विभक्तः पन्थाः ।

It is as follows :—The Cognition of "cow" as a word, "cow" as an object and "cow" as an idea,—although different from one another,—is seen to take place conjointly. Being analysed, the characteristics of the word are different, the characteristics of the object are different, and the characteristics of the idea are different. This is their separate way.[1]

तत्र समापन्नस्य योगिनो यो गवाद्यर्थः समाधिप्रज्ञायां समारूढः स चेच्छब्दार्थज्ञानविकल्पानुविद्ध उपावर्तते सा संकीर्णा समापत्तिः सवितर्केत्युच्यते ।

There if the object cow, etc., which is present in the Absorbent Cognition of the Yogi who is possessed of thought-transformation, stands intermixed with the option of word, object and idea, this mixed up thought-transformation is called 'Suppositional'.[2]

यदा पुनः शब्दसंकेतस्मृतिपरिशुद्धौ श्रुतानुमानज्ञानविकल्पशून्यायां समाधिप्रज्ञायां स्वरूपमात्रेणावस्थितोऽर्थस्तत्स्वरूपाकारमात्रतयैवावच्छिद्यते सा च निर्वितर्का समापत्तिस्तत्परं प्रत्यक्षम् । तच्च श्रुतानुमानयोर्बीजम् । ततः श्रुतानुमाने प्रभवतः । न च श्रुतानुमानज्ञानसहभूतं तद्दर्शनम् । तस्मादसंकीर्णं प्रमाणान्तरेण योगिनो निर्वितर्कसमाधिजं दर्शनमिति ॥ ४२ ॥

When however on the complete purification of the retentive power regarding the verbal convention, the object,—which exists in its pure nature in the Absorbent Cognition devoid of the option of verbal and inferential ideas,—is distinguished by the pure show of its own manifestation, then this is termed the 'clear (distinctive) thought-transformation'.[3] This is the Highest Perception and is the Seed of the verbal and inferential knowledge. The verbal and inferential knowledge are born of that Highest Per-

---

1. The word, the object and the idea refer to the three means of Real Cognition. These have been termed, in the seventh aphorism of this chapter, the "verbal cognition", "perception" and "inference" respectively. The other three extra means of Real Cognition adopted in the Vedānta Darśana, of course, fall under the category of "Inference".

2. There is no cause for our confusion simply from the apparent diversity of the words. The same four-fold division of the suppressive faculty is going to be described by different names in different contexts and in different ways. This subject has been mentioned in connection with the successive steps of "means" described in the seventeenth aphorism of this chapter. The same is the four-fold mode of manifesting the truth of Praṇava in aphorism 20. The same comes in the context of mental embellishment in aphorisms 35-38. The same is the operative transformation in aphorism 41. Again the commentator describes the same subject under the head of Absorbent Cognition in the aphorisms 42-44. Last of all, he concludes the subject by establishing in aphorism 46 that the Seeded (Cognitive) Spiritual Absorption is of four kinds only. In the case of the Suppositional thought-transformation, the Absorbent Cognition of the Yogi appears with some gross form, because the gross form is then the only object of his meditation. So his mental operation is changed according as the different words viz:—Hari, Rāma, cow, horse, tree, jar, etc., are spoken to him.

3. This portion of the Commentary serves as an introduction to the following aphorism. In this case, the Yogi's mind enters into the Intellective or inhibitive faculty by suppressing the intellectual or exhibitive habits and acquires the subtle appearance of the Absorbent Cognition. Before the rise of this faculty, the mind works only with the intellectual functions; but on the manifestation

ception. Further this Observation is not co-existent with the verbal and the inferential knowledge. Hence the Yogi's Observation, born of the Clear Spiritual Absorption, is not mixed up with any other means of knowledge.[1]

स्मृतिपरिशुद्धौ स्वरूपशून्येवार्थमात्रनिर्भासा निर्वितर्का ॥ ४३ ॥

On the complete purification of the retentive power, the appearance of the truth alone, as if devoid of its own nature, is the Clear Thought-transformation—43

निर्वितर्कायाः समापत्तेरस्याः सूत्रेण लक्षणं द्योत्यते —स्मृतिपरिशुद्धौ स्वरूपशून्येवार्थमात्रनिर्भासा निर्वितर्का। या शब्दसंकेतश्रुतानुमानज्ञानविकल्पस्मृतिपरिशुद्धौ ग्राह्यस्वरूपोपरक्ता प्रज्ञा स्वमिव प्रज्ञास्वरूपं ग्रहणात्मकं त्यक्त्वा पदार्थमात्रस्वरूपा ग्राह्यस्वरूपापन्नेव भवति सा तदा निर्वितर्का समापत्तिः। तथा च व्याख्यातम्।

The definition of this Clear Thought-transformation is being given in this aphorism. On the complete purification of the retentive power, the appearance of the truth alone, as if devoid of its own nature,[2] is the Clear Thought-transformation. On the complete purification of the retentive power about the fictions of verbal and inferential ideas of the verbal convention, that Absorbent Cognition,—which being coloured by the nature of the receivable object as if gives itself up, i.e., gives up the cognitional (exhibitive) manifestation of receiving character, and simply becomes transformed into the nature of the receivable object in the form of the (inhibitive) manifestation of its truth alone,—is then called the Clear Thought-transformation. And this has similarly been explained (in the preceding aphorism).

तस्या एकबुद्ध्युपक्रमो ह्यर्थात्मा अणुप्रचयविशेषात्मा गवादिर्घटादिर्वा लोकः। स च संस्थानविशेषो भूतसूक्ष्माणां साधारणो धर्म आत्मभूतः फलेन व्यक्तेनानुमितः स्वव्यञ्जकाञ्जनः प्रादुर्भूतो भवति। धर्मान्तरस्य उदये च तिरोभवति।

This (Clear Thought-transformation) gets the introduction[3] of the Single Intellect (the Single Soul) which is indeed the real character of the object and is the true nature of the special collection of atoms such as the cow, etc., the jar, etc., or the world. Further, "This" (Single Soul) is distinct from the special aggregation of atoms and is the common characteristic of the subtle elements. 'This' is peculiar to Himself and is inferred from the evident result. 'This', being possessed of His own manifestative cause, becomes visible (in the cognitive Sphere) and on the rise of another characteristic 'This' disappears (in the Ultra-Cognitive Absorption).

स एष धर्मोऽवयवीत्युच्यते। योऽसावेकश्च महांश्चाणीयांश्च स्पर्शवांश्च क्रियाधर्मकश्चानित्यश्च। तेनावयविना व्यवहाराः क्रियन्ते। यस्य पुनरवस्तुकः स प्रचयविशेषः सूक्ष्मं च कारणमनुपलभ्यं तस्यावयव्यभावादतद्रूपप्रतिष्ठं मिथ्याज्ञानमिति। प्रायेण

---

of this Cognition, the Yogī obtains the Intellective Vision; he is not confused by any other means. So this vision is called the Highest Perception (*pūrṇa niścaya*). This Perception is not the haughtiness of the so-called Vedāntin who simply goes through the sectarial teachings of the Vedānta theory or through the theoretical arguments (*prakriyā*) of the Vedānta Darśana and gets proud of the fiction of *Ahaṁ Brahmāsmi* (I am Brahma).

1. This aphorism, being also connected with the following one, denotes the practice of the "A" aspect (*ākāramātrā*) of the Praṇava, the gross and the subtle appearances, or the *Ādhibhūta* of the *Gītā*.

2. In this case the gross form of the object of meditation disappears and the Subtle Manifestation appears which is the inherent truth of all the gross objects such as Hari, Rāma, cow, jar, etc. Henceforth the mind gives up its exhibitive habit or the intellectual function and enters into the strong suppressive faculty or the Intellective Revelation. It has already been explained in the first aphorism in connection with the subject of mental planes that the mind alone travels through the whole system of creation. This thought-transformation is the beginning step of the fourth plane known as the one-pointedness of the mind, so the term "as if" has been used here. Hence it is clear that the mind does not give up its own inhibitive nature, simply it acquires the shining light of Yoga.

3. The term "introduction" denotes that the mind does not become fully saturated with that light; sometimes it becomes overpowered by the exhibitive habit. This is the subtle manifestation of the Absorbent Cognition. The rest is clear from the commentary itself.

सर्वमेव प्राप्तं मिथ्याज्ञानमिति । तदा च सम्यग्ज्ञानमपि किं स्याद्विषयाभावात् ?

This is the Characteristic which is called the Whole (*Avayavī*). It is He who is one, or large, or small, or tangible, or possessing the characteristics of the active force or non-eternal; all functions are performed by this Whole[1] In the case of him however who holds that this Particular Collection is the product of something non-existent and that the Subtle Cause is inadmissible; for him, owing to the absence of the Whole, all knowledge, being established in an appearance which is not its own, is false; almost whatever is obtained, is but false knowledge; and then owing to the absence of the object, what can be the Perfect Knowledge (for him)?

यद्यदुपलभ्यते तत्तदवयवित्वेनाघ्रातम् । तस्मादस्त्यवयवी यो महत्तत्त्वादिव्यवहारापन्नः समापत्तेर्निर्वितर्काया विषयी भवति ॥ ४३ ॥

Whatever is perceived is learnt through the reality of the Whole. Therefore there is the Whole (*Avayavī*) which is fallen into the function of the Great Principle, etc.; This becomes the Subject of the Clear Thought-transformation.[2]

एतयैव सविचारा निर्विचारा च सूक्ष्मविषया व्याख्याता ॥ ४४ ॥

By this the Reflective and the Ultra-Reflective (thought-transformations) also, possessed of subtle sphere, have indeed been described—44

एतयैव सविचारा निर्विचारा च सूक्ष्मविषया व्याख्याता । तत्र भूतसूक्ष्मकेष्वभिव्यक्तधर्मकेषु देशकालनिमित्तानुभवावच्छिन्नेषु या समापत्तिः सा सविचारेत्युच्यते । तत्राप्येकबुद्धिनिर्ग्राह्यमेवोदितधर्मविशिष्टं भूतसूक्ष्ममालम्बनीभूतं समाधिप्रज्ञायामुपतिष्ठते ।

There that thought-transformation is called Reflective which is transformed into the manifestation of the subtle elements of the manifested characteristics differentiated by the experience of time, space and exciting cause. There also the subtle element determined by[3] the Single Intellect alone and qualified by the present characteristic, becomes the support and appears in the Spiritual Absorbent Cognition.

1. Here the term "whole" signifies the Single Soul which is the Subjective Manifestation of the Absorbent Cognition and is the Pure Traceable Step of the Principal Material Cause, and this "whole" is beyond the reach of the modern material science (Y.S.II 19).

2. The commentator presents here the treasury before the reader; but the key is still with Him. This key is nowhere opened out in any text; it is always being communicated from ear to ear.

The following four terms or conditions indicate the requisite qualifications for getting the clue:

(i) The aspirant must keep it most secret just like the wealth of a miser. It must not be opened out before any assembly, nor can it be put into black and white. Since the creation of the world, it is coming from ear to ear and in the same way it will go on from ear to ear forever.

(ii) He must be faithful to the Vedic Scriptures with an open and sincere heart. Here there is no question of conversion; because the Scriptures never teach us to destroy the peace of the world on the lame excuse of conversion. On the contrary, they teach us to embrace all in accordance with the mutual relationship prescribed by them. Further they lay down that the Vedas are the roots, the Vedic Religion is the trunk, all other religious sects are the branches, the sub-branches, the leaves and the twigs of one and the same tree (*Manu Smṛti*, Chapters V-44; X 43-45). The grandsons and the granddaughters may not take any care of their Grandmother; moreover, they call her an old hag; but the grandmother always looks after her naughty darlings by thinking them to be so many particles of her own blood.

(iii) He should try his best to go through the *Manu Smṛti* in order to know the mutual relation of all beings whether of the superhuman world, or of the human world beginning from causation upto cessation, and also he should try to obey the laws as far as possible in order to fulfil the obedience to the mutual relationship.

(iv) He must not quarrel with the followers of other doctrines about the worship of images or any other gods and goddesses.

N.B.—He should not take this clue with a crooked heart, or the Almighty Father will punish him heavily.

3. The terms "determined by the Single Intellect" denote that in this case the mind becomes fully saturated with the light of Yoga and attains the full suppressive habit or the Intellective Function. This Reflective thought-transformation is the joyful manifestation of aphorism 17,—the grasp of the knowledge of dream in aphorism 38,—the instrumental manifestation (*karaṇa-grāhya*) in the second aspect "U" (*Ukāra Mātrā*) of the Praṇava and the *Adhidaiva* of the *Gītā*. When the Yogi

या पुनः सर्वथा सर्वतः शान्तोदिताव्यपदेश्यधर्मानवच्छिन्नेषु सर्वधर्मानुपातिषु सर्वधर्मात्मकेषु समापत्तिः सा निर्विचारेत्युच्यते। एवंस्वरूपं हि तद् भूतसूक्ष्मम् एतेनैव स्वरूपेणालम्बनीभूतमेव समाधिप्रज्ञास्वरूपमुपरञ्जयति। प्रज्ञा च स्वरूपशून्येवार्थमात्रा यदा भवति तदा निर्विचारेत्युच्यते।

On the other hand, that (thought-transformation) is called Ultra-Reflective[1] which is transformed by all means and in all respects into the manifestation of all the characteristics that follow all specific qualities unlimited by the past, present and unpredicable properties. Such manifestation is in fact that Subtle Element. And it being only supported by this manifestation alone, colours the character of the Absorbent Cognition. Further when the cognition becomes as if devoid of its own nature and becomes the Truth itself,[2] then it is called Ultra-Reflective.

तत्र महद्वस्तुविषया सवितर्का निर्वितर्का च। सूक्ष्मवस्तुविषया सविचारा निर्विचारा च। एवमुभयोरेतयैव निर्वितर्कया विकल्पहानिर्व्याख्यातेति ॥ ४४ ॥

There the Suppositional and the Clear (thought-transformations) have the spheres of the gross Substance; the Reflective and the Ultra-reflective have the spheres of the subtle Substance. Thus the cessation of doubt of these two (i.e., the Reflective and the Ultra-Reflective) has been described by this Clear (thought-transformation) alone.[3]

---

reaches this state, he always sees his own existence fully separated from his own body as we see ourselves separated from our dwelling houses. In the dreaming state, we fully understand the differences of time, space and the operative cause with reference to all objects even though this state is fully independent of the objects of the waking state. The Yogi conquers this dreaming state. In other words, this dreaming state becomes the waking for him while the external phenomenal world appears to him as an object of dream. This has been called the thought of complete disappearance of attachment described in aphorism 37 (*B.G.* II-69).

1. The Ultra-Reflective thought-transformation is the purely Egoistic manifestation of aphorism 17—the grasp of the knowledge of sleep in aphorism 38,—the third aspect "M" (*Makāra Mātrā*) of the Praṇava, the Subjective manifestation of the Cognitive Spiritual Absorption (*Ahaṁgrāhya*) and the *Adhiyajña* of the *Gītā*. In the sleeping state, we forget all differences of time, space and operative cause and enjoy the state of equanimity. Similarly this sleeping state becomes the object of sport for the Yogi when he attains this fourth step of Spiritual Absorption. This is the state where the Yogi sees the real character of death and being free from all afflictions and actions, becomes immortal. In the *Gītā*, this state has been described as the Finishing Limit of Action.

2. The commentator again puts here the terms "as if" which denote that in the Reflective Spiritual Absorption, the mind remains in active state which is of the suppressive habit, but here in the Ultra-Reflective Spiritual Absorption the mind gives up even that active nature and enters into the state of equanimity like that of the sleeping state. Hence this absorption has been described here "as if devoid of its own nature".

3. In the first step of Spiritual Absorption, some gross form becomes the object of meditation. In the second the light of Yoga first appears; so these two are dependent upon the Specific Step of the Pradhāna. The third and the fourth have no connection with the physical phenomenon; so they have simply the sphere of the subtle portion of this Pradhāna known as the Substance.

In the first step of Spiritual Absorption, the Yogi begins his work with supposition; there he does not get any clear idea, so it is called Suppositional (thought-transformation). In the second, he clearly sees the manifestation of the truth. He becomes doubtless and does not feel any fatigue on his further journey. The Yogi gets many temptations of some occult power in the second and in the beginning of the third. If he gets proud of his success and becomes the victim of sensuality, he loses all of his acquirements. Simply non-attachment is the only resource on which he will count for his solid success (*Y.S.* III-50).

This is the idea with many people that the Spiritual Absorption is a thing which cannot be had at all times, it comes only at the time of prayer or meditation; again it goes back when the prayer is over. But in reality that is not the case. Of course, there remain some gaps in the continuity of the Absorbent Cognition with reference to the first, the second and the beginning step of the third. But when the Yogi attains fully the fourth stage of Absorption, whatever may be his condition he is always established in his Spiritual Absorbent Cognition (*B.G.* V 7-9; VI 31). On the contrary, there are many people who pretend to be liberated and on the excuse of this instance, take the pose of King Janaka. They do not judge how far they have conquered the dreaming and the sleeping states and how far they have attained the manifested and the unmanifested qualities of Yoga, i.e., the perfections of body and mind (*B.G.* XVIII 35). That cannot be called a Spiritual Absorption in which there is no permanent succession of the suppressive change in the habits of the mind until it reaches the state of the Ultra-Cognitive Absorption which is the end of the mind. In

सूक्ष्मविषयत्वं चालिङ्गपर्यवसानम् ॥ ४५ ॥

Further, the nature of the Subtle Sphere has its termination in the Untraceable Step—45

सूक्ष्मविषयत्वं चालिङ्गपर्यवसानम् । पार्थिवस्याणोर्गन्धतन्मात्रं सूक्ष्मो विषयः । आप्यस्यापि रसतन्मात्रम् । तैजसस्य रूपतन्मात्रम् । वायवीयस्य स्पर्शतन्मात्रम् । आकाशस्य शब्दतन्मात्रमिति । तेषामहंकारः । अस्यापि लिङ्गतन्मात्रं सूक्ष्मो विषयः । लिङ्गमात्रस्याप्यलिङ्गं सूक्ष्मो विषयः । न चालिङ्गात्परं सूक्ष्ममस्ति । नन्वस्ति पुरुषः सूक्ष्म इति । सत्यम् । यथा लिङ्गात्परमलिङ्गस्य सौक्ष्म्यं न चैवं पुरुषस्य । किंतु लिङ्गस्यान्वयि कारणं पुरुषो न भवति, हेतुस्तु भवतीति । अतः प्रधाने सौक्ष्म्यं निरतिशयं व्याख्यातम् ॥ ४५ ॥

The subtile rudiment of smell (*gandha-tanmātra*) is the subtle sphere of the atom of earth; the subtile rudiment of taste (*rasa-tanmātra*) is of the atom of water; the subtile rudiment of light (*rūpa-tanmātra*) is of the atom of fire; the subtile rudiment of touch (*sparśa-tanmātra*) is of the atom of air; and the subtile rudiment of sound (*śabda-tanmātra*) is of the atom of ether. The egoism is (the subtile sphere) of them all; again the Pure Traceable Step (*liṅga-mātra*) is also the subtle sphere of this egoism; and the Untraceable Step (*aliṅga*) is the subtle sphere of that too[1]. Further, there is nothing subtle beyond the Untraceable. A doubt may arise whether the Puruṣa is subtle (or not). It is true. As the Untraceable Step has subtlety beyond the Traceable, the Puruṣa has no further subtlety similar to that; because the Puruṣa is not the material cause of the Traceable Step but He is the Efficient Cause of it. Hence the extreme subtlety has been described in relation to the Pradhāna (the Principal Material Cause).[2]

ता एव सबीजः समाधिः ॥ ४६ ॥

They are indeed the seeded Spiritual Absorption—46

ता एव सबीजः समाधिः । ताश्चतस्रः समापत्तयो बहिर्वस्तुबीजा इति समाधिरपि सबीजः । तत्र स्थूलेऽर्थे सवितर्कः निर्वितर्कः । सूक्ष्मेऽर्थे सविचारो निर्विचार इति । स चतुर्धोपसंख्यातः समाधिरिति ॥४६ ॥

These four thought-transformations have their seed in the phenomenal Substance[3]. So the Spiritual Absorption is also 'seeded'. There the Suppositional and the Clear (thought-transformations) are in the gross object; the Reflecitve and the Ultra-Reflective are in the subtle

---

other words, in this state the mind loses itself in its Original Cause after gradually giving up the exhibitive operations by acquiring inhibitive potency in the succession of the Inhibitive Change (*Y.S.* III 9-13).

Here we find a specific beauty in the description of the Spiritual Absorption. Our commentator holds that the mental grasp of the gross form of an object is the first stage of Spiritual Absorption. Hence comes the utility of idol worship. Our Great Seers have prescribed that a beginner should at first take an ideal of God, say an image, or an emblem, or any symbol for concentrating his mind upon it. When he gets practised in concentration, he will rise by gradual steps and ultimately come to realise the true nature of God. There can be no other alternative means of attaining success in this attempt. As for example, if I ask anybody whether his wife is with form (*Sākāra*) or without form (*Nirākāra*). If he answers in the affirmative, then when she dies, why does he remove her body as soon as possible ? The form is present before him, why does he not love that form any longer ? On the other hand, he is terribly afraid of seeing the same body. If again he says that she is without form, then why does he take care of her body for his household purposes? Such is the case with Īśvara. His true nature cannot be described with exclusive aim and must be explained by division. For the fulfilment of our enjoyment, He is with-form and after the attainment of Emancipation, He is without form. Further, without achieving the fulfilment of Enjoyment which is the beginning step, nobody can attain Emancipation, the last step.

1. The Subtle Sphere of the Reflective and the Ultra-Reflective Absorptions have been described in the preceding aphorism. Now by this the commentator shows the full system of dissolution known as the successive change of the Absorbent cognition begininng from the gross form of the mental grasp upto the end of the mind itself.

2. The Untraceable Step is the Principal Active Material Cause and the Puruṣa—the Inactive Efficient Cause. Here the commentator leaves this subject to the Vedānta Darśana, because this Science deals with the subject of making the Puruṣa free from Non-Science, and the Vedānta tries to reveal His True nature.

3. The "Substance" means the Objective Reality, i.e., the Pradhāna.

object. Thus this Spiritual Absorption is described to be four-fold.[1]

निर्विचारवैशारद्येऽध्यात्मप्रसादः ॥ ४७ ॥

On the perfect establishment of the Ultra-Reflective (thought-transformation), the Spiritual Transparency appears—47

निर्विचारवैशारद्येऽध्यात्मप्रसादः । अशुद्ध्यावरणमलापेतस्य प्रकाशात्मनो बुद्धिसत्त्वस्य रजस्तमोभ्यामनभिभूतः स्वच्छः स्थितिप्रवाहो वैशारद्यम् । यदा निर्विचारस्य समाधेर्वैशारद्यमिदं जायते तदा योगिनो भवत्यध्यात्मप्रसादः भूतार्थविषयः क्रमाननुरोधी स्फुटः प्रज्ञालोकः । तथा चोक्तम्—

"प्रज्ञाप्रासादमारुह्य अशोच्यः शोचतो जनान् ।
भूमिष्ठानिव शैलस्थः सर्वान्प्राज्ञोऽनुपश्यति ॥" ॥ ४७ ॥

Of the Intellective Essence which is the Self of Illumination and is freed from the covering dirt of impurity, the transparent flow of steadfastness, not overpowered by the active and the inert Energies, is (called) the Perfect Establishment. When this perfect establishment of the Ultra-Reflective Spiritual Absorption is born, then comes to the Yogi the Spiritual Transparency, i.e., the clear Intellective Vision possessed of the sphere of the Existing Reality not regarding any succession. So it has also been said :—On ascending the palace of the Intellective Vision, the Yogi who is beyond the province of compassion, pities the afflicted persons like a man who being on the height of a mountain, sees those on the ground.

ऋतंभरा तत्र प्रज्ञा ॥ ४८ ॥

There, the Intellective Vision is "full of Truth" (Ṛtambharā) —48

ऋतंभरा तत्र प्रज्ञा । तस्मिन्त्समाहितचित्तस्य या प्रज्ञा जायते तस्या ऋतंभरेति संज्ञा भवति । अन्वर्था च सा सत्यमेव बिभर्ति । न च तत्र विपर्यासज्ञानगन्धोऽप्यस्तीति । तथा चोक्तम्—"आगमेनानुमानेन ध्यानाभ्यासरसेन च । त्रिधा प्रकल्पयन्प्रज्ञां लभते योगमुत्तमम् ॥" इति ॥ ४८ ॥

That Intellective Vision which is born of the mind steadfast in that state, is termed "full of truth" (Ṛtambharā). Further the term bears the right meaning, as it conveys the truth alone; moreover, there is not even the trace of false knowledge. So it has also been said :—The Yogi, accomplishing the Intellective Vision by these three means—the Scriptures, the Inference and the pleasure arising out of the practice of Meditation,[2] attains the highest stage of Yoga.

श्रुतानुमानप्रज्ञाभ्यामन्यविषया विशेषार्थत्वात् ॥ ४९ ॥

It is possessed of the sphere other than those of the verbal and the inferential cognitions on account of its having the cognition of the Special Truth—49

सा पुनः—श्रुतानुमानप्रज्ञाभ्यामन्यविषया विशेषार्थत्वात् । श्रुतमागमविज्ञानं तत्सामान्यविषयम् । न ह्यागमेन शक्यो विशेषोऽभिधातुम् । कस्मात् ? न हि विशेषेण कृतसंकेतः शब्द इति ।

Further, this Intellective Vision is possessed of the sphere other than those of the verbal and the inferential cognitions on account of its having the cognition of the Special Truth. The verbal cognition is the knowledge of the scriptures. It has the sphere of the generic objects; because it is not possible to point out a particular thing by the Scriptures. Why ? Because the word is not equipped with the specific object.

तथानुमानं सामान्यविषयमेव यत्र प्राप्तिस्तत्र गतिर्यत्राप्राप्तिस्तत्र न भवति गतिरित्युक्तम् । अनुमानेन च सामान्येनोपसंहारः । तस्माच्छ्रुतानुमानविषयो न विशेषः कश्चिदस्तीति । न चास्य सूक्ष्मव्यवहित-

1. The same Cognitive Spiritual Absorption is described here to be 'seeded', because the mind still exists in its cognitive nature with the Inhibitive Habit. Further, the commentator himself concludes here by establishing that "this Spiritual Absorption is described to be fourfold". Thus we should not be confused by different synonyms in connection with the descriptions of these four steps of the Cognitive Spiritual Absorption.

2. The commentator shows here the means of solid success, because each Science requires the said three means for the achievement of its full result. The further consequence, which the Yogi attains by adopting this regular course, is described in the next aphorism.

विप्रकृष्टस्य वस्तुनो लोकप्रत्यक्षेण ग्रहणमस्ति। न चास्य विशेषस्याप्रामाणिकस्याभावोऽस्तीति । समाधिप्रज्ञानिर्ग्राह्य एव स विशेषो भवति—भूतसूक्ष्मगतो वा पुरुषगतो वा । तस्माच्छ्रुतानुमानप्रज्ञाभ्यामन्यविषया सा प्रज्ञा विशेषार्थत्वादिति ॥ ४९ ॥

Similarly, inference has only the sphere of the generic objects. It is said that where there is access, there is motion; where there is no access, there is no motion. Further, the conclusion drawn through inference, deals with general objects. Therefore the sphere of verbal and inferential cognitions has no specific object at all.[1] Also there is no cognition of this subtle, intervened and distant Substance through the worldly perception.[2] Further, this Special Truth, which cannot be perceived by the means of real cognition, is not without existence. This special truth can only be determined by the Spiritual Absorbent Cognition whether it is inherent in the subtle element or is inherent in the Puruṣa. Hence this Intellective Vision is possessed of the sphere other than those of the verbal and inferential cognitions on account of its having the cognition of the Special Truth.

तज्जः संस्कारोऽन्यसंस्कारप्रतिबन्धी ॥ ५० ॥

The habitual potency born therefrom becomes adverse to other habitual potencies.—50.

समाधिप्रज्ञाप्रतिलम्भे योगिनः प्रज्ञाकृतः संस्कारो नवो नवो जायते । तज्जः संस्कारोऽन्यसंस्कारप्रतिबन्धी। समाधिप्रज्ञाप्रभवः संस्कारो व्युत्थानसंस्काराशयं बाधते । व्युत्थानसंस्काराभिभवात्तत्प्रभवाः प्रत्यया न भवन्ति । प्रत्ययनिरोधे समाधिरुपतिष्ठते । ततः समाधिजा प्रज्ञा ततः प्रज्ञाकृताः संस्कारा इति नवो नवः संस्काराशयो जायते ।

On the attainment of the Spiritual Absorbent Cognition, the habitual potency, caused by the Intellective Vision, is born to the Yogi newer and newer. The habitual potency born therefrom becomes adverse to other habitual potencies. The habitual potency produced from the Spiritual Absorption destroys the vehicle of the exhibitive habitual potencies. From the disappearance of the exhibitive habitual potencies, the cognitions born thereof do not arise. On the restraint of the cognitions, the Spiritual Absorption appears. Thence comes the Intellective Vision born of Spiritual Absorption, thence come habitual potencies caused by the Intellective Vision; in this way the vehicle of the (inhibitive) habitual potency is produced newer and newer.

ततश्च प्रज्ञा ततश्च संस्कारा इति कथमसौ संस्काराशयश्चित्तं साधिकारं न करिष्यतीति?

Further, the Intellective Vision is born thereof; also the habitual potencies come therefrom and so on. Such being the case, why will not this vehicle of the (inhibitive) habitual potency make the mind duty-bound?

न ते प्रज्ञाकृताः संस्काराः क्लेशक्षयहेतुत्वाच्चित्तमधिकारविशिष्टं कुर्वन्ति । चित्तं हि ते स्वकार्यादवसादयन्ति । ख्यातिपर्यवसानं हि चित्तचेष्टितमिति ॥ ५० ॥

---

1. It requires no proof to establish that the verbal and the inferential knowledge can never bring home to any one the real nature of what a thing is in itself. For example, our boys get from their school texts some idea of the shape and form and the nature of the tiger. They know for certain that the tiger is a ferocious animal. Still they are not afraid of seeing many pictures of that animal in their books. But when they are taken to some zoological garden in a city, they are astonished to see what a tiger is. The same is the case with us. Neither the wiseacre philosophers, although they may be well-versed in the Western and the Eastern philosophies, nor the modern scientists can appreciate through the knowledge of books the character of the Truth which appears in the state of one-pointedness of the mind (vide the *Kaṭhopaniṣad* Chapter I valli II-7 and *Gītā* Chapter II-29).

2. Perception alone can determine the specific nature of an object, but this ordinary perception can never reach this subtle Substance. Hence these three means of real cognition though indispensably necessary in the beginning, cannot go a great way to reveal the real nature of this Truth. It is superfluous to say in this connection that the other three means of real cognition, adopted by the Vedānta Darśana, come under the head of 'inference'. It has already been said that this Science is the cultivating ground which is the sphere of Action, and the Vedānta will show the real nature of the harvest. So the subject of the Vedānta Darśana is much more scrupulous than that of this Science which is the stepping ground for that highest Science.

Those habitual potencies produced by the Intellective Vision, being the cause for the destruction of the afflictions, do not make the mind charged with further duties, because they only release the mind from its duties. In fact, the Completion of the Revelation is the working of the mind.

तस्यापि निरोधे सर्वनिरोधान्निर्बीजः समाधिः ॥ ५१ ॥

On the restraint of that even all being restrained, comes the Seedless Spiritual Absorption.—51.

किं चास्य भवति? तस्यापि निरोधे सर्वनिरोधान्निर्बीजः समाधिः । स न केवलं समाधिप्रज्ञाविरोधी, प्रज्ञाकृतानामपि संस्काराणां प्रतिबन्धी भवति । कस्मान्निरोधजः संस्कारः समाधिजान्संस्कारान्बाधत इति । निरोधस्थितिकालक्रमानुभवेन निरोधचित्तकृतसंस्कारास्तित्वमनुमेयम् । व्युत्थाननिरोधसमाधिप्रभवैः सह कैवल्यभागीयैः संस्कारैश्चित्तं स्वस्यां प्रकृताववस्थितायां प्रविलीयते । तस्मात् ते संस्काराश्चित्तस्याधिकारविरोधिनो न स्थितिहेतवो भवन्तीति । यस्मादवसिताधिकारं सह कैवल्यभागीयैः संस्कारैश्चित्तं निवर्तते । तस्मिन्निवृत्ते पुरुषः स्वरूपमात्रप्रतिष्ठोऽतः शुद्धः केवलो मुक्त इत्युच्यत इति ॥ ५१ ॥

What more comes to the inhibitive habitual potency ? On the restraint of that even, all being restrained, comes the Seedless Spiritual Absorption. That (suppressive habitual potency) is not only the opponent of the Spiritual Absorbent Cognition, but also becomes opposed to the habitual potencies produced by the Intellective Vision. How ? The habitual potency born of Restraint opposes the habitual potencies born of Spiritual Absorption. The existence of the habitual potency brought about by the inhibitive mind, is inferred from the experience of the succession at the time of the suppressive rest. The mind disappears in its own Existent Determinative Cause along with the habitual potencies leading to Absoluteness and born of the Spiritual Absorption by the suppression of the exhibitive habits. Therefore (these) habitual potencies, the opponents of the duties of the mind, do not become the cause for its (further) continuance; because the mind, being freed from its duties, ceases along with the habitual potencies leading to Absoluteness. On the cessation of that mind, the Puruṣa is completely self-established. Hence He is called pure, absolute and liberated.

इति श्रीपातञ्जले सांख्यप्रवचने योगशास्त्रे प्रथमः समाधिपादः समाप्तः ॥१॥

---

1. This Seedless Spiritual Absorption is the same as the Ultra-Cognitive Spiritual Absorption described in I. 18. Here also the commentator fully explains the same idea. This Spiritual Absorption is not a child's toy that it can be achieved and dissolved every now and then. If the mind, being freed from all its habitual potencies, disappears in its Determinative Cause, how can it come back again? Let us compare these last two aphorisms with the *Asamprajñāta Samādhi* (Ultra-Cognitive Spiritual Absorption) patronised by the so-called Yogirājas of the modern days. They reach this state every now and then, and come back to enjoy the worldly pleasures in imitation of the King Janaka (the liberated soul). They do not know even the character of the lowest form of Spiritual-Absorption, not to say of the attainment of the highest end of it.

Here ends the first chapter known as the Subject of Spiritual Absorption with regard to the Science of Yoga Composed by Patañjali in the Excellent Teaching of the Sāṅkhya.

CHAPTER II

ON THE PRACTICE OF YOGA

तपःस्वाध्यायेश्वरप्रणिधानानि क्रियायोगः ॥ १ ॥

Penance, Study and full aspiration-after-Īśvara are the Yoga of Action—1

उद्दिष्टः समाहितचित्तस्य योगः। कथं व्युत्थितचित्तोऽपि योगयुक्तः स्यादित्येतदारभ्यते। तपःस्वाध्यायेश्वरप्रणिधानानि क्रियायोगः। नातपस्विनो योगः सिध्यति। अनादिकर्मक्लेशवासनाचित्रा प्रत्युपस्थितविषयजाला चाशुद्धिर्नान्तरेण तपः संभेदमापद्यत इति तपस उपादानम्। तच्च चित्तप्रसादनमबाध्यमानमनेनासेव्यमिति मन्यते।

The Yoga of the composed mind has been described above (in the first chapter). How can an exhibitive mind also be possessed of Yoga? (With this purpose) this (chapter) is taken up. The Yoga of Action consists in Penance, Study and full aspiration after Īśvara.[1] The Yoga does not become firm in him who is not given to Penance. The impurity,—variegated by the beginningless residua of actions and *afflictions* and coming from the contact with the net-work of sense-objects,—can never get dissipated without Penance. So Penance has been included in the Yoga of Action. Further it is considered that this (Penance) should be practised by a Yogi when it is not adverse to mental composure[2].

स्वाध्यायः प्रणवादिपवित्राणां जपो मोक्षशास्त्राध्ययनं वा। ईश्वरप्रणिधानं सर्वक्रियाणां परमगुरावर्पणम्। तत्फलसंन्यासो वा ॥ १ ॥

"Study" means the *repetition* of the purifying truths such as the Praṇava (*Aum*) etc., and the reading of the Scriptures leading to Emancipation[3]. "Full

1. Some of us may doubt from the arrangements of these three commandments that "Full aspiration after Īśvara" is of lower value, as it is placed last of all. This is not the case. It is rather the most essential subject for the commencement of Yoga. When the Yogi has got "Full aspiration after God," it automatically leads him to study: again the study leads him to penance which renders the Yogi qualified for the attainment of Īśvara. This is the beauty of composition of the great Author. He places the achievable object in the first place; and the rest follow in its train as gradual steps for the achievement of the first. So it happens that Yoga begins with "Full aspiration after Īśvara" and ends in the "profound Meditation upon Īśvara".

2. By this it is clear that without Penance the mind cannot be purified, nor can there be any success. Further it should be taken up according to one's own ability. The performance of one's own duties enjoined by the Scriptures in accordance with the division of caste and life-order, is Penance. The nature and varieties of Penance should be ascertained from the *Pūrva-mīmāṁsā*, the *Vedas* and the *Smṛtis*.

3. The *Praṇava*, etc., denotes that the mere utterance of *Aum* is not helpful; it should be added to the name of one's own desired deity which is the special manifestation of Īśvara (Y.S. I-25). Further, all at once we can never make friends with a king without the help of a particular officer of his. Similarly Īśvara is absolute, we can never attain Him unless we satisfy our respective desired deities through regular services. Accordingly the term "repetition" has previously been explained as the seeking after and the constant engagement in the means of revelation of the Truth signified by the Praṇava (Y.S.I-28).

aspiration after Īśvara" means the dedication of all actions to the Highest Preceptor[1] or the renunciation of their fruits.[2]

समाधिभावनार्थः क्लेशतनूकरणार्थश्च ॥ २ ॥

With the aim of producing Spiritual Absorption and with the intention of minimising the afflictions —2.

स हि क्रियायोगः—समाधिभावनार्थः क्लेशतनूकरणार्थश्च । स ह्यासेव्यमानः समाधिं भावयति, क्लेशांश्च प्रतनूकरोति । प्रतनूकृतान्क्लेशान्प्रसंख्यानाग्निना दग्धबीजकल्पानप्रसवधर्मिणः करिष्यतीति ।

This "Yoga of Action" must be performed with the aim of producing Spiritual Absorption and with the intention of minimising the afflictions, because this (Yoga of Action) being fully practised produces Spiritual Absorption and diminishes the afflictions; further it will render the minimised afflictions unproductive by the fire of meditation like parched-up seeds.

तेषां तनूकरणात्पुनः क्लेशैरपरामृष्टा सत्त्वपुरुषान्यतामात्रख्यातिः सूक्ष्मा प्रज्ञा समाप्ताधिकारा प्रतिप्रसवाय कल्पयिष्यत इति ॥ २ ॥

After their perfect attenuation the subtle Intellective Vision, manifesting the only distinction between the (objective) Essence and the Puruṣa, is not touched again by the afflictions and its duties being over, becomes suitable for disappearance.

अविद्यास्मितारागद्वेषाभिनिवेशाः क्लेशाः ॥३॥

Non-Science, Egoism, Attachment, Aversion and Clinging-to-life are the afflictions.—3.

अथ के क्लेशाः कियन्तो वेति? अविद्यास्मितारागद्वेषाभिनिवेशाः क्लेशाः । क्लेशा इति पञ्चविपर्यया इत्यर्थः । ते स्पन्दमाना गुणाधिकारं दृढयन्ति परिणाममवस्थापयन्ति कार्यकारणस्रोतमुन्नमयन्ति परस्परानुग्रहतन्त्रीभूत्वा कर्मविपाकं चाभिनिर्हरन्ति ॥ ३ ॥

Now, what are the afflictions and how many are they? Non-Science, Egoism, Attachment, Aversion and Clinging to Life are the afflictions. The afflictions signify the five perversive cognitions; this is the meaning. They, when full of motion, confirm the functions of the Energies,—establish change,—open up the current of cause and effect, and being the chain of mutual support, bring about the fruition of actions.

अविद्या क्षेत्रमुत्तरेषां प्रसुप्ततनुविच्छिन्नोदाराणाम् ॥ ४ ॥

Non-Science is the field of the following whether dormant, feeble, separated or fully active—-4

अविद्या क्षेत्रमुत्तरेषां प्रसुप्ततनुविच्छिन्नोदाराणाम् । अत्राविद्या क्षेत्रं प्रसवभूमिरुत्तरेषामस्मितादीनां चतुर्विधकल्पानां प्रसुप्ततनुविच्छिन्नोदाराणाम् । तत्र का प्रसुप्तिः? चेतसि शक्तिमात्रप्रतिष्ठानां बीजभावोपगमः । तस्य प्रबोध आलम्बने सम्मुखीभावः । प्रसंख्यानवतो दग्धक्लेशबीजस्य सम्मुखीभूतेप्यालम्बने नासौ पुनरस्ति । दग्धबीजस्य कुतः प्ररोह इति । अतः क्षीणक्लेशः कुशलश्चरमदेह इत्युच्यते । तत्रैव सा दग्धबीजभावा पञ्चमी क्लेशावस्था नान्यत्रेति । सतां क्लेशानां तदा बीजसामर्थ्यं दग्धमिति । विषयस्य सम्मुखीभावेऽपि सति न भवत्येषां प्रबोध इत्युक्ता प्रसुप्तिर्दग्धबीजानां चाप्ररोहश्च ।

Non-Science is the field, i.e., the breeding ground of the following viz : the egoism, etc., possessed of fourfold potential capacity whether Dormant, Feeble, Separated or fully Active. There, what then is Dormancy ? It is the existence in germinal state of those that are established in power alone in the mind. On awakening, it turns its face towards its support. In the case of him who is possessed of "Meditation" and the seed of whose

1. He who being fully displeased with the worldly enjoyments becomes self-contented, is qualified for dedicating all the Vedic Rites to Īśvara by not performing the Ritual Action prescribed by the Scriptures. This Yogi is fit for entering into the stage of the Great Vow.

2. This alternative is for the beginners who are in the Agreeable End. They should perform all the Vedic rites by renouncing the fruits of the Actions for Desirable End to the Highest Preceptor Īśvara. This is the standard of Ordinary Vow.

afflictions has been parched up, this awakening no longer takes place even when confronted with any exciting cause. Where is the germination of a parched-up-seed? Hence the adept (Yogi) whose afflictions have been destroyed, is said to be possessed of his last body. So it is in this case only that the state of parched-up-seed is the fifth state of the afflictions and nowhere else. At that time the germinative power of the existing afflictions is burnt up; the awakening of the afflictions does not take place even when confronted with the sense-objects; thus have been described the Dormancy and the unproductivity[1] of the burnt-up-seed.

तनुत्वमुच्यते, प्रतिपक्षभावनोपहताः क्लेशास्तनवो भवन्ति ।

Now the feebleness is being described. The afflictions, being overpowered by the development of the contraries, become feeble.

तथा विच्छिद्य विच्छिद्य तेन तेनात्मना पुनः पुनः समुदाचरन्तीति विच्छिन्नाः । कथं? रागकाले क्रोधस्यादर्शनात् । न हि रागकाले क्रोधः समुदाचरति । रागश्च क्वचित् दृश्यमानो न विषयान्तरे नास्ति । नैकस्यां स्त्रियां चैत्रो रक्त इत्यन्यासु स्त्रीषु विरक्तः, किंतु तत्र रागो लब्धवृत्तिरन्यत्र तु भविष्यद्वृत्तिरिति । स हि तदा प्रसुप्ततनुविच्छिन्नो भवति ।

Similarly they are separated when they intentionally work again and again at intervals with their respective characters. How ? Because anger is not seen at the time of attachment; nor indeed does anger practically work at the time of attachment. Also attachment, being seen with reference to some object, does not cease to exist in another object. It does not mean that because Caitra (a person) is attached to one woman, he must be averse to other women. The fact is that in the former the operation is prevalent whereas in the latter it is to take place in future. Thus, it (the potential capacity of the afflictions) becomes, in fact, Dormant, Feeble and Separated.

विषये यो लब्धवृत्तिः स उदारः । सर्व एवैते क्लेशविषयत्वं नातिक्रामन्ति । कस्तर्हि विच्छिन्नः प्रसुप्तस्तनुरुदारो वा क्लेश इत्युच्यते? सत्यमेवैतत् । किंतु विशिष्टानामेवैतेषां विच्छिन्नादित्वम् ।

When it (the potential capacity) is prevalent in operation in regard to the sense-objects, then it is (called) fully active. All these indeed do not cross over the sphere of the afflictions. Why then are the afflictions separately designated as dormant, feeble, separated and fully active ? It is true; but the state of being separated, etc., (of the afflictions) is for those only that are afflicted thereby.

यथैव प्रतिपक्षभावनातो निवृत्तस्तथैव स्वव्यञ्जकाञ्जनेनाभिव्यक्त इति ।

As all this is destroyed by the production of the contraries, so also it is developed by the colour of its own manifestative cause.

सर्व एवामी क्लेशा अविद्याभेदाः । कस्मात्? सर्वेष्वविद्यैवाभिप्लवते । यद्यदविद्यया वस्त्वाकार्यते तदेवानुशेरते क्लेशा विपर्यासप्रत्ययकाल उपलभ्यन्ते क्षीयमाणां चाविद्यामनुक्षीयन्त इति ॥ ४ ॥

All these afflictions are the varieties of Non-Science alone. Why ? (Because) Non-Science alone pervades them all. Whatever the Substance is falsely created by Non-Science, the afflictions underlie the same. They are found at the time of perversive cognition and get destroyed with the destruction of Non-Science.

अनित्याशुचिदुःखानात्मसु नित्यशुचिसुखात्मख्यातिरविद्या ॥ ५ ॥

Non-Science is the (wrong) cognition of everlastingness, purity, pleasingness and self in the non-eternal, the impure, the painful and in the non-self respectively—5

तत्राविद्यास्वरूपमुच्यते — अनित्याशुचिदुःखानात्मसु नित्यशुचिसुखात्मख्यातिरविद्या ।

Now the character of Non-Science is being described. Non-Science is the

---

1. By this it is clear that the dormant state is of two descriptions,—with seed-power and having the seed-power parched up. The first case occurs in regard to those so-called Yogis who believe that the state of torpor or the laxity of mind is the same as Spiritual Absorption and think it to be the highest goal. The Second is for them who are possessed of Meditation (*prasaṁkhyānavataḥ*) and whose seed of afflictions has been parched up (*dagdha-kleśa-bījaḥ*). This is the fifth state of afflictions, i.e., their total destruction.

(wrong) cognition of everlastingness, purity, pleasingness and self in the non-eternal, the impure, the painful and in the non-self respectively.

अनित्ये कार्ये नित्यख्यातिस्तद्यथा—ध्रुवा पृथिवी, ध्रुवा सचन्द्रतारका द्यौः, अमृता दिवौकस इति ।

The cognition of everlastingness in the transient phenomena is as follows : the earth is eternal; the sky with the moon and the stars is eternal; the gods are immortal.

तथाशुचौ परमबीभत्से काये शुचिख्यातिः । उक्तं च—

'स्थानाद् बीजादुपष्टम्भान्निःस्यन्दान्निधनादपि ।
कायमाधेयशौचत्वात्पण्डिता ह्यशुचिं विदुः' ॥ इति ।

अशुचौ शुचिख्यातिर्दृश्यते—नवेव शशाङ्कलेखा कमनीयेयं कन्या मध्वमृतावयवनिर्मितेव चन्द्रं भित्त्वा निःसृतेव ज्ञायते । नीलोत्पलपत्रायताक्षी हावगर्भाभ्यां लोचनाभ्यां जीवलोकमाश्वासयन्तीवेति, कस्य केनाभिसंबन्धः । भवति चेयमशुचौ शुचिविपर्यासप्रत्यय इति । एतेनापुण्ये पुण्यप्रत्ययस्तथैवानर्थे चार्थप्रत्ययो व्याख्यातः ।

Similar is the cognition of purity in the impure and most loathsome body. As it is said :—The wise know for certain the body to be impure on account of its source, seed, sustenance, perspiration, destruction and the necessity of keeping it constantly clean.[1] The cognition of the pure in the impure is seen—This girl is attractive like the new phase of the moon, as if her limbs are made up of honey and nectar, she seems to have made her appearance after breaking through the moon, her eyes are of the dimension of the blue-lotus-petals, she imparts life as it were to the human-world by the gestures of her looks. Now which is related to what ?[2] This is however the perversive cognition of purity in the impure. By this, the cognition of virtue in vice and also the cognition of good in evil have been described.

तद्यथा दुःखे सुखख्यातिं वक्ष्यति—"परिणामतापसंस्कारदुःखैर्गुणवृत्तिविरोधाच्च दुःखमेव सर्वं विवेकिनः" इति । तत्र सुखख्यातिरविद्या ।

Similarly this (aphorism) that "all is indeed, pain for the sagacious Soul[3] on account of the pain of after-effect, anxiety and habitual potency as also the counter-action in the functions of the Energies (chapters II-15)" will describe the cognition of pleasure in pain. There the cognition of pleasure is Non-science.

तथानात्मन्यात्मख्यातिर्बाह्योपकरणेषु चेतनाचेतनेषु भोगाधिष्ठाने वा शरीरे पुरुषोपकरणे वा मनस्यनात्मन्यात्मख्यातिरिति । तथैतदत्रोक्तम्—"व्यक्तमव्यक्तं वा सत्त्वमात्मत्वेनाभिप्रतीत्य तस्य सम्पदमनुनन्दत्यात्मसम्पदं मन्वानस्तस्य व्यापदमनुशोचत्यात्मव्यापदं मन्वानः, स सर्वोऽप्रतिबुद्धः" । इति ।

Similar is the cognition of self in non-self among the conscious and unconscious instruments in the form of the material supports[4]; all this is the cognition of self in the non-self, whether it be the mind, the instrument of the Puruṣa, or it be the body—the vehicle of enjoyments. Similarly it has been said on this point, "he who believing the manifested or the unmanifested Essence to be the self, rejoices in the growth thereof by

1. This is with reference to one's own body.

2. This is with reference to another's body. People very often compare the beauty of a girl with that of the moon. This shows the opinion of the commentator that it is foolishness to compare this impure body of blood and flesh, this store of excreta and urine, with the pure moon.

3. The term 'Sagacious Soul' signifies the Yogi who is in the grade of Great Vow, i.e., whose mind has been freed from its gross impurities.

4. The conscious instruments are the mental phenomena and the unconscious instruments are the bodily adjuncts. According to this Science, the intellective Essence has three aspects :—*Buddhi* (the Intellect or the Single Soul), *Ahaṁkāra* (Egoism) or *Citta* (the intellectual faculty or the lower self) and *Manaḥ* (the mind). Further, the *Citta* and the *Manaḥ* both come within the Intellectual faculty, i.e., the Created Aspect. So this *Citta* has been translated as mind everywhere as there is no such subtle division in English. According to Indian Philosophy, the mind is taken as one of the senses while the *Citta* is considered as the instrument of the Puruṣa. The teaching of this Science is to raise one from the intellectual to the Intellective sphere, i.e., from the Created Aspects to the Creative Manifestation.

thinking it to be his own development, or grieves for its decrease on thinking it to be his own destruction, is wholly mistaken."

एषा चतुष्पदा भवत्यविद्या मूलमस्य क्लेशसन्तानस्य कर्माशयस्य च सविपाकस्येति । तस्याश्चामित्रागोष्पदवद्वस्तु सतत्त्वं विज्ञेयम् । यथा नामित्रो मित्राभावो न मित्रमात्रं किंतु तद्विरुद्धः सपत्नः । यथा चागोष्पदो न गोष्पदाभावो न गोष्पदमात्रं किंतु देश एव ताभ्यामन्यद्वस्त्वन्तरम् । एवमविद्या न प्रमाणं न प्रमाणाभावः । किंतु विद्याविपरीतं ज्ञानान्तरमविद्येति ॥ ५ ॥

This Non-science has thus four steps. It is the root of this series of affliction and of the vehicle-of-action with its fruition. This Non-Science is to be understood to have some objective reality like the word "non-friend" (Amitra) and "non-cow foot-print" (*Agoṣpada*). As the (term) "non-friend" means neither the absence of a friend nor a particular friend but some one opposite to a friend viz : an enemy; or as the (term) "non-cow-foot-print" means neither the absence of cow-foot-print nor a particular cow-foot-print but a place (deep forest) different from both of them. Thus the Non-science is neither the real cognition nor the absence of cognition but another form of cognition[1] opposite to the real Science (Con-science).

दृग्दर्शनशक्त्योरेकात्मतेवास्मिता ॥ ६ ॥

Egoism is the apparent identity of the powers of the Pure Perceptivity and the Perceiving Instrument.—6.

दृग्दर्शनशक्त्योरेकात्मतेवास्मिता । पुरुषो दृक्शक्तिर्बुद्धिर्दर्शनशक्तिरित्येतयोरेकस्वरूपापत्तिरिवास्मिता क्लेश उच्यते ।

The Puruṣa is the power of the Pure Perceptivity and the Intellect is the power of Perceiving Instrument. The transformation of these two into an apparent-identity is said to be the affliction called Egoism[2].

भोक्तृभोग्यशक्त्योरत्यन्तविभक्तयोरत्यन्तासंकीर्णयोरविभागप्राप्ताविव सत्यां भोगः कल्पते । स्वरूपप्रतिलम्भे तु तयोः कैवल्यमेव भवति कुतो भोग इति । तथा चोक्तम् —"बुद्धितः परं पुरुषमाकारशीलविद्यादिभिर्विभक्तमपश्यन्कुर्यात्तत्रात्मबुद्धिं मोहेन" इति ॥ ६ ॥

On the occurrence of the false inseparable acceptance of the powers of the enjoyer and the enjoyable which are vastly different and extremely distinct from each other, the Experience (*bhoga*) becomes possible. On the other hand, on the re-attainment of their own characters, comes Absoluteness between them. Whence then can there be Experience, (*bhoga*) ? So also it has been said:—not seeing the Puruṣa to be beyond and distinct from the intellect by appearance, conduct and knowledge, one forms the idea of 'Self' therein through preversive knowledge[3].

सुखानुशयी रागः ॥ ७ ॥

Attachment follows the experience of pleasure.—7.

सुखानुशयी रागः । सुखाभिज्ञस्य सुखानुस्मृतिपूर्वः सुखे तत्साधने वा यो गर्द्धस्तृष्णालोभः स राग इति ॥ ७ ॥

That which is the desire, thirst and greed for pleasure or for the means thereof of a person who knows pleasure through the remembrance of previous enjoyment, is Attachment.

दुःखानुशयी द्वेषः ॥ ८ ॥

Aversion follows the experience of pain.—8.

दुःखानुशयी द्वेषः । दुःखाभिज्ञस्य दुःखानुस्मृतिपूर्वो

---

1. This is the "Indefinable Cognition" (*Anirvacanīya Khyāti*) of the Vedānta Darśana. Here the commentator leaves the subject to that Philosophical Text.

2. Power of Pure Perceptivity is Perception (*Dṛk-śakti* is Dṛṣṭi) ; Power of Perceiving Instrument is Perception (*darśana-śakti* is *Dṛṣṭi*). Hence, Egoism is the Simple Perception. The Subject, possessed of perception, is the Perceiver; the Object, possessed of perception, is the Perceivable or perceptible. Hence, though the Subject and th Object are quite different, they become one through power (vide the Terminology).

Causation and Cessation exist in the powe alone but not in the Pure Substance. As here Experience (*bhoga*) begins from oneness, so Ema cipation will come after oneness (Y.S.III 54).

3. Here the term 'appearance' shows I rity, 'conduct' shows Indifference, and 'knowledge' refers to Con-Science. The personified application of these three terms denotes that He is the thing of direct perception.

दुःखे तत्साधने वा यः प्रतिघो मन्युर्जिघांसा क्रोधः स द्वेषः ॥ ८ ॥

That which is the resistence, sorrow, wish to destroy and anger at Pain or at the means thereof preceded by the remembrance of pain of a person who has experienced pain, is Aversion.

स्वरसवाही विदुषोऽपि तथारूढोऽभिनिवेशः ॥ ९ ॥

Clinging-to-life is the sentiment which causes its own potency to flow equally even in the wise.—9.

स्वरसवाही विदुषोऽपि तथारूढोऽभिनिवेशः। सर्वस्य प्राणिन इयमात्माशीर्नित्या भवति मा न भूवं भूयासमिति। न चाननुभूतमरणधर्मकस्यैषा भवत्यात्माशीः। एतया च पूर्वजन्मानुभवः प्रतीयते स चायमभिनिवेशः क्लेशः।

The eternal self-benediction of all living beings is "may I not cease to exist, may I live on", and such self-benediction can never come to a being who has not experienced death. Further, by this, the experience of previous births is inferred; it is this affliction, the clinging-to-life.

स्वरसवाही क्रमेरपि जातमात्रस्य प्रत्यक्षानुमानागमैरसंभावितो मरणत्रास उच्छेददृष्ट्यात्मकः पूर्वजन्मानुभूतं मरणदुःखमनुमापयति।

The fear of death,—in the form of the idea of annihilation of Self,—which cannot be expressed by perception, inference and textual teaching, carrying its own potency even in the just born insect, informs the pain of death experienced in previous births[1].

यथा चायमत्यन्तमूढेषु दृश्यते क्लेशस्तथा विदुषोऽपि विज्ञातपूर्वापरान्तस्य रूढः। कस्मात्? समाना हि तयोः कुशलाकुशलयोर्मरणदुःखानुभवादियं वासना ॥ ९ ॥

As this affliction is seen to exist even in the extremely ignorant, so also it is present even in the wise who have fully understood the starting and the finishing ends of life[2]. Why? Because this habitual Potency caused by the experience of the pain of death is the same in both the wise and the ignorant[3].

ते प्रतिप्रसवहेयाः सूक्ष्माः ॥ १० ॥

They when subtle are destroyed with the disappearance (of the mind).—10.

ते प्रतिप्रसवहेयाः सूक्ष्माः। ते पञ्च क्लेशा दग्धबीजकल्पा योगिनश्चरिताधिकारे चेतसि प्रलीने सह तेनैवास्तं गच्छन्ति ॥ १० ॥

They,—the five afflictions whose seed-power has been parched up,—are destroyed along with the disappearance of the Yogi's *mind*, the duties whereof are at an end.

ध्यानहेयास्तद्वृत्तयः ॥ ११ ॥

Their operations are to be got rid of by Meditation.—11.

स्थितानां तु बीजभावोपगतानाम्—ध्यानहेयास्तद्वृत्तयः। क्लेशानां या वृत्तयः स्थूलास्ताः क्रियायोगेन तनूकृताः सत्यः प्रसंख्यानेन ध्यानेन हातव्या यावत्सूक्ष्मीकृता यावद्दग्धबीजकल्पा इति। यथा च वस्त्राणां स्थूलो मलः पूर्वं निर्धूयते पश्चात्सूक्ष्मो यत्नेनोपायेन वा अपनीयते, तथा स्वल्पप्रतिपक्षाः स्थूला वृत्तयः क्लेशानां सूक्ष्मास्तु महाप्रतिपक्षा इति ॥ ११ ॥

On the other hand, in the case of those (afflictions) that remain in the state of seed, their operations are to be got rid of by Meditation. Of the afflictions those operations which are gross, being attenuated by the Yoga-of-Action, should be got rid of by Meditation known as Prasaṁkhyāna until they are made subtle and until they become like the parched-up-seed. As the gross impurities of cloth are at first washed off and the fine ones are removed afterwards by effort and means, so the gross operation of the afflictions, are the minor enemies[4] and the subtle ones are the great enemies[5].

---

1. This statement is quite sufficient for an intelligent student who is free from all sorts of prejudices, to understand the theory of rebirth.

2. These two terminations are the *Pūrva-mīmāṁsā* and the *Uttara-mīmāṁsā*, i.e., the two-fold *Niṣṭhās* of the *Gītā* (vide B.G. III 3).

3. See *Y.S.* IV-27 in order to understand how the habitual potency exercises its influence even upon the wise.

4. The gross impurities are to be removed by the achievements of the five external component parts of Yoga, i.e., by the accomplishment of the Material Actions.

5. The subtle impurities, on the other hand, are to be destroyed by the practice of the three internal component parts of Yoga, i.e., by the practice of the Spiritual Action (Y.S. II-29).

क्लेशमूलः कर्माशयो दृष्टादृष्टजन्मवेदनीयः ॥ १२ ॥

The vehicle-of-action, having its root in the afflictions, is to be experienced in the Seen Birth or in the Unseen Births—12

क्लेशमूलः कर्माशयो दृष्टादृष्टजन्मवेदनीयः। तत्र पुण्यापुण्यकर्माशयः कामलोभमोहक्रोधप्रभवः। स दृष्टजन्मवेदनीयश्चादृष्टजन्मवेदनीयश्च। तत्र तीव्रसंवेगेन मन्त्रतपःसमाधिभिर्निर्वर्तित ईश्वरदेवता-महर्षिमहानुभावानामाराधनाद्वा यः परिनिष्पन्नः स सद्यः परिपच्यते पुण्यकर्माशय इति। तथा तीव्रक्लेशेन भीतव्याधितकृपणेषु विश्वासोपगतेषु वा महानुभावेषु वा तपस्विषु कृतः पुनः पुनरपकारः स चापि पापकर्माशयः सद्य एव परिपच्यते। यथा नन्दीश्वरः कुमारो मनुष्यपरिणामं हित्वा देवत्वेन परिणतः तथा नहुषोऽपि देवानामिन्द्रः स्वकं परिणामं हित्वा तिर्यक्त्वेन परिणत इति।

There the vehicle of good and bad actions is born of lust, avarice, forgetfulness and anger. It is to be experienced in the Seen Birth (*Dṛṣṭa Janma*) or is to be experienced in the unseen births (*Adṛṣṭa Janma*). There the vehicle of good actions, which is accomplished with intense capacity by means of incantations, austerities and Spiritual-Absorption, or which is formed by the worship of Īśvara, gods, great seers and good-souls, ripens at once. Similarly, the vehicle of bad actions, produced by repeated evil done to men who are suffering from intense affliction due to fear or disease or weakness, or done to men who place confidence in him, or to the good souls or ascetics, also ripens all at once. As the noble boy Nandīśvara, leaving his human form, was changed into a god, so *Nahuṣa* the ruler of the gods, leaving the form acquired by his own virtue, was transformed into a snake.

तत्र नारकाणां नास्ति दृष्टजन्मवेदनीयः कर्माशयः। क्षीणक्लेशानामपि नास्त्यदृष्टजन्मवेदनीयः कर्माशय इति ॥ १२ ॥

There the evil-doers have no vehicle-of-action (*kramāśaya*) to be experienced in the Seen-Birth[1]; and also they, whose afflictions have been destroyed, have no vehicle-of-actions to be experienced in the unseen-births[2].

सति मूले तद्विपाको जात्यायुर्भोगाः ॥ १३ ॥

The root existing, the fruition (of the vehicle-of-action) brings about life-state (*jāti*), life-period (*āyuḥ*) and life-experience (bhoga).—13.

सति मूले तद्विपाको जात्यायुर्भोगाः। सत्सु क्लेशेषु कर्माशयो विपाकारम्भी भवति नोच्छिन्नक्लेशमूलः। यथा तुषावनद्धाः शालितण्डुला अदग्धबीजभावाः प्ररोहसमर्था भवन्ति नापनीततुषा दग्धबीजभावा वा।

As long as the afflictions exist, the vehicle-of-action continues to fructify but not when the root of afflictions has been destroyed. For example, the grains of paddy which have husks attached to them or are not in the state of parched up-seed, are capable of germinating but not so when the husk is taken out or they attain the state of parched-up-seed.

तथा क्लेशावनद्धः कर्माशयो विपाकप्ररोही भवति नापनीतक्लेशो न प्रसंख्यानदग्धक्लेशबीजभावो वेति। स च विपाकस्त्रिविधो जातिरायुर्भोग इति।

Similarly, the vehicle-of-action, being attached to the afflictions becomes capable of fructifying but not so when its afflictions are taken out[3] or when its seed of afflictions attains the parched-up-state by Meditation[4]; and that fruition is threefold,—the life-state, the life-period and the life-experience.

1. The Seen-Birth means the last birth. The Yogī who sees his death, i.e., the full course of his life after conquering the dreaming and the sleeping states as have been explained in the foot-note of chapter I-44, is not to come back to rebirth.

2. The "un-seen births" refers to the cycle of rebirth, because the ignorant person can never conquer his three successive states—the waking, the dreaming and the sleeping, so he cannot experience the full course of his life. Accordingly he comes to birth again.

3. This indicates the attainment of the state of a god (*videha*) by the performance of the Vedic Rites as have been explained in the foot-note of Ch. 1. Aph. 19 1-2. This is similar to the rice separated from husks.

4. This is the state of Emancipation similar to a seed parched-up by the fire of meditation through the practice of Yoga.

तत्रेदं विचार्यते—किमेकं कर्म एकस्य जन्मनः कारणम्, अथैकं कर्मानेकं जन्माक्षिपतीति ।

Now whether a single action becomes the cause of one birth or a single action causes many births, is to be considered in this connection.

द्वितीया विचारणा—किमनेकं कर्मानेकं जन्म निर्वर्तयति, अथानेकं कर्मैकं जन्म निर्वर्तयतीति ।

The second consideration is whether manifold action produces manifold birth or manifold action produces one birth.

न तावदेकं कर्मैकस्य जन्मनः कारणम्। कस्मात्? अनादिकालप्रचितस्यासंख्येयस्यावशिष्टस्य कर्मणः सांप्रतिकस्य च फलक्रमानियमादनाश्वासो लोकस्य प्रसक्तः, स चानिष्ट इति ।

It is not that a single action is the cause of one birth. Why ? Because there would be no safety for a man on account of the irregularity in the succession of the fruition of innumerable remaining actions accumulated from beginningless time and also of those that are being accumulated at present. Accordingly it is not agreeable.

न चैकं कर्मानेकस्य जन्मनः कारणम् । कस्मात्? अनेकेषु कर्मसु एकैकमेव कर्मानेकस्य जन्मनः कारणमित्यवशिष्टस्य विपाककालाभावः प्रसक्तः, स चाप्यनिष्ट इति ।

Further, a single action is not the cause of manifold birth. Why ? Because if each and every action out of many actions be the cause of manifold birth, then the absence of the period of fruition of the remaining actions comes in So it is also disagreeable.

न चानेकं कर्मानेकस्य जन्मनः कारणम्। कस्मात्? तदनेकं जन्म युगपन्न संभवतीति क्रमेणैव वाच्यम् । तथा च पूर्वदोषानुषङ्गः । तस्माज्जन्मप्रायणान्तरे कृतः पुण्यापुण्यकर्माशयप्रचयो विचित्रः प्रधानोपसर्जनभावेनावस्थितप्रायेणाभिव्यक्त एकप्रघट्टकेन मरणं प्रसाध्य संमूर्च्छित एकमेव जन्म करोति, तच्च जन्म तेनैव कर्मणा लब्धायुष्कं भवति । तस्मिन्नायुषि तेनैव कर्मणा भोगः संपद्यत इति ।

Nor again is manifold action the cause of manifold birth. Why ? Because that manifold birth cannot take place simultaneously. It must be said to happen by succession. So in this case also, the above defect comes in. Therefore, the collection of the vehicle of good and bad actions, performed between births and deaths, is variegated and is firm with the state of being subservient to the principal (cause)[1]. It (the collection) becomes manifested at the time of death and after causing death by one combined effort becomes united ; it produces but one birth, and that birth becomes subject to the life-period procured by that action alone. During that period, the life-experience is fulfilled by that action only.

असौ कर्माशयो जन्मायुर्भोगहेतुत्वाच्च त्रिविपाकोऽभिधीयत इति । अत एकभविकः कर्माशय उक्त इति ।

That vehicle of action is said to possess three-fold fruition due to the causation of life-state (birth), life-period and life-experience. Hence, the vehicle-of-action is said to be Productive of Single Life (*Ekabhavika*)[2].

दृष्टजन्मवेदनीयस्त्वेकविपाकारम्भी भोगहेतुत्वाद्, द्विविपाकारम्भी वा भोगायुर्हेतुत्वान्नन्दीश्वरवन्नहुषवद्वेति ।

That however, which is to be experienced in the seen-birth (*dṛṣṭa-janma*), becomes the beginner either of single fruition due to life-experience or of double fruition due to life-experience and life-period like Nandīśvara or Nahuṣa.[3]

---

1. This Principal Cause has been termed "nature" which being united with the functions of the Energies takes the form of the "Intensive Cause" (Y.S. IV-2).

2. The theories of Single-birth current among the other sects take their rise from this view of the Vedic Scriptures. But the followers of those theories do not fully grasp the inner significance of this view. The term "Productive of Single Life" (*Ekabhavika*) denotes that we can break this chain of birth and death at a single birth through proper obedience to the Vedic Laws. We are not to wait for many births for getting out of its clutches. If we cannot break the chain in this life which is the best chance, God knows what would be in store for us. It will go on producing birth after birth some times in hell and some times in human lives.

3. The single fruition is illustrated in the case of the noble boy Nandiśvara who, at the age of eight attained the life-state of a god on the strength of his virtuous action as has been described in the preceding aphorism. His life-period was not fixed; he simply obtained the life-experience of a god.

क्लेशकर्मविपाकानुभवनिर्वर्तिताभिस्तु वासनाभिरनादिकालसंमूर्च्छितमिदं चित्तं विचित्रीकृतमिव सर्वतो मत्स्यजालं ग्रन्थिभिरिवाततमित्येता अनेकभवपूर्विका वासनाः । यस्त्वयं कर्माशय एष एवैकभविक उक्त इति ।

This mind however, being saturated from beginningless time with the (habitual) residua accomplished by the experience of affliction, action and fruition, seems to be variously coloured like a fishing-net stretched out all over with knots. So these residua must have been produced through many previous births. This vehicle-of-action is indeed called "Ekabhavika" (Productive of Single Life).

ये संस्काराः स्मृतिहेतवो वासनास्ताश्चानादिकालीना इति ।

The habitual potencies which cause memory, are the residua and are lying concealed from beginningless time[1].

यस्त्वसावेकभविककर्माशयः स नियतविपाकश्चानियतविपाकश्च । तत्र दृष्टजन्मवेदनीयस्य नियतविपाकस्यैवायं नियमो न त्वदृष्टजन्मवेदनीयस्यानियतविपाकस्यैव । कस्मात्? यो ह्यदृष्टजन्मवेदनीयोऽनियतविपाकस्तस्य त्रयी गतिः । कृतस्याविपक्वस्य विनाशः प्रधानकर्मण्यावापगमनं वा नियतविपाकप्रधानकर्मणाभिभूतस्य वा चिरमवस्थानमिति ।

That vehicle-of-action, which is however Productive of Single Life, is (partly) regulated-fruitive (*niyata-vipāka*) and (partly) unregulated-fruitive (aniyata-vipāka). The above rule (relating to Nandīśvara and Nahuṣa) applies only to the regulated-fruitive which is to be experienced in the seen-birth but not to the unregulated-fruitive which is to be experienced in the unseen-births. Why? Because that vehicle-of-action which is unregulated fruitive and which is to be experienced in the unseen-births, has three-fold mode of operation—either the destruction of the produced unfruitive, or merging into the principal action, or long existence by being overpowered by the principal action of the regulated-fruitive.

तत्र कृतस्याविपक्वस्य नाशो, यथा शुक्लकर्मोदयादिहैव नाशः कृष्णस्य । यत्रेदमुक्तम्—"द्वे द्वे ह वै कर्मणी वेदितव्ये पापकस्यैको राशिः पुण्यकृतोऽपहन्ति तदिच्छस्व कर्माणि सुकृतानि कर्तुमिहैव ते कर्म कवयो वेदयन्ते" ।

There the destruction of the produced unfruitive (action) is as the destruction of the black action by the rise of the white one in this birth[2]. It is said in this connection "two and only two actions are to be understood; a heap of evil actions is destroyed by a virtuous one; so you should desire to perform the virtuous actions in this life; the wise prescribe this Course of Action."

प्रधानकर्मण्यावापगमनम् । यत्रेदमुक्तं—"स्यात्स्वल्पः संकरः सपरिहारः सप्रत्यवमर्शः कुशलस्य नापकर्षायालम् । कस्मात्? कुशलं हि मे बह्वन्यदस्ति यत्रायमावापं गतः स्वर्गेऽप्यपकर्षमल्पं करिष्यति" इति ।

The merging into the principal action, it is said in this connection, is thus : "If there be indeed a little mixture (of evil), it may be removed or tolerated; it is not capable of affecting adversely the virtuous one." Why? Because I have many of the virtuous actions where it is merged; it

---

The double fruition is illustrated in the case of Nahuṣa who was degraded by the curses of the Seer Agastya from the life-state of the ruler of the gods which he had attained by virtue of his own good actions, to the life-state of a serpent with the life-experience and life-period suitable to that state until Arjuna came to rescue him.

By this it is also clear that there is always a chance of failure even after the success attained by virtuous material actions, but there is no such chance in the case of the Yogi who fully finishes his course by the help of Spiritual Action.

1. By this it is explained that the vehicle-of-action is the same as the Productive of Single Life accompanied by the memory, the habitual potencies and the (habitual) residua which are termed the "Regulated-fruitive action" (*Prārabdha*), the "Present action" (*Kriyamāṇa*) and the "Stored up actions" (*Sañcita*) respectively.

2. The actions, which are performed against the commandments of the Vedic Scriptures either through perversive knowledge or through mishap, are to be destroyed in this life by proper purificatory actions (*Prāyaścitta*) prescribed by the Scriptures.

will seldom cause any diminution even in heaven[1].

नियतविपाकप्रधानकर्मणाभिभूतस्य वा चिरमवस्थानं, कथमिति? अदृष्टजन्मवेदनीयस्यैव नियतविपाकस्य कर्मणः समानं मरणमभिव्यक्तिकारणमुक्तम् । न त्वदृष्टजन्मवेदनीयस्यानियतविपाकस्य वा । यत्त्वदृष्टजन्मवेदनीयं कर्मानियतविपाकं तन्नश्येदावापं वा गच्छेदभिभूतं वा चिरमप्युपासीत, यावत्समानं कर्माभिव्यञ्जकं निमित्तमस्य न विपाकाभिमुखं करोतीति ।

Of what kind is the long existence of that which is over-powered by the principal action of the regulated fruitive ? Death has been said to be the common cause of manifestation of the action of Regulated-fruitive which is to be experienced in the unseen-births, but not of the Unregulated-fruitive to be experienced in the unseen-births[2]. However the Unregulated fruitive action which is to be experienced in the unseen-births, may be destroyed or may get merged, or being overpowered may live long until some similar action as an exciting cause for manifestation does move it towards fruition[3].

तद्विपाकस्यैव देशकालनिमित्तानवधारणादियं कर्मगतिश्चित्रा दुर्विज्ञाना चेति । न चोत्सर्गस्यापवादान्निवृत्तिरित्येकभविकः कर्माशयोऽनुज्ञायत इति ॥ १३ ॥

Further on account of the absence of determination for space, time and exciting cause, the working of that fruition is various and difficult to be known[4]. Moreover that "there is no negation of a rule by its exception" is indicated by the vehicle-of-action which is Productive of Single Life[5].

ते ह्लादपरितापफलाः पुण्यापुण्यहेतुत्वात् ॥१४॥

They are possessed of the fruits of pleasure and pain on account of their origination in virtue and vice.—14.

ते ह्लादपरितापफलाः पुण्यापुण्यहेतुत्वात् । ते जन्मायुर्भोगाः पुण्यहेतुकाः सुखफलाः, अपुण्यहेतुका दुःखफला इति । यथा चेदं दुःखं प्रतिकूलात्मकमेवं विषयसुखकालेऽपि दुःखमस्त्येव प्रतिकूलात्मकं योगिनः ॥ १४ ॥

They,—the birth, the life-period and the life-experience,—when produced by virtue are possessed of the pleasurable fruit. And they are possessed of the painful fruit when they are produced by

1. It is the description of those actions which are the bounden duties to be performed according to the commandments of the Scriptures such as sacrifice of Jyotiṣṭoma, the performance of paternal rites (*śrāddha*), the worship of gods, the entertainment of noble guests, etc., where the performer is duty-bound to kill animals for the completion of those rites. These actions are mixed with little evil which being merged into the principal factor, cannot move to fruition independently. This kind of evil has a specific taste like a little tamarind mixed with sugar.

2. "Death is the common cause" means that it is the junction where the regulated fruition comes to an end and some other actions being connected with a principal factor, get rise out of the preserved residua for the fruition of the next birth.

3. This subject will be fully explained in IV 2-9.

4. "Difficult to be known" does not mean that the working of action is exclusively unknowable. The Yogi can see the working of action after opening his Intellective Vision.

Some may think that this sort of assertion is a mere allurement. But it is not so. Let us look into the material science. Nobody can deny the existence of mind and matter. If there be so many scientific inventions of matter, then can there be nothing of the mind ? The Yoga-Sūtra is the only Science for elucidating the scientific inventions of the mind. A full account of those inventions will be given in the third Chapter.

There is no achievement without the proper means. Nobody can get a proper idea about Astronomy without the help of telescope and other instruments. Astronomy is a material science, so the material instruments are helpful. Thirst of the dreaming state can be quenched by visionary water, and the thirst of the waking state can be quenched by actual water but not vice versa. Similarly the mind is spiritual, so the spiritual instruments are necessary for its perfect knowledge but not the material ones. Let us try to develop spiritualism through regular course and we are sure to see everything just before our eyes.

5. The material action is the principal cause of human life. So this is the idea of the commentator that the rule of material action cannot be fully abolished by the material action alone. Though this material action is indispensable in the beginning, yet at the end the Spiritual action is essential for the cessation of all actions (Y.S. II-2. IV-6).

vice. As this pain is counteractive, so even at the time of enjoying the sense-objects, there indeed exists pain which is counteractive for the Yogi.

परिणामतापसंस्कारदुःखैर्गुणवृत्तिविरोधाच्च दुःखमेव सर्वं विवेकिनः ॥ १५ ॥

On account of the pain of after-effect, anxiety and habitual potency as also on account of the opposition in the functions of the Energies, all is mere pain for a sagacious soul.—15.

कथं तदुपपद्यते? परिणामतापसंस्कारदुःखैर्गुणवृत्तिविरोधाच्च दुःखमेव सर्वं विवेकिनः। सर्वस्यायं रागानुविद्धश्चेतनाचेतनसाधनाधीनः सुखानुभव इति तत्रास्ति रागजः कर्माशयः।

How is it possible? On account of the pain of after-effect, anxiety and habitual potency as also on account of the opposition in the functions of the Energies, all is mere pain for a sagacious soul (Yogi). This feeling of pleasure being intermixed with attachment is in the case of every body dependent upon the conscious and the unconscious instruments[1]. So there exists the vehicle-of-action born of attachment.

तथा च द्वेष्टि दुःखसाधनानि मुह्यति चेति। द्वेषमोहकृतोऽप्यस्ति कर्माशयः। तथा चोक्तम्—"नानुपहत्य भूतान्युपभोगः संभवति"। इति हिंसाकृतोऽप्यस्ति शारीरः कर्माशय इति। विषयसुखं चाविद्येत्युक्तम्।

Again as one hates the means of pain and also becomes a prey to ignorance, so also there is the vehicle-of-action produced by aversion and ignorance. Further it has been said that enjoyment is not possible without injuring living beings. There is also the physical vehicle-of-action produced by causing pain to others. Moreover, the pleasure of sense-objects is said to be Non-science.

या भोगेष्विन्द्रियाणां तृप्तेरुपशान्तिस्तत्सुखम्। या लौल्यादनुपशान्तिस्तद् दुःखम्। न चेन्द्रियाणां भोगाभ्यासेन वैतृष्ण्यं कर्तुं शक्यम्। कस्मात्? यतो भोगाभ्यासमनुविवर्धन्ते रागाः, कौशलानि चेन्द्रियाणामिति। तस्मादनुपायः सुखस्य भोगाभ्यास इति।

The quietude of the senses, which ensues from gratification after enjoyment of objects, is pleasure; the want of satisfaction due to passion, is pain. Further, it is not possible to bring about the perversity of taste in regard to the senses by the practice of enjoyment. Why? Because the practice of enjoyment increases attachment and skilfulness of the senses. Therefore, the practice of enjoyment is not the way to pleasure.

स खल्वयं वृश्चिकविषभीत इवाशीविषेण दष्टो यः सुखार्थी विषयानुवासितो महति दुःखपंके निमग्न इति। एषा परिणामदुःखता नाम प्रतिकूला सुखावस्थायामपि योगिनमेव क्लिश्नाति।

He who being surcharged with the desire of sense-objects longs for pleasure, is indeed involved in the great mire of pain like a person who being afraid of the scorpion-poison, is bitten by a cobra. This painfulness of after-effect, which is indeed counteractive, afflicts the Yogi alone even while enjoying pleasure.

अथ का तापदुःखता? सर्वस्य द्वेषानुविद्धश्चेतनाचेतनसाधनाधीनस्तापानुभव इति। तत्रास्ति द्वेषजः कर्माशयः। सुखसाधनानि च प्रार्थयमानः कायेन वाचा मनसा च परिस्पन्दते। ततः परमनुगृह्णात्युपहन्ति चेति परानुग्रहपीडाभ्यां धर्माधर्मावुपचिनोति स कर्माशयो लोभान्मोहाच्च भवतीत्येषा तापदुःखतोच्यते।

Now what is the painfulness of anxiety? The feeling of sorrow being intermixed with aversion is in the case of all dependent upon the conscious and the unconscious instruments. There also exists the vehicle-of-action born of aversion. Further, one longing for the means of pleasure moves with the body, speech and mind; thereby one favours and injures others. So one accumulates virtue and vice from favouring and injuring others. This vehicle of action comes from avarice and ignorance. This is called the painfulness of anxiety.

---

1. The conscious instrument is the internal sphere *i.e.*, the mind, and the unconscious instrument is the external sphere, *i.e.*, the body.

का पुनः संस्कारदुःखता? सुखानुभवात्सुखसंस्काराशयो दुःखानुभवादपि दुःखसंस्काराशय इति। एवं कर्मभ्यो विपाकेऽनुभूयमाने सुखे दुःखे वा पुनः कर्माशयप्रचय इति।

What is again the painfulness of habitual potency? The vehicle of the habitual potency of pleasure comes from the experience of pleasure and the vehicle of the habitual potency of pain comes from the experience of pain. Thus through pleasure and pain which are experienced in fruition, the collection of the vehicle-of-action comes from actions again.

एवमिदमनादिदुःखस्रोतो विप्रसृतं योगिनमेव प्रतिकूलात्मकत्वादुद्वेजयति। कस्मात्? अक्षिपात्रकल्पो हि विद्वानिति। यथोर्णातन्तुरक्षिपात्रे न्यस्तः स्पर्शेन दुःखयति न चान्येषु गात्रावयवेषु, एवमेतानि दुःखान्यक्षिपात्रकल्पं योगिनमेव क्लिश्नन्ति नेतरं प्रतिपत्तारम्।

Thus this beginningless stream of pain, on account of its counteraction, troubles the Advanced Yogi alone[1]. Why? Because a wise man is as sensitive as the eye-ball. As the silk-thread being put into the eye-ball troubles it by mere touch but does not affect the other parts of the body, so these pains also afflict the Yogi alone who is similar to the eye-ball, but no other enjoyer.

इतरं तु स्वकर्मोपहृतं दुःखमुपात्तमुपात्तं त्यजन्तं त्यक्तं त्यक्तमुपाददानमनादिवासनाविचित्रया चित्तवृत्त्या समन्ततोऽनुविद्धमिवाविद्यया हातव्य एवाहंकारममकारानुपातिनं जातं जातं बाह्याध्यात्मिकोभयनिमित्तास्त्रिपर्वाणस्तापा अनुप्लवन्ते। तदेवमनादिना दुःखस्रोतसा व्यूह्यमानमात्मानं भूतग्रामं च दृष्ट्वा योगी सर्वदुःखक्षयकारणं सम्यग्दर्शनं शरणं प्रपद्यत इति।

On the contrary, the three-knotted pains which are caused by both the material and the spiritual means[2], flow over the one (other than the Yogi) who, after repeatedly receiving pain earned through his own labour, gives it up and after giving it up again and again takes it up, who is as it were thoroughly pervaded by Non-Science with the mental function variegated by beginningless residua, and who, simply following the "I-ness" and "My-ness" in objects which should be discarded, is repeatedly born. It is thus that the Yogi, seeing himself and the whole of the living beings to be surrounded by the beginningless stream of pain, takes refuge in the Integral Vision which is the destructive cause of all pains.

गुणवृत्तिविरोधाच्च दुःखमेव सर्वं विवेकिनः, प्रख्याप्रवृत्तिस्थितिरूपा बुद्धिगुणाः परस्परानुग्रहतन्त्रीभूत्वा शान्तं घोरं मूढं वा प्रत्ययं त्रिगुणमेवारभन्ते। चलं च गुणवृत्तमिति क्षिप्रपरिणामि चित्तमुक्तम्। रूपातिशया वृत्त्यतिशयाश्च परस्परेण विरुध्यन्ते, सामान्यानि त्वतिशयैः सह प्रवर्तन्ते। एवमेते गुणा इतरेतराश्रयेणोपार्जितसुखदुःखमोहप्रत्ययाः सर्वे सर्वरूपा भवन्तीति गुणप्रधानभावकृतस्त्वेषां विशेष इति। तस्माद् दुःखमेव सर्वं विवेकिन इति तदस्य महतो दुःखसमुदायस्य प्रभवबीजमविद्या। तस्याश्च सम्यग्दर्शनमभावहेतुः।

Now "as also on account of the opposition in the functions of the Energies all is mere pain for a sagacious soul" means that the Energies of the intellect being possessed of the form of illumination, activity and inertia become the chain of mutual support, and begin the notion of three qualities either calm, or disturbed or dull. Further since the function of the Energies is ever changeful, the mind is said to change quickly. They (Energies) having predominance of forms and activities, become opposed to one another; the ordinary functions however work with the intense ones. Thus these Energies, being possessed of the notions of pleasure, pain and stupidity acquired by (their) mutual support, become all and assume the forms of all; their distinction is however made by the manifestation of the dominant Energy. Therefore all is mere pain for the sagacious soul (Yogi). It is the Non-Science which is the productive seed of this great heap of

1. Here 'Advanced Yogi' refers to a person who is qualified for the standard of Great Vow. This subject has been explained in the *Gītā* (*Y.S.* II-31).

2. The terms "material and spiritual means" denote the same as the unconscious and the conscious instruments. For the three-knotted pains, Vide I-31.

pain, and the Integral Vision is the cause for its cessation.

यथा चिकित्साशास्त्रं चतुर्व्यूहम्—रोगी रोगहेतुरारोग्यं भैषज्यमिति, एवमिदमपि शास्त्रं चतुर्व्यूहमेव तद्यथा—संसारः संसारहेतुर्मोक्षो मोक्षोपाय एवेति। तत्र दुःखबहुलः संसारो हेयः। प्रधानपुरुषयोः संयोगो हेयहेतुः। संयोगस्यात्यन्तिकी निवृत्तिर्हानम्। हानोपायः सम्यग्दर्शनम्।

As the medical science consists of four departments—Disease, Cause of disease, Recovery and Medicine, this Science also is possessed of four departments (arrays). They are as follows :—the Mundane Existence, the Cause of the Mundane Existence, Emancipation and the Means of Emancipation. There the Mundane Existence being full of pain is "Avoidable"; the Conjunction of the Pradhāna and the Puruṣa is the "Cause of the Avoidable"; the complete cessation of the Conjunction is the "Avoidance" and the Integral Vision is the "Means of the Avoidance"[1]

तत्र हातुः स्वरूपमुपादेयं वा हेयं वा न भवितुमर्हतीति। हाने तस्योच्छेदवादप्रसङ्गः। उपादाने च हेतुवादः। उभयप्रत्याख्याने शाश्वतवाद इत्येतत्सम्यग्दर्शनम्। तदेतच्छास्त्रं चतुर्व्यूहमित्यभिधीयते ॥ १५ ॥

There the individuality of one who avoids is neither proper to be "Avoidable" nor proper to be acceptable. In the case of Avoidance, the question of his annihilation comes in. In the case of acceptance the statement of (some other) primitive cause becomes obvious. On the removal of both, the statement of Eternity remains. So this is termed the "Integral Vision"[2]. Hence this Science is said to possess four departments.

हेयं दुःखमनागतम् ॥ १६ ॥

The pain which is not yet come is the "Avoidable".—16.

हेयं दुःखमनागतम्। दुःखमतीतमुपभोगेनातिवाहितं न हेयपक्षे वर्तते। वर्तमानं च स्वक्षणोपभोगारूढमिति न तत्क्षणान्तरे हेयतामापद्यते। तस्माद्यदेवानागतं दुःखं तदेवाक्षिपात्रकल्पं योगिनं क्लिश्नाति नेतरं प्रतिपत्तारं, तदेव हेयतामापद्यते। तस्माद्यदेव हेयमित्युच्यते तस्यैव कारणं प्रतिनिर्दिश्यते ॥ १६ ॥

The pain which is past and has been spent up by experience, cannot stand on the side of the Avoidable. The present (pain) is mounted on its own moment of being experienced, so in the next moment it cannot come under the category of the "Avoidable". Therefore that pain which is not yet come, afflicts the Yogi alone who is similar to the eye-ball but afflicts no other enjoyer; simply that (pain) stands on the side of the "Avoidable."[3] Therefore, the cause of that (pain) only which is really said to be the "Avoidable," is specified.

द्रष्टृदृश्ययोः संयोगो हेयहेतुः ॥ १७ ॥

The conjunction of the Perceiver and the Perceivable is the cause of the "Avoidable".—17.

द्रष्टृदृश्ययोः संयोगो हेयहेतुः। द्रष्टा बुद्धेः प्रतिसंवेदी पुरुषः। दृश्या बुद्धिसत्त्वोपारूढाः सर्वे धर्माः। तदेतद् दृश्यमयस्कान्तमणिकल्पं सन्निधिमात्रोपकारि दृश्यत्वेन स्वं भवति पुरुषस्य दृशिरूपस्य स्वामिनः।

The Perceiver is the Puruṣa who is the reflective knower of the intellect. The Perceivable is all the characteristics present in the intellective Essence. So this Perceivable like a load-stone by its perceptibility becomes the helping mate owing to its direct proximity to its Lord,

1. These are the technical terms for this science :—The Avoidable (*heya*), the Cause of the Avoidable (*heya-hetu*), the Avoidance (*hāna*) and the means of the Avoidance (*hānopāya*) are used for the Worldly life, the Cause of the worldly life, Emancipation and the Means of Emancipation respectively.

2. Here the commentator leaves this subject for the Vedānta Darśana by referring to the statement of Indefinable Cognition adopted by that text; because the individuality of the actor is the Absolute Substantial Truth. We should always bear in mind the gradual steps prescribed by the Scriptures for the Final Emancipation of the human soul. This Science of Yoga-Sūtra deals with the sphere of Action and the Vedānta Darśana shows the Substance in its pure and simple form beyond Action. 'Avoidance' and 'Acceptance' being dependent upon Action cannot exist in the pure and simple Substance (*Brahma*).

3. Here the commentator makes us aware of being prepared for the future birth which has been termed 'pain'.

the Puruṣa who is the external form of "Perceptivity".

अनुभवकर्मविषयतामापन्नं यतोऽयःस्वरूपेण प्रतिपन्नमन्यस्वरूपप्रतिलब्धात्मकं स्वतन्त्रमपि परार्थत्वात्परतन्त्रम् । तयोर्दृग्दर्शनशक्त्योरनादिरर्थकृतः संयोगो हेयहेतुर्दुःखस्य कारणमित्यर्थः ।

By obtaining the nature of the sphere of the act of perception as it (the Perceivable) is accomplished in its own nature like iron, it becomes of the nature obtained from that of the Other by reflection. Although it is independent, yet it becomes dependent on the Other, because it fulfils the Interests of that Other. The conjunction of the powers of the "Pure Perceptivity" and the "Perceiving Instrument", brought about by the beginningless Purposefulness, is the cause of the "Avoidable (*heya*) *i.e.*, the cause of pain. This is the meaning.[1]

तथा चोक्तम् —"तत्संयोगहेतुर्विवर्जनात्स्यादयमात्यन्तिको दुःखप्रतीकारः ।" कस्मात्? दुःखहेतोः परिहार्यस्य प्रतीकारदर्शनात् । तद्यथा पादतलस्य भेद्यता कण्टकस्य भेत्तृत्वं परिहारः कण्टकस्य पादानधिष्ठानं पादत्राणव्यवहितेन चाधिष्ठानम् ।

So also it has been said that this complete remedy of pain must come from the full avoidance of the cause of that Conjunction. Why? Because the prevention of the avoidable cause of pain is seen. This is as follows :—The sole of a foot has the capacity of being pierced through and the thorn has the power of pricking, so the prevention consists in not-placing the foot on the thorn, or in placing it separated by a shoe.

एतत्त्रयं यो वेद लोके स तत्र प्रतिकारमारभमाणो भेदजं दुःखं नाप्नोति । कस्मात्? त्रित्वोपलब्धिसामर्थ्यादिति ।"

He, who knows this trio in the world, by adopting the prevention mentioned in this connection, does not get pain born of the prick. Why? On account of the faculty of realising the three-fold truth.

अत्रापि तापकस्य रजसः सत्त्वमेव तप्यम् । कस्मात् ? तपिक्रियायाः कर्मस्थत्वात्सत्त्वे कर्मणि तपिक्रिया नापरिणामिनि निष्क्रिये क्षेत्रज्ञे दर्शितविषयत्वात् । सत्त्वे तु तप्यमाने तदाकारानुरोधी पुरुषोऽनुतप्यत इति ॥ १७ ॥

Here also the active Energy (Rajas) has the afflictive power; and the Essence (Sattva) indeed is to be afflicted. Why? Because the verb "Tap" (to afflict) rests in its object, so the act of afflicting exists in the Object,—Essence (Intellective Essence). It cannot exist in (the Subject) the unchanging inactive knower of the field[2] on account of (his) possession of the represented objects. When however the Essence is afflicted, in compliance with that appearance the Puruṣa is reflectively afflicted.

प्रकाशक्रियास्थितिशीलं भूतेन्द्रियात्मकं भोगापवर्गार्थं दृश्यम् ॥ १८ ॥

The Perceivable is of the nature of illumination, activity and inertia; it consists of the realities of the elements and the senses; it is possessed of the interests of Experience and Emancipation.—18.

दृश्यस्वरूपमुच्यते—प्रकाशक्रियास्थितिशीलं भूतेन्द्रियात्मकं भोगापवर्गार्थं दृश्यम् । प्रकाशशीलं सत्त्वम् । क्रियाशीलं रजः । स्थितिशीलं तम इति ।

---

1. Here, in this science, the commentator describes the Conjunction to be brought about by "Purpose" but the Vedānta-Darśana holds the creation as accidental. Hence, some of us may think these theories to be contradictory. But that is not the case.

It is evident from the Terminology that the Supreme Spirit (*Brahma*) is neuter but being accidently attributed with the Power of Generation (*māyā*) becomes masculine as the Universal Spirit (*Brahmā*). Then purposefulness for being manifold comes to Him. And He then takes the form of Cosmic Consciousness (*Dṛṣṭi*) as the Active Creator of the perishable Created Minds (*Citta*).

Accordingly we must not forget that the Yoga-Sūtra deals with the Spirit of Meditation (*Dhyeya Brahma*) showing the sphere of Action and the Vedānta-Darśana exhibits the Pure and Simple Substance (*Jñeya-brahma*) beyond the Sphere of Action. Thus it follows that on the fulfilment of both the interests i.e., on the full achievement of the four sorts of practices, the Yogi will see the whole Creation accidental, but not at the time of practice (The First Being desired to be manifold for creation, etc., the Śrutis).

2. For the "field" vide the *Gītā* XIII 6-7. It is, in short, the Perceivable known as the Pradhāna with all its changes.

एते गुणाः परस्परोपरक्तप्रविभागाः परिणामिनः संयोगवियोगधर्माण इतरेतरोपाश्रयेणोपार्जितमूर्तयः परस्पराङ्गाङ्गित्वेऽप्यसंभिन्नशक्तिप्रविभागास्तुल्यजातीयातुल्यजातीयशक्तिभेदानुपातिनः प्रधानवेलायामुपदर्शितसन्निधानानुगुणत्वेऽपि व्यापारमात्रेण च प्रधानान्तर्णीतानुमिताऽस्तिताः पुरुषार्थकर्तव्यतया प्रयुक्तसामर्थ्याः सन्निधिमात्रोपकारिणोऽयस्कान्तमणिकल्पाः प्रत्ययमन्तरेणैकतमस्य वृत्तिमनुवर्तमानाः प्रधानशब्दवाच्या भवन्ति । एतद्दृश्यमित्युच्यते ।

The nature of the Perceivable is being described. The Perceivable is of the nature of illumination, activity and inertia; it consists of the realities of the elements and the senses; it is possessed of the interests of Experience and Emancipation. The essential Energy (*Sattva*) is of the nature of illumination; the active Energy (*Rajas*) is of the nature of activity; and the inert Energy (*Tamas*) is of the nature of inertia. These Energies have the partitions of mutual colour; they are changeful and possess the characteristics of conjunction and separation. They acquire manifestations by mutual proximate support. Although they have the relation of part and whole, they are the divisions of one united power; they follow the differences of the power of the same and different classes. They show their presence in the province of the principal factor. Although they have the kindred nature, they are supposed to exist in opposition to the principal factor by each function. They have the power of being employed in obedience to the Puruṣa's interests. They become beneficial by direct proximity like the load stone. They gratify the function of one of them without any exciting cause and are called by the term "Pradhāna" (the Principal Material Cause). This is called the Perceivable[1].

तदेतद्भूतेन्द्रियात्मकं--भूयभावेन पृथिव्यादिना सूक्ष्मस्थूलेन परिणमते । तथेन्द्रियभावेन श्रोत्रादिना सूक्ष्मस्थूलेन परिणमत इति । तत्तु नाप्रयोजनं, प्रयोजनमुररीकृत्य प्रवर्तत इति । भोगापवर्गार्थं हि तद् दृश्यं पुरुषस्येति । तत्रेष्टानिष्टगुणस्वरूपावधारणमविभागापन्नं भोगो, भोक्तुः स्वरूपावधारणमपवर्ग इति । द्वयोरतिरिक्तमन्यद्दर्शनं नास्ति । तथा चोक्तम्—"अयं तु खलु त्रिषु गुणेषु कर्त्तृष्वकर्त्तरि च पुरुषे तुल्यातुल्यजातीये चतुर्थे तत्क्रियासाक्षिण्युपनीयमानान्त्सर्वभावानुपपन्नाननुपश्यन्नदर्शनमन्यच्छङ्कते" इति ।

This (Perceivable) consists of the realities of the elements and the senses. As the elemental state, it changes into the subtle and gross earth, etc. Similarly as the state of the senses, it changes into the subtle and gross ear, etc.,[2] This (Perceivable) is not purposeless but it thrives with a set purpose before it, because this Perceivable is possessed of the purpose of fulfilling the Experience (*bhoga*) and Emancipation (*Apavarga*) of the Puruṣa. Here the Experience consists in the determination of the character of good and evil merits to be inseparable, and the Emancipation is the ascertainment of the character of the Enjoyer (the Puruṣa). Beyond these two there is no other Observation. So also it has been said that this, however, suspects some ignorance other than to identify all the manifested phenomena to be present in the three Energies which are the actors and also indeed in the inactive Puruṣa, the fourth, the same and not yet the same in class[3] and the witness of their actions.

---

1. These three Energies are the inhabitants of a common abode called the Pradhāna. So they are one in habitation but at the time of functioning they act as mutual friends and foes just like twin brothers. The same rule holds good even in the animal kingdom which is but the product of the three Energies. The animals live in groups in ties of love and friendship, but again they quarrel over objects relating to their personal interest. The nature of these Energies is very beautifully described in the commentary.

2. The terms "Subtle" and "Gross" denote the subtile rudiments and the gross forms with reference to the elements; and also with regard to the senses, they refer to the subtle power of sensation and the gross organs of senses.

3. By this the commentator refers to the Indefinable character of the Self-expressive Principle (*Anirvacanīya Khyāti*) which is the basis of the Vedānta Darśana. For example, ice is nothing but gas, again the same ice is not the gas in its pure and simple form. Thus 'Indefinable' means 'incapable of being described with exclusive aim'.

तावेतौ भोगापवर्गौ बुद्धिकृतौ बुद्धावेव वर्तमानौ कथं पुरुषे व्यपदिश्येते इति? यथा जयः पराजयो वा योद्धृषु वर्तमानः स्वामिनि व्यपदिश्यते स हि तत्फलस्य भोक्तेति। एवं बन्धमोक्षौ बुद्धावेव वर्तमानौ पुरुषे व्यपदिश्येते स हि तत्फलस्य भोक्तेति। बुद्धेरेव पुरुषार्थापरिसमाप्तिर्बन्धस्तदर्थावसायो मोक्ष इति।

How can these two,—Experience[1] and Emancipation,—which are brought about by the intellect and which exist in the intellect alone, be ascribed to the Puruṣa ? As the victory or the defeat of the soldiers is ascribed to their commander, because he is the enjoyer of that fruit; so the bondage and freedom, being present in the intellect itself, are attributed to the Puruṣa, because He is the enjoyer of that fruit. The intellect itself is bound till the non-fulfilment of the Puruṣa's interest and it gets freed by the completion of that interest.

एतेन ग्रहणधारणोहापोहतत्त्वज्ञानाभिनिवेशा बुद्धौ वर्तमानाः पुरुषेऽध्यारोपितसद्भावाः, स हि तत्फलस्य भोक्तेति॥ १८॥

By this, it is established that Recognition (*Grahaṇa*), Retention (*Dhāraṇā*), Reasoning (*Ūha*), Exclusion of illusion (*Apoha*), Knowledge of the Reality (*Tattva-Jñāna*) and the Determined Resolution (*Abhiniveśa*) are present in the intellect but their existence is falsely attributed to the Puruṣa[2], because He is the enjoyer of that fruit.

विशेषाविशेषलिङ्गमात्रालिङ्गानि गुणपर्वाणि ॥ १९॥

The Specific, the Unspecific, the Pure Traceable and the Untraceable are the steps of the Energies—19

दृश्यानां तु गुणानां स्वरूपभेदावधारणार्थमिदमारभ्यते-विशेषाविशेषलिङ्गमात्रालिङ्गानि गुणपर्वाणि। तत्राकाशवाय्वग्न्युदकभूमयो भूतानि शब्दस्पर्शरूपरसगन्धतन्मात्राणामविशेषाणां विशेषाः।

This aphorism is taken up with the purpose of ascertaining the difference of the character of the perceivables, i.e., of the Energies. The Specific, the Unspecific, the Pure Traceable and the Untraceable are the Steps of the Energies. There ether (ākāśa), air (vāyu), fire (agni), water (udaka) and earth (bhūmi) are the specific forms of the Unspecific subtile rudiments such as sound, touch, light, taste and smell.

तथा श्रोत्रत्वक्चक्षुर्जिह्वाघ्राणानि बुद्धीन्द्रियाणि। वाक्पाणिपादपायूपस्थानि कर्मेन्द्रियाणि, एकादशं मनः सर्वार्थमित्येतान्यस्मितालक्षणस्याविशेषस्य विशेषाः। गुणानामेष षोडशको विशेषपरिणामः।

Similarly the ear, the skin, the eye, the tongue and the nose are the senses of knowledge. The mouth, the hand, the foot, the rectum and the sex organs are the senses of action. The eleventh is the mind which is Omniobjective, i.e. fulfils all the Interests[3]. These are the Specific forms of the Unspecific Egoism. This is the sixteen-fold Specific change of the Energies.

षडविशेषाः तद्यथा शब्दतन्मात्रं स्पर्शतन्मात्रं रूपतन्मात्रं रसतन्मात्रं गन्धतन्मात्रं चेति। एकद्वित्रिचतुष्पञ्चलक्षणाः शब्दादयः पञ्चाविशेषाः।

---

1. "Experience" means "enjoyment and suffering" both.

2. The modern sectarian teachers take the Puruṣa (*Īśvara*) to be soaked in these six beatific qualities (*Kalyāṇa Guṇas*) which however have clearly been indicated to be the qualities of Buddhi, by the commentator. Their false representation has become the subject of dispute among the numerous sects of the present days. If we could carefully grasp this idea of the commentator in this commentary, would there be any ground for those selfish sectarial theories ?

3. The "mind is Omniobjective" means that the mind runs through all the steps beginning from the Specific to the Untraceable. This mind is the external manifestation of the Substance termed "Pradhāna". In one aspect, it becomes the subject, in the other it becomes the object, and again in another it becomes the instrument. All the different forms of the different states are centred in the mind. This mind comes from the Substance with all its varieties by the process of evolution, and again after withdrawing them all in itself, it goes back to its origin at the time of Emancipation. In other words, when the mind is present with its exhibitive habits, it serves the interest of Experience. On the other hand, when it becomes accomplished with the inhibitive habitual potency, it fulfils the interest of Emancipation. Further, this Specific Step is the object of the Suppositional and Clear thought-transformations, the gross form of the mental grasp and the subtle manifestation of the Spiritual Absorbent Cognition known as *Adhibhūta* of the Gītā.

षष्ठश्चाविशेषोऽस्मितामात्र इति । एते सत्तामात्रस्यात्मनो महतः षडविशेषपरिणामाः ।

The six Unspecifics are the subtile rudiment of sound, the subtile rudiment of touch, the subtile rudiment of light, the subtile rudiment of water and the subtile rudiment of earth. These five Unspecifics are possessed of one, two, three, four and five features respectively such as sound, etc.,[1]. The sixth Unspecific is the Egoism only[2]. These are the six Unspecific changes of the purely existing Great Self.

यत्तत्परमविशेषेभ्यो लिङ्गमात्रं महत्तत्त्वं तस्मिन्नेते सत्तामात्रे महत्यात्मन्यवस्थाय विवृद्धिकाष्ठामनुभवन्ति । प्रतिसंसृज्यमानाश्च तस्मिन्नेव सत्तामात्रे महत्यात्मन्यवस्थाय यत्तन्निःसत्तासत्तं निःसदसन्निरसदव्यक्तमलिङ्गं प्रधानं तत्प्रतियन्ति । एष तेषां लिङ्गमात्रः परिणामो निःसत्तासत्तं चालिङ्गपरिणाम इति ।

That which is beyond the Unspecific and is the purely Traceable, is the Great Principle[3]. These all existing in that pure existence, the Great Self, reach their culmination of growth. When they are dissolved, they simply existing in that pure existence the Great Self, pass back to what is neither existing nor non-existing, neither real nor unreal but not unreal, yet unmanifested, untraceable Principal Cause (*Pradhāna*)[4]. This (the Great Principle) is their (of the Energies) Pure Traceable change and that which is neither existing nor non-existing, is their Untraceable change.

अलिङ्गावस्थायां न पुरुषार्थो हेतुर्नालिङ्गावस्थायामादौ पुरुषार्थता कारणं भवतीति । न तस्याः पुरुषार्थता कारणं भवतीति । नासौ पुरुषार्थकृतेति नित्याख्यायते ।

In the untraceable state (which is accidental), the Puruṣa's interest does not become the cause of change as the Purposefulness of the Puruṣa does not become the cause in the original state of the Untraceable. The Purposefulness of the Puruṣa can never be the cause of that (untraceable state). This is not brought about by the Puruṣa's interest; so it is called Eternal[5].

त्रयाणां त्ववस्थाविशेषाणामादौ पुरुषार्थता कारणं भवति । स चार्थे हेतुर्निमित्तकारणं भवतीत्यनित्याख्यायते ।

On the other hand, in the beginning of the other three distinctive states, the Puruṣa's interest becomes the cause. Further, this purposefulness appears in the form of efficient, exciting and material causes. So He is called non-eternal[6].

---

1. The subtile rudiment of ether is possessed of one feature, i.e., sound; that of air has two, i.e., sound and touch; that of light has three, i.e., sound, touch and form; that of water has four, i.e., sound, touch, form and taste; and that of earth has five, i.e., sound, touch, form, taste and smell.

2. The modern science may reach upto this Unspecific Step of the Energies. The scientists may call these five kinds of subtile rudiments as Electrons and the Egoism as Proton. So this Unspecific step is the last limit of the material science. Further, this step is the object of the Reflective thought-transformation, the instrumental or the joyful manifestation of the Spiritual Absorption, the grasp of the knowledge of dream, the *Karaṇagrāhya* or the *Adhidaiva* of the Gītā and also the beginning step of the subjective manifestation.

3. This Pure Traceable Step is the object of the Ultra-Reflective-thought-transformation, the lower Subjective or the unified manifestation of the Cognitive Spiritual Absorption, the *Ahaṁgrāhya*, the grasp of the knowledge of sleep and the *Adhiyajña* of the Gītā. Further, in the Vedānta-Darśana, this Great Principle is called the Single Soul (*Ekajīva*) or the Creator of this world. He can never be realised or attained to by the exhibitive habit of the mind. So he is beyond the province of the modern scientists and is the Basis of the creation.

4. This Untraceable Step is the Objective Substance according to the Indian System of Philosophy. It is also called Essence or the Root Matter.

5. This stage will be considered as the Power or the Attribute of the Puruṣa in the Vedānta Darśana, and there the Puruṣa will be considered as the Substance, because the commentator has described this Untraceable Step as a "change" of the Energies with a view to showing the relation of the Yoga-Sūtra with the Vedānta. Further it has already been explained in the first chapter in connection with the definition of Īśvara that the power or attribute of a substance may increase or decrease, but the substance by itself remains the same.

6. The Purposefulness of the Puruṣa by Conjunction is defined to be the cause of the Active Īśvara of the Vedānta Darśana. So according to that theory, the Īśvara is called Super-imposed (*Kalpita*) or non-eternal. But the sectarial dualistic theories cannot advance beyond this Pure Traceable Step. This is their last limit.

गुणास्तु सर्वधर्मानुपातिनो न प्रत्यस्तमयन्ते नोपजायन्ते । व्यक्तिभिरेवातीतानागतव्ययागमवतीभिर्गुणान्वयिनीभिरुपजननापायधर्मका इव प्रत्यवभासन्ते ।

The Energies, however, following all the characteristics, neither get disappearance, nor are they born. They appear to be subject to the characteristics of birth and death accompanied by the relative qualities pertaining to the past, future, decreasing and increasing manifestations alone.

यथा देवदत्तो दरिद्राति । कस्मात्? यतोऽस्य म्रियन्ते गाव इति । गवामेव मरणात्तस्य दरिद्राणं न स्वरूपहानादिति ।

Suppose Devadatta (a person) has become poor. Why ? Because his cows are dead. His poverty is due simply to the death of his cows but not to the destruction of himself.

समः समाधिर्लिङ्गमात्रमलिङ्गस्य प्रत्यासन्नं तत्र तत्संसृष्टं विविच्यते क्रमानतिवृत्तेः । तथा षडविशेषा लिङ्गमात्रे संसृष्टा विविच्यन्ते परिणामक्रमनियमात् । तथा तेष्वविशेषेषु भूतेन्द्रियाणि संसृष्टानि विविच्यन्ते ।

Similar is the consideration here[1]. The Pure Traceable state is next to the Untraceable. It is united with that and is distinguished therefrom, because the succession is unsurpassed. Similarly the six Unspecifics, being united with the Pure Traceable, are distinguished from that; because the succession of change is regulated[2]. Similarly the elements and the senses, being united with the Unspecifics, are distinguished therefrom.

तथा चोक्तं—"पुरस्तात् न विशेषेभ्यः परं तत्त्वान्तरमस्ति" इति विशेषाणां नास्ति तत्त्वान्तरपरिणामः । तेषां तु धर्मलक्षणावस्थापरिणामा व्याख्यायिष्यन्ते ।। १९ ।।

So also it has been said that there is no other lower (element) truth below the Specifics. So there is no other elemental change of the Specifics. The change of their (of the Specifics) Characteristics, Symptoms and Conditions will be described again (in Chapter III.13).

द्रष्टा दृशिमात्रः शुद्धोऽपि प्रत्ययानुपश्यः ।। २० ।।*

The Perceiver is the Perceptivity itself; although pure, he becomes the agent of notion—20

व्याख्यातं दृश्यम् । अथ द्रष्टुः स्वरूपावधारणार्थमिदमारभ्यते—द्रष्टा दृशिमात्रः शुद्धोऽपि प्रत्ययानुपश्यः । दृशिमात्र इति दृक्शक्तिरेव विशेषणापरामृष्टेत्यर्थः। स पुरुषो बुद्धेः प्रतिसंवेदी, स बुद्धेर्न सरूपो नात्यन्तं विरूप इति ।

The Perceivable has been described. Now it is taken up with the purpose of ascertaining the character of the Perceiver. The Perceiver is the Perceptivity itself; although pure, he becomes the agent of notion. "The Perceptivity itself" means the power of the "Pure

1. This illustration signifies the constant fullness of the substance known as the untraceable Pradhāna. Simply its characteristics, symptoms and conditions are liable to change (Vide Y.S. III.13). Thousands of lamps may be lighted from one lamp but the illuminative power of the original lamp gets no decrease.

2. "The succession of change is regulated" denotes that the succession is inviolable. As for example :—water has three stages,—the solid, the liquid and the gaseous. If it is to go from its solid stage to the gaseous one, it must have to pass through the liquid stage either slowly or quickly and vice versa.

Similarly, at the time of dissolution, this creation shall also have to pass through the regular succession of steps by which it has evolved. In other words, the Spiritual Absorbent Cognition must begin from the gross object and pass through the subjective manifestation, i.e., this cognition must have to pass through the gross, subtle, instrumental and the subjective manifestations successively.

The so-called spiritualists, being stimulated by the intoxication of their fictitious theories, may strongly deprecate the images of gods. But it is highly regrettable that they have no intelligence to appreciate the object which our Perfect Seers had in view in introducing the worship of idols. Since there can be no other alternative than to recommend this sort of worship for bringing home to the minds of the beginners the idea of Absolute God, our Perfect Seers prescribed the idol-worship.

* Here the commentator describes the indefinable nature of the "intellect," because this intellect has two aspects,—the Material and the Spiritual. When it is used in the sense of the

Perceptivity," i.e., untouched by attribute (relativity). This is the meaning. This Puruṣa is the reflective knower of the "intellect". Neither He is similar nor extremely dissimilar to the "intellect".

न तावत्सरूपः। कस्मात्? ज्ञाताज्ञातविषयत्वात्परिणामिनी हि बुद्धिः, तस्याश्च विषयो गवादिर्घटादिश्च ज्ञातश्चाज्ञातश्चेति परिणामित्वं दर्शयति। सदा ज्ञातविषयत्वं तु पुरुषस्यापरिणामित्वं परिदीपयति। कस्मात्? न हि बुद्धिश्च नाम पुरुषविषयश्च स्यादगृहीता गृहीता चेति सिद्धं पुरुषस्य सदा ज्ञातविषयत्वं, ततश्चापरिणामित्वमिति।

He is not similar. Why ? On account of the nature of the cognitive and the incognitive spheres, the intellect is indeed changeful. Further, its sphere,—the cow, etc., the jar, etc., i.e., the cognitive and the incognitive,—shows its changefulness. On the other hand, the nature of the cognitive sphere elucidates for all time the unchangefulness of the Puruṣa. Why ? Because the intellect indeed can never be the Non-Receiver, and the sphere of the Puruṣa can never be the Receiver. Hence, in regard to the Puruṣa the nature of the Cognitive sphere is ever established, thence also the unchangefulness (is established).

किञ्च? परार्था बुद्धिः संहत्यकारित्वात्, स्वार्थः पुरुष इति। तथा सर्वार्थाध्यवसायकत्वात् त्रिगुणा बुद्धिस्त्रिगुणत्वादचेतनेति। गुणानां तूपद्रष्टा पुरुष इत्यतो न सरूपः।

What more ? The intellect is possessed of the interest of the Other on account of its action by combination, the Puruṣa is possessed of the interest of his own. Similarly on account of having the nature of the determinative cause of all objects, the intellect consists of the three Energies, and having the quality of the three Energies, it is unconscious. On the other hand, the Puruṣa is the supervisor of the Energies. So He is not similar.

अस्तु तर्हि विरूप इति। नात्यन्तं विरूपः। कस्मात्? शुद्धोऽप्यसौ प्रत्ययानुपश्यः। यतः प्रत्ययं बौद्धमनुपश्यति तमनुपश्यन्नतदात्मापि तदात्मक इव प्रत्यवभासते। तथा चोक्तम्—"अपरिणामिनी हि भोक्तृशक्तिरप्रतिसङ्क्रमा च परिणामिन्यर्थे प्रतिसङ्क्रान्तेव तद्वृत्तिमनुपतति। तस्याश्च प्राप्तचैतन्योपग्रहरूपाया बुद्धिवृत्तेरनुकारमात्रतया बुद्धिवृत्त्यविशिष्टा हि ज्ञानवृत्तिरित्याख्यायते" ॥ २० ॥

Then let Him be dissimilar. No, He is not extremely dissimilar. Why ? Although he is pure, he becomes the agent of notion. As the notion enters into the intellectual (phenomenon), the Puruṣa, instrumentally seeing it, appears to be of that nature although he is not the same. So also it has been said :—"In fact[1], the power of the Enjoyer is unchangeful and unmoving; further, with the relation to the changeful object, that (power) follows this (changeful) function as it were changed into this (function). Moreover,[2] this is said to be the operation of the Consciousness and is in fact unqualified by the intellectual function, (but) simply imitates the operation of the intellect that has obtained the favourite form of the Consciousness".

तदर्थ एव दृश्यस्यात्मा ॥ २१ ॥[3]

His purpose is the very self of the Perceivable—21

तदर्थ एव दृश्यस्यात्मा। दृशिरूपस्य पुरुषस्य कर्मरूपतामापन्नं दृश्यमिति तदर्थ एव दृश्यस्यात्मा भवति, स्वरूपं भवतीत्यर्थः। तत्स्वरूपं तु पररूपेण प्रतिलब्धात्मकं भोगापवर्गार्थतायां कृतायां पुरुषेण न दृश्यत इति। स्वरूपहानादस्य नाशः प्राप्तो न तु विनश्यति ॥ २१ ॥

The Perceivable is made to take the nature of the form of action on behalf of

---

Spiritual aspect, it signifies the Great Principle or the Receiver Puruṣa known as the Consciousness in the Terminology (vide *Gītā II*-49). Again when this "intellect is used in the Material sense, it is considered to be the modification of the Objective Matter (vide *Gītā* VII-4).

1. This sentence refers to the exhibitive operation of the Intellect.

2. This sentence refers to the inhibitive function of the Intellect.

3. The Vedānta Darśana admits manifoldness of ignorance even though it has its monistic theory.

It has been already explained that the subject of this science showing Action is to make the Puruṣa free from ignorance. So the manifoldness of the Puruṣa is established in this Science. For this reason, the commentary shows clearly that though the Perceivable loses its nature, yet in essence it is not destroyed. Why ? The next aphorism will supply the answer.

the Puruṣa who is the external form of Perceptivity. His (of the Puruṣa) purpose is the very self of the Perceivable, i.e., is its very nature; this is the meaning. Its nature however, consisting of the shape obtained by reflection from the form of the Other, is not perceived by the Puruṣa when the interest of Experience and Emancipation is fulfilled. So from the loss of its own nature, it gets cessation but is not fully destroyed.

कृतार्थं प्रति नष्टमप्यनष्टं तदन्यसाधारणत्वात्
॥ २२ ॥

Although destroyed in relation to him whose interest has been fulfilled, it is not destroyed on account of its commonness to others—22

कस्मात्? कृतार्थं प्रति नष्टमप्यनष्टं तदन्यसाधारणत्वात् । कृतार्थमेकं पुरुषं प्रति दृश्यं नष्टमपि नाशं प्राप्तमप्यनष्टं तदन्यपुरुषसाधारणत्वात् । कुशलं पुरुषं प्रति नाशं प्राप्तमप्यकुशलान्पुरुषान्प्रति न कृतार्थमिति तेषां दृशेः कर्मविषयतामापन्नं लभत एवं पररूपेणात्मरूपमिति । अतश्च दृग्दर्शनशक्त्योर्नित्यत्वादनादिः संयोगो व्याख्यात इति । तथा चोक्तम् "धर्मिणामनादिसंयोगाद्धर्ममात्राणामप्यनादिः संयोगः" इति ॥ २२ ॥

Why? Although destroyed for him whose interest has been fulfilled, it is not destroyed on account of its commonness to others. Although the Perceivable is destroyed, i.e., gets destruction with reference to one Puruṣa whose interest has been fulfilled, it is not destroyed on account of its commonness to other Puruṣas. Though it gets destroyed for the skilful Puruṣa (who has obtained perfection in Yoga), yet it has not fulfilled its duties in relation to the unskilful Puruṣas. So it gets fallen into the nature of the sphere of action on behalf of their Perceptivity[1]. Thus it gets its own form from that of the Other. Hence on account of the eternity of the powers of both the Pure Perceptivity and the Perceiving Instrument, the beginningless conjunction has been described. So also it has been said :—"By reason of the beginningless conjunction of the characterized substances there is also the beginningless conjunction of each of the characteristics."

स्वस्वामिशक्त्योः स्वरूपोपलब्धिहेतुः संयोगः
॥ २३ ॥

Conjunction is the cause of the acknowledgment of the character of the powers both of its own and its lord—23

संयोगस्वरूपाभिधित्सयेदं सूत्रं प्रववृते—स्वस्वामिशक्त्योः स्वरूपोपलब्धिहेतुः संयोगः । पुरुषः स्वामी दृश्येन स्वेन दर्शनार्थं संयुक्तस्तस्मात्संयोगाद् दृश्यस्योपलब्धिर्या स भोगः । या तु द्रष्टुः स्वरूपोपलब्धिः सोऽपवर्गः दर्शनकार्यावसानः संयोग इति । दर्शनं वियोगस्य कारणमुक्तम् । दर्शनमदर्शनस्य प्रतिद्वन्द्वीत्यदर्शनं संयोगनिमित्तमुक्तम् । नात्र दर्शनं मोक्षकारणमदर्शनाभावादेव बन्धाभावः स

---

1. Here the commentator puts the term "Perceptivity" in the singular number and the term *Puruṣas* in the plural. Hence, it is clear that Perceptivity (*dṛśiḥ*) is one but its reflection is manifold. As for example :—A fishing net is stretched out under the sun. The individual portions of the rays of the sun, being proud of the dimensions of their respective holes, regard themselves to be high or low, big or small, fat or thin, etc. So they are always busy in increasing their spheres of individuality. When, however, any of the holes is closed or cut off by special effort, the individual portion of the sun-rays in relation to that hole, sees its personal individuality to be coincident with the all-pervading sun-shine, because its self-identification with the hole has been removed by the destruction of its compounding limit. At this stage the all-pervading sun-shine realises that it is nothing but the sun itself.

Similarly the Attributed Brahmā or Con-Science is the sun, the *Kūṭastha Puruṣa* known as the Single Soul or Consciousness is the all-pervading sun-shine, and the holes which divide the sun-shine are the Jīvas or the Created Mind known as Citta. This Citta is manifold and is termed "Cognition" or lower self. All these terms should be ascertained from the Terminology. We are to note here that the teaching of this Science is to emancipate the Puruṣas, fastened to the mind and body, from the limitations thereof. The stage which follows it will be discussed in the *Vedānta Darśana*. Accordingly in the *Sāṅkhya-Tattva-Kaumudī*, the manifoldness of the Puruṣa is defined thus :—"On account of the reflexive subjection to birth, death and instruments and also due to individual manifestation, the manifoldness of the Puruṣa is established." On the other hand, the Vedānta defines "Jīva" to be unborn, immortal, Pure, eternal, free, wise, etc. Why? Because the full achievement of this Science is the stepping ground of the Vedānta-Darśana.

मोक्ष इति । दर्शनस्य भावे बन्धकारणस्यादर्शनस्य नाश इत्यतो दर्शनं ज्ञानं कैवल्यकारणमुक्तम् ।

This aphorism begins with the intention of defining the character of the Conjunction :—Conjunction is the cause of acknowledgment of the character of the powers both of its own and its lord. The Puruṣa, the Lord, is conjoined with his own Perceivable for the purpose of Perceiving Action. The acknowledgment of the Perceivable, ensuing from that Conjunction, is Experience. Again that which is the acknowledgment of the character of the Perceiver, is Emancipation. In other words, Conjunction has its cessation by the action of Observation. So Observation is said to be the cause of separation. Observation is opposed to Non-Observation (Non-Science). So Non-Observation is said to be the cause of Conjunction. Here the observation is not the cause of Emancipation; the absence of bondage comes simply from the absence of Non-Science. That is Emancipation.[1] On the advent of Observation Non-Science, the cause of bondage, gets destroyed. Hence Observation or Con-Science is said to be the cause of Absoluteness.

किं चेदमदर्शनं नाम? किं गुणानामधिकारः ? आहोस्विद् दृशिरूपस्य स्वामिनो दर्शितविषयस्य प्रधानचित्तस्यानुत्पादः स्वस्मिन्दृश्ये विद्यमाने यो दर्शनाभावः?

Again what is indeed this Non-observation ? Is it the function of the Energies ? Or is it the unproduction of the Principal Cognition (Single Soul), the Lord who is the external form of Perceptivity and to whom all objects are presented, i.e., the absence of Perceiving Action even in the presence of his own Perceivable ?

किमर्थवत्त्वं गुणानाम्? अथाविद्या स्वचित्तेन सह निरुद्धा स्वचित्तस्योत्पत्तिबीजम् ।

Is it the Purposefulness of the Energies? Or is it Non-Science which is latent along with its own *mind* and is the seed for the growth of its own *mind* ?

किं स्थितिसंस्कारक्षये गतिसंस्काराभिव्यक्तिः?

Is it the manifestation of the potency of motion on the exhaustion of the potency of rest ?

यत्रेदमुक्तं—"प्रधानं स्थित्यैव वर्तमानं विकाराकरणादप्रधानं स्यात् । तथा गत्यैव वर्तमानं विकारनित्यत्वादप्रधानं स्यात् ।" उभयथा चास्य वृत्तिः प्रधानव्यवहारं लभते नान्यथा । कारणान्तरेष्वपि कल्पितेष्वेव समानश्चर्चः ।

It has been said there :—"The Pradhāna, lying only in rest, cannot be the chief actor for not causing any change. Similarly being only in motion, it cannot be the first in rank on account of the eternity of change." Further its conduct, tending to both these states, gets the function of the Principal Cause (*Pradhāna*) but not otherwise. The same consideration should also be applied to other alternative causes[2] which have been set forth.

दर्शनशक्तिरेवादर्शनमित्येके, प्रधानस्यात्मख्यापनार्था प्रवृत्तिरिति श्रुतेः । सर्वबोध्यबोधसमर्थः प्राक्प्रवृत्तेः पुरुषो न पश्यति, सर्वकार्यकरणसमर्थं दृश्यं तदा न दृश्यत इति ।

Some say that the observing power itself is non-observation, because the Śrutis assert that the rise of the Pradhāna is to express itself. So the Puruṣa who is able to perceive all perceivables does not perceive before the manifestation of the Pradhāna, and the Perceivable which is able to accomplish all actions is not perceived at that time.

---

1. Here the commentator says that the absence of Non-Science is the direct cause of Emancipation but observation is not the cause thereof. What is the inner significance of this assertion ? This is to warn us against the idea of getting Emancipation simply by the theoretical learning of the philosophies. The knowledge of books by itself cannot destroy Non-Science, because restlessness of mind, unsteadiness of body, quick-breathing, sensuality, dream, sleep, stupid imagination, etc., are brought about by this Non-Science. He in whom these can never be found and who has acquired the manifested and the unmanifested qualities of the Spiritual-Absorption, is considered to be the emancipated. In other words, he is seen to shine with the necessary perfections of the body and the mind.

2. These alternatives are the different synonyms used in different texts for conveying the same idea with regard to Motion and Rest.

उभयस्याप्यदर्शनं धर्म इत्येके । तत्रेदं दृश्यस्य स्वात्मभूतमपि पुरुषप्रत्ययापेक्षं दर्शनं दृश्यधर्मत्वेन भवति । तथा पुरुषस्यानात्मभूतमपि दृश्यप्रत्ययापेक्षं पुरुषधर्मत्वेनेवादर्शनमवभासते ।

Others say that the Non-Observation is the characteristic of both of them. In that case, this observation,—though the very self of the Perceivable yet depending as it does upon the Puruṣa's cognition,—becomes an essence of the Perceivable's characteristic. Similarly the non-observation,—though of the opposite nature of the Puruṣa, yet depending upon the illumination of the Perceivable,—appears as an essence of the Puruṣa's characteristic.

दर्शनं ज्ञानमेवादर्शनमिति केचिदभिदधति ।

Some others explain that observation or (exhibitive) knowledge itself is Non-observation.

इत्येते शास्त्रगता विकल्पाः । तत्र विकल्पबहुत्वमेतत्सर्वपुरुषाणां गुणानां संयोगे साधारणविषयम् ॥ २३ ॥

So these are the textual options[1]. There the multiplicity of options is the common subject for the Conjunction of all Puruṣas with the Energies.

तस्य हेतुरविद्या ॥ २४ ॥

Non-Science is its cause—24

यस्तु प्रत्यक्चेतनस्य स्वबुद्धिसंयोगः, तस्य हेतुरविद्या । विपर्ययज्ञानवासनेत्यर्थः । विपर्ययज्ञानवासनावासिता च न कार्यनिष्ठां पुरुषख्यातिं बुद्धिः प्राप्नोति साधिकारा पुनरावर्तते सा तु पुरुषख्यातिपर्यवसानां कार्यनिष्ठां प्राप्नोति । चरिताधिकारा निवृत्तादर्शना बन्धकारणभावान्न पुनरावर्तते ।

Non-Science is the cause of that, however, which is the conjunction of the inner Consciousness (Con-Science) with its own intellect. The meaning is that Non-Science is the residua of perversive cognition. Further, the intellect being possessed of the residua of perversive cognition, does not get the termination of its work. i.e., the revelation of the Puruṣa; so it comes back with its duty. On the contrary, when it gets the end of its work terminated by the Revelation of the Puruṣa, then it being freed from its duty and ignorance does not come back on account of the absence of the cause of bondage.

अत्र कश्चित्षण्डकोपाख्यानेनोद्घाटयति । मुग्धया भार्ययाभिधीयते षण्डकः—आर्यपुत्र! अपत्यवती मे भगिनी, किमर्थं नाम नाहमिति । स तामाह मृतस्तेऽहमपत्यमुत्पादयिष्यामीति ।

Some one clears this position by the story of an impotent husband. The impotent is thus addressed by his stupid wife, "My lord ! My sister[2] has got a child; why indeed have I none ?" He replies to her thus :—"I shall produce child in you when I am dead."

तथेदं विद्यमानं ज्ञानं चित्तनिवृत्तिं न करोति, विनष्टं करिष्यतीति का प्रत्याशा?

Similarly this prese ıt knowledge cannot bring about the cess ion of the mind. What hope is there tha his will cause its destruction ?

तत्राचार्यदेशीयो वक्ति, "ननु बुद्धिनिवृत्तिरेव मोक्षोऽदर्शनकारणाभावाद् बुद्धिनिवृत्तिः । तच्चादर्शनं बन्धकारणं दर्शनान्निवर्तते" ।

An imperfect teacher says on this point :—"Is it not that Emancipation is but the cessation of the intellect, because the cessation of the intellect comes from the absence of its cause known a Non-Science ? Further this Non-Science, the cause of bondage ceases by Observation."

तत्र चित्तनिवृत्तिरेव मोक्षः । किमर्थमस्थान एवास्य मतिविभ्रमः ? ॥२४॥

There (in refutation of the above remark, we can say) the cessation of the *mind* (*citta*) alone is Emancipation. Why does he (the imperfect teacher) get such mental confusion in an improper place[3] ?

---

1. "Textual options" means the different methods of teaching adopted in different Spiritual Systems.

2. 'Stupid wife' refers to the intellect having perversive cognition and 'sister' denotes the Intellect possessed of the Revelation of Puruṣa. And the term 'impotent husband' represents the egoism or the lower self (अहंकार).

3. By this it is clear that the mind is at first restrained from its action, then it gets destroyed. The meaning is that the Pure Traceable Step of the Energies becomes the cause for the appearance of the mind; so also at the time of receding it first gives up its exhibitive habit; then by gradual

तदभावात्संयोगाभावो हानं तद् दृशेः कैवल्यम् ॥ २५ ॥

From its absence comes the absence of Conjunction; this is the Avoidance, the Absoluteness of Perceptivity—25

हेयं दुःखं, हेयकारणं च संयोगाख्यं सनिमित्तमुक्तम् । अतः परं हानं वक्तव्यम्—तदभावात्संयोगाभावो हानं तद्दृशेः कैवल्यम् । तस्यादर्शनस्याभावाद् बुद्धिपुरुषसंयोगाभाव आत्यन्तिको बन्धनोपरम इत्यर्थः ।

The Avoidable pain and the cause of that Avoidable by the name of Conjunction have been described together with the sphere of action. Now the complete Avoidance is to be described :—From its absence comes the absence of Conjunction. This is the Avoidance,—the Absoluteness of Perceptivity. From the absence of that Non-Science, comes the absence of the Conjunction of the intellect with the Puruṣa, i.e., comes the complete cessation of bondage; this is the meaning.

एतद्धानं तद्दृशेः कैवल्यं, पुरुषस्यामिश्रीभावः पुनरसंयोगो गुणैरित्यर्थः ॥ २५ ॥

It is the Avoidance which is the Absoluteness of Perceptivity, the unmixed state of the Puruṣa, i.e., his state of being not conjoined again with the Energies : this is the meaning.

विवेकख्यातिरविप्लवा हानोपायः ॥ २६ ॥

The Intellective-Revelation unwavering is the means of Avoidance—26

दुःखकारणनिवृत्तौ दुःखोपरमो हानं, तदा स्वरूपप्रतिष्ठः पुरुष इत्युक्तम् । अथ हानस्य कः प्राप्त्युपाय इति ? —विवेकख्यातिरविप्लवा हानोपायः । सत्त्वपुरुषान्यताप्रत्ययो विवेकख्यातिः । सा त्वनिवृत्तमिथ्याज्ञाना प्लवते । यदा मिथ्याज्ञानं दग्धबीजभावं वन्ध्यप्रसवं सम्पद्यते तदा विधूतक्लेशरजसः सत्त्वस्य परे वैशारद्ये परस्यां वशीकारसंज्ञायां वर्तमानस्य विवेकप्रत्ययप्रवाहो निर्मलो भवति । सा विवेकख्यातिरविप्लवा हानोपायः । ततो मिथ्याज्ञानस्य दग्धबीजभावोपगमः पुनश्चाप्रसव इत्येष मोक्षस्य मार्गो हानस्योपाय इति ॥ २६ ॥

On the cessation of the cause of Pain comes the absence of Pain and this is termed "Avoidance"; so it has been said that the Puruṣa becomes self-established at that time. Now, what is the means of achieving Avoidance ? The Intellective-Revelation unwavering is the means of Avoidance. The cognition of the distinction between the Essence and the Puruṣa is the Intellective-Revelation. It, however, fluctuates when not freed from false knowledge. When false knowledge is caused to attain the state of the parched-up-seed and becomes barren of germination, then the flow of the distinguishing cognition of the (intellective) Essence,—of which the dirt of affliction has been fully washed off and which exists in its highest splendour and in the supreme consciousness of control,—becomes pure. This Intellective Revelation, being unwavering, is the means of the Avoidance. Therefrom comes the state of parched-up-seed to the false knowledge, i.e., it becomes unreproductive; this is the path of Emancipation or the means of the Avoidance.

तस्य सप्तधा प्रान्तभूमिः प्रज्ञा ॥ २७ ॥

His intellective vision possessed of final ground is seven-fold—27

तस्य सप्तधा प्रान्तभूमिः प्रज्ञा । तस्येति प्रत्युदितख्यातेः प्रत्याम्नायः सप्तधेति । अशुद्ध्यावरणमलापगमाच्चित्तस्य प्रत्ययान्तरानुत्पादे सति सप्तधैव सप्तप्रकारैव प्रज्ञा विवेकिनो भवति ।

---

steps it comes with suppressive habit to the Pure Traceable Step which is called "Intellect". This is the cessation of the mind (*Citta*). Again the cessation of intellect comes in when the Ultra Cognitive Spiritual Absorption or the Untraceable Step appears. Some may think that knowledge consists in knowing the Truth only by the study of philosophical works. In order to do away with this doubt, the commentator says that when this present knowledge known as the exhibitive habit of cognition cannot even relieve the mind of its work, then it is quite clear that this knowledge can never lead to Emancipation which consists in the revelation of the Intellect or in the cessation of the mind. Further, this cessation of the mind is the Emancipation of the Puruṣa from the bonds of Action. This is the subject of this Science. And the cessation of the Intellect in the form of Final Emancipation, is the subject-matter of the Vedānta-Darśana.

"His" means "of the Yogi" qualified with the rise of Intellective Revelation:—The Spiritual-Absorbent-Cognition is seven-fold. When from the absence of the dirt forming a covering of the impurities, other (exhibitive) notions of the mind are not produced, the Absorbent-Cognition of the intellective Yogi becomes sevenfold only, i.e., simply of seven descriptions.

तद्यथा—परिज्ञातं हेयं नास्य पुनः परिज्ञेयमस्ति। क्षीणा हेयहेतवो न पुनरेतेषां क्षेतव्यमस्ति। साक्षात्कृतं निरोधसमाधिना हानम्। भावितो विवेकख्यातिरूपो हानोपाय इत्येषा चतुष्टयी कार्यविमुक्तिः प्रज्ञायाः।

These are as follows:—The Avoidable has been fully understood; nothing more of it is left to be known. The causes of the Avoidable have been destroyed, there is nothing more of them to be destroyed. The Avoidance has been seen by the help of the inhibitive Spiritual-Absorption. The means of the Avoidance in the form of the Intellective-Revelation has been developed. Thus, this is the fourfold material freedom of the Intellective-Vision[1].

चित्तविमुक्तिस्तु त्रयी चरिताधिकारा बुद्धिः, गुणा गिरिशिखरतटच्युता इव ग्रावाणो निरवस्थानाः स्वकारणे प्रलयाभिमुखाः सह तेनास्तं गच्छन्ति। न चैषां प्रविलीनानां पुनरस्त्युत्पादः प्रयोजनाभावादिति। एतस्यामवस्थायां गुणसंबन्धातीतः स्वरूपमात्रज्योतिरमलः केवली पुरुषः।

The Spiritual Freedom is threefold:—The intellect has finished its duties. The Energies,—just like stones detached from the edge of a mountain-peak,—getting no support and being ready for entering into their own cause, get lost along with the *mind* (citta). There is no more production of the fully exhausted Energies on account of the absence of necessity. In this state, the Puruṣa goes beyond the relation of the Energies and being the only light of His own manifestation, becomes pure and absolute[2].

इत्येतां सप्तविधां प्रान्तभूमिप्रज्ञामनुपश्यन्पुरुषः कुशल इत्याख्यायते। प्रतिप्रसवेऽपि च चित्तस्य मुक्तः कुशल इत्येव भवति गुणातीतत्वादिति ॥ २७ ॥

Thus the Puruṣa, having reflectively seen this sevenfold Intellective-Vision possessed of final ground[3], is said to be skilful (*kuśala*). Moreover, He remains in fact free and skilful even in the absence of the mind (lower egoism or *citta*); because his position is beyond the Energies.

योगाङ्गानुष्ठानादशुद्धिक्षये ज्ञानदीप्तिराविवेकख्यातेः ॥ २८ ॥

On the destruction of impurity by the gradual achievement of the component parts of Yoga, the light of knowledge goes upto the Intellective Revelation—28

सिद्धा भवति विवेकख्यातिर्हानोपाय इति। न च सिद्धिरन्तरेण साधनमित्येतदारभ्यते—योगाङ्गानुष्ठानादशुद्धिक्षये ज्ञानदीप्तिराविवेकख्यातेः। योगाङ्गान्यष्टावभिधायिष्यमाणानि, तेषामनुष्ठानात्पञ्चपर्वणो विपर्ययस्याशुद्धिरूपस्य क्षयो नाशस्तत्क्षये सम्यग्ज्ञानस्याभिव्यक्तिः। यथा यथा च साधनान्यनुष्ठीयन्ते तथा तथा तनुत्वमशुद्धिरापद्यते। यथा यथा च क्षीयते तथा तथा च क्षयक्रमानुरोधिनी ज्ञानस्यापि दीप्तिर्विवर्धते। सा खल्वेषा विवृद्धिः प्रकर्षमनुभवत्याविवेकख्यातेः। आगुणपुरुषस्वरूपविज्ञानादित्यर्थः।

It has been established that the Intellective-Revelation is the means of Avoidance. Further, there is no success without a course of procedure. So this being taken up:—On the destruction of impurity by the gradual achievement of the component parts of Yoga, the light of knowledge goes upto the Intellective-Revelation. The component parts of Yoga are eight and are about to be described. By their gradual achievement, the five-knotted perversive-cognition (Non-Science) in the form of impurity gets ruined, i.e., gets destroyed. On its destruction the perfect knowledge is

1. The material freedom (*Kārya-vimukti*) is the subject of this Science.
2. The Vedānta Darśana will show the Spiritual freedom (*Citta-vimukti*).
3. "Final ground" denotes that this Intellective Vision has its cessation; so this happiness also should be avoided by the highest Non-attachment (*Y.S.* Chs. I.16;III 18).

manifested. The more are the means of achievement practised, the more attenuated gets the impurity. And as it is destroyed more and more, the light of knowledge increases more and more according to the degree of the destruction. This growth (of knowledge) indeed reaches its excellence upto the Intellective-Revelation, i.e., upto the practical experience of the real character of the Puruṣa and the Energies.

योगाङ्गानुष्ठानमशुद्धेर्वियोगकारणम्, यथा परशुश्छेद्यस्य: विवेकख्यातेस्तु प्राप्तिकारणं यथा धर्मः सुखस्य नान्यथा कारणम् ।

The 'gradual achievement of the component parts of Yoga' becomes the cause of separation of the impurity, as the axe is to a thing to be cut off thereby. Again this is also the cause of the attainment of the Intellective-Revelation, as virtue is of happiness[1]; in no other way does this become the cause.

कति चैतानि कारणानि शास्त्रे भवन्ति। नवैवेत्याह—तद्यथा 'उत्पत्तिस्थित्यभिव्यक्तिविकारप्रत्ययाप्तयः । वियोगान्यत्वधृतयः कारणं नवधा स्मृतम् ॥' इति ।

How many causes are there in the Scriptures ? They are nine only and are as follows:—Generation, Continuance, Manifestation, Modification, Confidence, Attainment, Separation, Differentiation and Support; this ninefold cause is prescribed by the text.

तत्रोत्पत्तिकारणं मनो भवति ज्ञानस्य ।

1. There, the mind is the cause of generation of the Consciousness[2].

स्थितिकारणं—मनसः पुरुषार्थता शरीरस्येवाहार इति ।

2. Obedience to the Puruṣa's interest is the cause of the continuance of the mind; as food is that of the body[3].

अभिव्यक्तिकारणं यथा रूपस्याऽलोकस्तथा रूपज्ञानम् ।

3. The cause of manifestation is as light is of the form; so is the Consciousness of the form[4].

विकारकारणं मनसो विषयान्तरम्, यथाग्निः पाक्यस्य ।

4. The cause of modification is the variation of the mind into different objects, as fire is that of the thing to be cooked[5].

प्रत्ययकारणं धूमज्ञानमग्निज्ञानस्य ।

5. The cause of confidence is as the knowledge of smoke is of the knowledge of fire[6].

प्राप्तिकारणं योगाङ्गानुष्ठानं विवेकख्यातेः ।

6. The cause of attainment is as the gradual achievement of the component parts of Yoga is of the Intellective-Revelation.[7]

वियोगकारणं तदेवाशुद्धेः ।

7. The cause of separation is as that (achievement of the component parts) is of impurity.[8]

---

1. It has already been explained that without the help of the Scriptures, nobody can ascertain the correct path. So the commentator indicates that dutiful submission to the authority of the Vedic Scriptures is the only way to solid happiness.

2. The Consciousness is absolute in its true nature, but in relation to the mind it gets reflexive subjection to birth and death, etc. So from the worldly point of view, the mind is said to be the cause of the generation of the Consciousness.

3. The body increases or decreases according to the quantity and quality of food supplied to it; it can never stay without food. Similarly the Puruṣa's Interest in the form of Experience and Emancipation is the cause of continuance of the mind.

4. The function of light is to illuminate the object on which it falls, and also it takes the shape of that object. Similarly, the Consciousness illuminates the body and receives the notion of its own dimension according to that of the body.

5. Wheat, being cooked by fire, is modified into gruel, cakes, biscuits, bread etc. Further, it becomes very difficult for a person ignorant of these preparations to ascertain the real nature of wheat of which these are the modifications. Similarly, through the modifications of the mind, it is very difficult for us to ascertain the real character of the Substance.

6. This existence of fire is inferred by smoke; similarly, we are confident of the existence of the Existing Reality through the function of the world. In short, nobody can deny his own existence; his very existence is sufficient proof of the Existing Reality.

7-8. The gradual practice of Yoga removes the dirt of the mind, and also reveals the existing Reality. So, it works only as a two-fold cause.

अन्यत्वकारणं यथा सुवर्णस्य सुवर्णकारः । एवमेकस्य स्त्रीप्रत्ययस्याविद्या मूढत्वे, द्वेषो दुःखत्वे, रागः सुखत्वे, तत्त्वज्ञानं माध्यस्थ्ये ।

8. The cause of differentiation is as the goldsmith is of gold. Thus, regarding the notion of the same woman, Non-Science becomes the cause of stupid imagination, aversion becomes the cause of painfulness, attachment becomes the cause of the feeling of pleasure and the knowledge of reality becomes the cause of neutrality.[1]

धृतिकारणं शरीरमिन्द्रियाणाम् । तानि च तस्य । महाभूतानि शरीराणां तानि च परस्परं सर्वेषाम् । तैर्यग्यौनमानुषदैवतानि च परस्परार्थत्वादिति ।

9. The cause of support is as the body is of the senses which in turn are of the body; and the main elements are that (support) of the bodies. Further, they (the bodies) are mutually the support of all the other bodies. Thus the bodies of the inferior animals, men and gods are supported by one another on account of the obedience to their mutual interest.[2]

एवं नव कारणानि । तानि च यथासम्भवं पदार्थान्तरेष्वपि योज्यानि ।

Hence, these are the nine causes. Further these should be applied also to other objects as far as possible.[3]

योगाङ्गानुष्ठानं तु द्विधैव कारणत्वं लभत इति ॥ २८ ॥

The gradual achievement of the component parts of Yoga, however, becomes the cause in two ways only.

यमनियमासनप्राणायामप्रत्याहारधारणा-ध्यानसमाधयोऽष्टावङ्गानि ॥ २९ ॥

Restraint, Observance, Posture, Breath-control, Abstraction, Concentration, Meditation and spiritual Absorption are the eight component parts of Yoga—29

तत्र योगाङ्गान्यवधार्यन्ते —यमनियमासनप्राणायामप्रत्याहारधारणाध्यानसमाधयोऽष्टावङ्गानि । यथाक्रममेषामनुष्ठानं स्वरूपं च वक्ष्यामः ॥ २९ ॥

There, the component parts of Yoga are being determined. Restraint, Observance, Posture, Breath-control, Abstraction, Concentration, Meditation and Spiritual Absorption are the eight component parts of Yoga. We shall describe their gradual achievement and character according to the order of arrangement.

तत्राहिंसासत्यास्तेयब्रह्मचर्यापरिग्रहा यमाः ॥ ३० ॥

There Harmlessness, Truthfulness, Abstinence from theft, Continence and Non-Acceptance of gift are the Restraints—30

तत्राहिंसासत्यास्तेयब्रह्मचर्यापरिग्रहा यमाः । तत्राहिंसा सर्वथा सर्वदा सर्वभूतानामनभिद्रोहः । उत्तरे च यमनियमास्तन्मूलास्तत्सिद्धिपरतयैव तत्प्रतिपादनाय प्रतिपाद्यन्ते । तदवदातरूपकरणायैवोपादीयन्ते । तथा चोक्तम्—स खल्वयं ब्राह्मणो यथा यथा व्रतानि बहूनि समादित्सते तथा तथा प्रमादकृतेभ्यो हिंसानिदानेभ्यो निवर्तमानस्तामेवावदातरूपामहिंसां करोति ।

There, Harmlessness is the absence of oppression towards all living beings by all means and for all times. The following Restraints and Observances are its root. Their main object is but its attain-

---

1. The goldsmith differentiates gold into various shapes, but the substance remains the same. Similarly the function of the Energies brings about so many varieties in the shape of internal and external phenomena, but the Substance itself is not changed.

2. The body is the support of the senses, and again the senses and the elements constitute the body. So these are mutually supported. Further, one body is the food of another body. Similarly, the bodies of animals are the food of men (see the list of the prescribed food ordained by the *Manusmṛti*). The Pitṛs and the gods are propitiated by the sacrifice of animals which are prescribed by the Scriptures (this subject has been fully explained in the *Gītā*). So the commentator puts here the term "obedience to mutual interest," in order to confirm the authority of the Scriptures.

3. The terms "Other objects" denote the unconscious stationary things such as trees, plants stones, mineral objects, etc. The trees and the plants which supply food to the animals and men are supported by the substances coming out of their very bodies such as blood, skin, bone, excreta, etc., which serve as manures, and contribute to the growth of the trees and plants. Similarly, the gods are supported by the trees and stones which are used for the completion of the Vedic rites (*pallava and pratīka*); again, the gods support them all by showering rain, etc., and by favourable natural help. Hence, the whole world is inter-dependent.

ment; they are accomplished for its achievement; they are taken up for making it perfect. So also it has been said:—He is indeed a Brāhmaṇa[1] who,—the more he wishes to accept many a vow, the more he turns away from the origins of injury caused through inadvertence,—simply makes that harmlessness perfect.

सत्यं यथार्थे वाङ्मनसे । यथा दृष्टं यथानुमितं यथा श्रुतं तथा वाङ्मनश्चेति । परत्र स्वबोधसङ्क्रान्तये वागुक्ता सा यदि न वञ्चिता भ्रान्ता वा प्रतिपत्तिवन्ध्या वा भवेदित्येषा सर्वभूतोपकारार्थं प्रवृत्ता न भूतोपघाताय ।

Truthfulness consists in true speech and mind, i. e., the speech and mind in accordance with that which is seen, inferred and heard. The speech is uttered for transferring one's own knowledge to another, if it is neither deceptive nor mistaken nor barren of observation and if it is engaged for the good of all living beings but not for their injury (that speech is truthful).

यदि चैवमप्यभिधीयमाना भूतोपघातपरैव स्यान्न सत्यं भवेत्, पापमेव भवेत् । तेन पुण्याभासेन पुण्यप्रतिरूपकेण कष्टं तमः प्राप्नुयात् । तस्मात्परीक्ष्य सर्वभूतहितं सत्यं ब्रूयात् ।

But in spite of being used with the best of intentions, if it turns to be the injury to living beings, it cannot be truthful; it must be but sin; the advocate of such Truth must go to painful darkness by that false show and false appearance of virtue. Therefore, after examining it carefully, one should speak the truth beneficial to all beings.

स्तेयमशास्त्रपूर्वकं द्रव्याणां परतः स्वीकरणं तत्प्रतिषेधः पुनरस्पृहारूपमस्तेयमिति ।

Theft is the acceptance of things from another against the laws of the Scriptures. Abstinence from theft consists in the negation thereof, as also in the absence of the desire for it.

ब्रह्मचर्यं गुप्तेन्द्रियस्योपस्थस्य संयमः ।

Continence is the full control of the sex-organ, the organ of generation.

विषयाणामर्जनरक्षणक्षयसङ्गहिंसादोषदर्शनादस्वीकरणमपरिग्रह इत्येते यमाः ॥ ३० ॥

Non-acceptance of gifts is the non-receiving of things after realising the blemishes of material goods in earning, preservation, loss, attachment and injury. These are the Restraints[2].

जातिदेशकालसमयानवच्छिन्नाः सार्वभौमा महाव्रतम् ॥ ३१ ॥

They, being universal when not limited by caste, place, time and circumstances, are termed the "Great Vow"—31

ते तु—जातिदेशकालसमयानवच्छिन्नाः सार्वभौमा महाव्रतम् । तत्राहिंसा जात्यवच्छिन्ना मत्स्यवधकस्य मत्स्येष्वेव नान्यत्र हिंसा । सैव देशावच्छिन्ना न तीर्थे हनिष्यामीति । सैव कालावच्छिन्ना न चतुर्दश्यां न पुण्येऽहनि हनिष्यामीति ।

1. Here, the term "Brāhmaṇa" refers to the Yogī who is in the grade of the Ordinary Vow. Some hints for the better understanding of the beauty of composition have been given in the footnote of the first aphorism in this second chapter. Here also we find the same thing. The author puts the main subject of this Science in the first chapter, and in the second he describes the means thereof. In the same way, he puts the object to be achieved in the first place of this aphorism and the rest become the gradual steps for its achievement. The commentator beautifully elucidates the process for solid success. He begins from the Observances which are the bounden duties to be performed in the grade of the Ordinary Vow. These are as follows :—The full-aspiration-after-Īśvara automatically leads a person to study: from study come austerities which consist in performing the actions according to the division of caste and life-order. Thence comes contentment and therefrom the purity of mind appears. This purity of mind destroys the desire for wealth. Subsequently the desire for woman also ceases to exist. He, who is free from carnal appetite, can never appropriate to himself by unlawful means the things belonging to others. On the absence of thievish nature, truthfulness must make its appearance. Last of all, Harmlessness takes a strong stand in him. This is the regular process for the achievement of Harmlessness.

A faithless creature, a person who is ignorant of the Vedic laws, a libertine, a greedy fellow, an impure rascal, a miser, a debauchee, a thief and a liar can never be harmless. If all of these rules are not observed, then this harmlessness is sure to take its opposite course.

2. The commentator extols the non-acceptance of gifts from others and deprecates the hoarding up of wealth, because it brings about the downfall of the yogī; and this statement is confirmed by all our Scriptures.

They, however being universal when not limited by caste, place, time and circumstances, are termed the "Great Vow." There, harmlessness is limited by caste;—The injury adopted by the fisherman should be inflicted upon fish alone and none else. The same (harmlessness) is limited by place too :—"I shall not kill at a sacred spot." The same is again limited by time also:—"I shall not kill on the fourteenth day of a fortnight and on a sacred day"[1].

सैव त्रिभिरुपरतस्य समयावच्छिन्ना देवब्राह्मणार्थे नान्यथा हनिष्यामीति। यथा च क्षत्रियाणां युद्ध एव हिंसा नान्यत्रेति ।

The same in the case of a person who desists from these three[2], is limited by circumstances also:—"I shall not kill except for the sake of gods and Brāhmaṇas." So also the injury inflicted by the Kṣatriyas should be in battle alone and nowhere else.

एभिर्जातिदेशकालसमयैरनवच्छिन्ना अहिंसादयः सर्वथैव परिपालनीयाः। सर्वभूमिषु सर्वविषयेषु सर्वथैवाविदितव्यभिचाराः सार्वभौमा महाव्रतमित्युच्यन्ते ॥ ३१ ॥

Thus, harmlessness and the rest must be observed by all means not limited by these distinctions of caste, place, time and circumstances. When they are performed everywhere, in all cases, by all means and without any exception, they being universal, are called the 'Great Vow'.

शौचसन्तोषतपःस्वाध्यायेश्वरप्रणिधानानि नियमाः ॥ ३२ ॥

The Observances are Purification, Contentment, Penance, Study, and Full-aspiration-after-Īśvara—32

शौचसंतोषतपःस्वाध्यायेश्वरप्रणिधानानि नियमाः। तत्र शौचं मृज्जलादिजनितं मेध्याभ्यवहरणादि च बाह्यम्। आभ्यन्तरं चित्तमलानामाक्षालनम्। संतोषः सन्निहितसाधनादधिकस्यानुपादित्सा। तपो द्वन्द्वसहनम्। द्वन्द्वं च जिघत्सापिपासे शीतोष्णे स्थानासने काष्ठमौनाकारमौने च। व्रतानि चैव यथायोगं कृच्छ्रचान्द्रायणसान्तपनादीनि। स्वाध्यायो मोक्षशास्त्राणामध्ययनं प्रणवजपो वा। ईश्वरप्रणिधानं तस्मिन्परमगुरौ सर्वकर्मार्पणम्।

शय्यासनस्थोऽथ पथि व्रजन्वा
स्वस्थः परिक्षीणवितर्कजालः।
संसारबीजक्षयमीक्षमाणः
स्यान्नित्यमुक्तोऽमृतभोगभागी ॥

यत्रेदमुक्तं ततः प्रत्यक्चेतनाधिगमोऽप्यन्तरायाभावश्चेति ॥ ३२ ॥

There, purification, caused by earth and water or by the eating and drinking of the consecrated things[3], is external. The internal purification is to wash away the mental impurities. Contentment is the absence of desire for procuring more things than what already belong to him. Penance is to tolerate the pairs of opposites. Further, the pairs of opposites are

1. Here, we find two-fold Vow : the Ordinary and the Great. The Ordinary Vow is the standard of Material Action and the Great Vow is that of the spiritual one, i.e., the *Pūrva-Mīmāṁsā* and the *Uttara-Mīmāṁsā* (the *Dharma-Sūtra* and the *Brahma-Sūtra*) respectively.

Keeping before our mind this view of the different grades of qualifications, if we judge the laws of the Scriptures regarding animal-sacrifice on the authority of any authoritative text, we can get a full solution of the contradictory theories presented by our modern teachers. It has been already described by the commentator that the whole creation is inter-dependent and all living beings have their obedience to mutual interest. So the Scriptures lay down the laws by which we can fulfil the interest of one another. Animal-sacrifice for the performance of the Vedic Rites is not at all a sin, on the contrary, it conduces to virtue; it is beneficial to both the sacrificer and the sacrificed.

Life depends on life. In other words, a living being can live only upon other living beings (MS. V. 28). A vegetarian also cannot deny that he subsists upon living beings. It has been definitely proved by the modern scientists that every particle of matter in this universe has got life.

Man is the highest being in this world. Our Scriptures assert that if the goat (or any animal) in the Vedic Sacrifice dies for the sake of gods, it will enjoy a higher life in the next world. The sacrificer also will be benefited by the propitiated gods.

2. The words "the person who desists from these three" signify that first of all, a man must be well-established in the ordinary vows, i.e., he must have a distaste for the carnal enjoyment. then he should desist from the Vedic sacrifices which are ordained for the sake of gods and Brāhmanas.

3. Here, there is no description of any particular kind of food whether roots or fruits, milk or water, air or fire. Simply consecrated food is indicated (vide *Gītā* XVII 8-10). Further, the significance of the "repetition of Praṇava" has been explained in the first chapter *Y.S.* I-28).

hunger and thirst, heat and cold, standing and sitting, dead-silence and gestural-silence, and also the vows performed with the appropriate rites such as Kṛchhra-cāndrāyana, Sāntapana, etc. Study is the reading of the Scriptures leading to Emancipation or the repetition of the Praṇava. The Full-aspiration-after-Īśvara is the Dedication of all (material) actions to Him, the Highest Preceptor. It has been said in this connection (showing the Finishing Limit of Action): "Whether placed on bed or on a seat or walking along a road, he the ever-freed and ever-established in himself, whose net-work of doubts has been destroyed and who is seeing the destruction of the seed of re-birth, becomes the sharer of immortality[1]." Thus it is that therefrom come in the attainment of the inner-soul and also the absence of impediments (*Y. S.* 1,29).

वितर्कबाधने प्रतिपक्षभावनम् ॥ ३३ ॥

For the prevention of evil ideas, (the habituation of the mind to) the development of contrary thoughts—33

एतेषां यमनियमानां वितर्कबाधने प्रतिपक्षभावनम् । यदास्य ब्राह्मणस्य हिंसादयो वितर्का जायेरन् । हनिष्याम्यहमपकारिणमनृतमपि वक्ष्यामि द्रव्यमप्यस्य स्वीकरिष्यामि दारेषु चास्य व्यवायी-भविष्यामि परिग्रहेषु चास्य स्वामी भविष्यामीति । एवमुन्मार्गप्रवणवितर्कज्वरेणातिदीप्तेन बाध्यमानस्तत्प्रतिपक्षान्भावयेत् । घोरेषु संसाराङ्गारेषु पच्यमानेन मया शरणमुपगतः सर्वभूताभयप्रदानेन योगधर्मः । स खल्वहं त्यक्त्वा वितर्कान्पुनस्तानाददानस्तुल्यः श्ववृत्तेनेति भावयेत् । यथा श्वा वान्तावलेही तथा त्यक्तस्य पुनराददान इति । एवमादि सूत्रान्तरेष्वपि योज्यम् ॥ ३३ ॥

For the prevention of evil ideas regarding these restraints and observances, (habituation of the mind to the) development of contrary thoughts is required. When the evil ideas in the form of injury, etc., come to this Brāhmaṇa[2] such as "I shall kill the evil doer, I shall also tell a lie, I shall also possess this man's things. I shall also be an adulterer of his wife, I shall also be its owner by the acceptance (of gift)" he, being thus afflicted by the high fever of wicked ideas tending to evil course, should develop the contrary thoughts :—"I, being burnt up by the horrible fire of rebirth, have taken refuge in the practice of Yoga after giving assurance of safety to all living beings. If that very I, who have once given up those evil thoughts, were to take them up again, I shall be equal to a dog in conduct." He should think in this way :—"As a dog licks up his own vomit, so is the man who takes up again the thing once given up by him." Thus, all this should be applied to other aphorisms also.

वितर्का हिंसादयः कृतकारितानुमोदिता लोभक्रोधमोहपूर्वका मृदुमध्याधिमात्रा दुःखाज्ञानानन्तफला इति प्रतिपक्षभावनम् ॥ ३४ ॥

The evil actions regarding injury, etc., are done, caused to be done and permitted to be done through avarice, anger and ignorance; they have mild, middle and intense degrees and are possessed of the infinite fruits of pain and darkness; such is the development of contrary thoughts—34

वितर्का हिंसादयः कृतकारितानुमोदिता लोभक्रोधमोहपूर्वका मृदुमध्याधिमात्रा दुःखाज्ञानानन्तफला इति प्रतिपक्षभावनम् । तत्र हिंसा तावत् कृतकारितानुमोदितेति त्रिधा । एकैका पुनस्त्रिविधा । लोभेन मांसचर्मार्थेन, क्रोधेनापकृतमनेनेति, मोहेन धर्मो मे भविष्यतीति । लोभक्रोधमोहाः पुनस्त्रिविधाः मृदुमध्याधिमात्रा इत्येवं सप्तविंशतिर्भेदा भवन्ति हिंसायाः ।

1. This dedication of all actions to the Highest Preceptor is the Finishing Limit of Action. It is purely practical and cannot be achieved only by the words of mouth as is generally done now-a-days. People commit sins throughout the whole day or week and then dedicate all their actions to God by parrot-like prayers for a few minutes. Īśvara is not an Entity to be pleased by flattery. This dedication is only possible when so many qualifications are acquired.

2. Here, the terms "this Brāhmaṇa" refer to the Yogī who is in the standard of the Great Vow. So this aphorism and the next are for him who is in the grade of Spiritual Action with the sole aim of Emancipation. This is clear from the commentary itself.

There, injury is thus done, caused to be done and permitted to be done; so it is threefold. Each of them again is threefold. "Through avarice" means "for flesh and skin"; "through anger" means "as evil is done by this" and "through ignorance" means "virtue will come to me". Again avarice, anger and ignorance, having mild, middle and intense degrees, are threefold. Thus this injury has twenty seven divisions.

मृदुमध्याधिमात्राः पुनस्त्रिविधाः मृदुमृदुर्मध्यमृदुस्तीव्रमृदुरिति । तथा मृदुमध्यो मध्यमध्यस्तीव्रमध्य इति । तथा मृदुतीव्रो मध्यतीव्रोऽधिमात्रतीव्र इति । एवमेकाशीतिभेदा हिंसा भवति ।

The mild, middle and intense degrees are again threefold :—mildly mild, mildly middle and mildly intense; similarly middlingly mild, middlingly middle and middlingly intense; similarly intensely mild, intensely middle and intensely intense. Thus injury becomes of eighty-one divisions.

सा पुनर्नियमविकल्पसमुच्चयभेदादसंख्येया, प्राणभृद्भेदस्यापरिसंख्येयत्वादिति । एवमनृतादिष्वपि योज्यम् ।

Again, this becomes innumerable according to the divisions of compulsion, option and conjunction[1] on account of numberlessness of the division of living beings. Similarly, this should also be applied to falsehood, etc.

ते खल्वमी वितर्का दुःखाज्ञानानन्तफला इति प्रतिपक्षभावनम् । दुःखमज्ञानं चानन्तं फलं येषामिति प्रतिपक्षभावनम् ।

"The development of contrary thoughts" means that these evil courses are indeed possessed of infinite fruits of pain and darkness, i.e., pain and darkness are the endless fruits of them; such is the development of the contrary thoughts.

तथा च हिंसकस्तावत्प्रथमं वध्यस्य वीर्यमाक्षिपति । ततश्च शस्त्रादिनिपातेन दुःखयति ततो जीवितादपि मोचयतीति । ततो वीर्याक्षेपादस्य चेतनाचेतनमुपकरणं क्षीणवीर्यं भवति । दुःखोत्पादान्नरकतिर्यक्प्रेतादिषु दुःखमनुभवति । जीवितव्यपरोपणात्प्रतिक्षणं च जीवितात्यये वर्तमानो मरणमिच्छन्नपि दुःखविपाकस्य नियतविपाकवेदनीयत्वात् कथंचिदेवोच्छ्वसिति । यदि च कथंचित्पुण्यावापगता हिंसा भवेत्तत्र सुखप्राप्तौ भवेदल्पायुरिति । एवमनृतादिष्वपि योज्यं यथासंभवम् ।

So also the killer at first over-powers the whole energy of the victim, then afflicts him with the blow of weapons, etc., and finally separates him even from his life. Thereby his (killer's) conscious and unconscious instruments become weak due to the expenditure of his strength. By causing pain he suffers pain by births in hell, in animals as also in the wombs of evil spirits, etc. And by killing the living beings he being tired of his life every moment, somehow lives even though longing for death; because the result of the regulated fruitive of the painful fruition must be experienced. If the injury be anyhow mixed up with virtue, in that case, he lives a short life for enjoying that pleasure. Thus it should be applied to falsehood, etc., also as far as possible.[2]

एवं वितर्काणां चामुमेवानुगतं विपाकमनिष्टं भावयन्न वितर्केषु मनः प्रणिदधीत । प्रतिपक्षभावनहेतोर्हेया वितर्काः । यदास्य स्युरप्रसवधर्माणस्तदा तत्कृतमैश्वर्यं योगिनः सिद्धिसूचकं भवति ॥ ३४ ॥

Thus by thinking of the evil fruition of the wicked ideas 'such is the result of such and such actions', the Yogi should

---

1. Compulsion is that where animals must be sacrificed for the completion of Rites such as *Jyotiṣṭoma*, *Anvahārya* मासिक *Śrāddha*, etc. Option is that where animals may or may not be sacrificed. Conjunction is that where both the stationary and the moving creatures are sacrificed.

2. The commentator puts falsehood and the rest in the same category as 'injury' because as animal-sacrifice is ordained in the Scriptures for the worldly prosperity (*abhyudaya*), so also telling lies, theft and the rest have also been prescribed for special occasions in order to keep peace and order in worldly life. These laws of the Scriptures apply only to those who are in the standard of the Ordinary Vow.

But the rule in the commentary is for him who solely depends upon the Yoga of the Great Vow with the full obedience to Restraints and Observances as have been described previously. He is allowed to give up the Material Sacrifices to the fullest extent. This harmlessness is not at all possible for a man who has not observed the laws of the Ordinary Vow.

not engage his mind in those thoughts. These evil ideas should be abandoned by means of developing the contrary thoughts. When they become unproductive for him, the power caused thereby becomes the sign of success for the Yogi.

अहिंसाप्रतिष्ठायां तत्सन्निधौ वैरत्यागः ॥३५॥

On the establishment of harmlessness, in his vicinity abandonment of enmity—35

तद्यथा—अहिंसाप्रतिष्ठायां तत्सन्निधौ वैरत्यागः सर्वप्राणिनां भवति ॥ ३५ ॥

These (perfections) are as follows :—On the establishment of harmlessness, abandonment of enmity comes to all beings in his vicinity.[1]

सत्यप्रतिष्ठायां क्रियाफलाश्रयत्वम् ॥ ३६ ॥

On the establishment of truthfulness masterfulness over action and fruition—36

सत्यप्रतिष्ठायां क्रियाफलाश्रयत्वम् । धार्मिको भूया इति भवति धार्मिकः । स्वर्गं प्राप्नुहीति स्वर्गं प्राप्नोति । अमोघास्य वाग्भवति ॥ ३६ ॥

(When he says) "Be virtuous" one becomes virtuous. (Again when he says) "Go to heaven," one goes to heaven. His speech becomes infallible.

अस्तेयप्रतिष्ठायां सर्वरत्नोपस्थानम् ॥ ३८ ॥

On the establishment of Abstinence from theft, presence of all excellent things—37

अस्तेयप्रष्ठिायां सर्वरत्नोपस्थानम् । सर्वदिक्स्थान्यस्योपतिष्ठन्ते रत्नानि ॥ ३७ ॥

All excellent things come to him from all sides.

ब्रह्मचर्यप्रतिष्ठायां वीर्यलाभः ॥ ३७ ॥

On the establishment of continence, attainment of vigour—38

ब्रह्मचर्यप्रतिष्ठायां वीर्यलाभः । यस्य लाभादप्रतिघान्गुणानुत्कर्षयति । सिद्धश्च विनेयेषु ज्ञानमाधातुं समर्थो भवतीति ॥ ३८ ॥

By the attainment of which, the irresistible virtues grow. Further, the Yogi being thus perfect, becomes able to impart knowledge to the disciples.

अपरिग्रहस्थैर्ये जन्मकथंतासंबोधः ॥ ३६ ॥

On the firmness of non-acceptance (of gift) comes the right perception of the how and why of birth—39

अपरिग्रहस्थैर्ये जन्मकथंतासंबोधः अस्य भवति कोऽहमासं कथमहमासं किंस्विदिदं कथंस्विदिदं के वा भविष्यामः कथं वा भविष्याम इत्येवमस्य पूर्वान्तापरान्तमध्येष्वात्म· भावजिज्ञासास्वरूपेणोपावर्तते । एता यमस्थैर्ये सिद्धयः, नियमेषु वक्ष्यामः ॥ ३६ ॥

On the firmness of non-acceptance (of gift) the right perception of the how and why of birth comes to him :—"who was I," "how was I," "what is this," "how is this," "what shall we be," "how shall we be." Thus the inquiry of self-existence pertaining to past, future and present, appears to him in its exact form. These are the perfections on the firmness of the Restraints. Now, we shall describe the perfections regarding the firmness of Observances.

शौचात्स्वाङ्गजुगुप्सा परैरसंसर्गः ॥ ४० ॥

From purification comes dislike for one's own body and unmixing with others—40

शौचात्स्वाङ्गजुगुप्सा परैरसंसर्गः । स्वाङ्गे जुगुप्सायां शौचमारभमाणः कायावद्यदर्शी कायानभिष्वङ्गो यतिर्भवति । किंच? परैरसंसर्गः । कायस्वभावावलोकी स्वमपि कायं जिहासुर्मृज्जलादिभिराक्षालयन्नपि कायाशुद्धिमपश्यन्कथं परकायैरत्यन्तमेवाप्रयतैः संसृज्येत ॥ ४० ॥

On the dislike for one's own body, the ascetic, undertaking purification, sees defects of the body and becomes unattached to it. What more? Unmixing with others. The knower of the corporal nature, seeing the impurity of body even

1. These are the perfections which are attained by the Yogi who can fully observe the rules as have been described in the preceding aphorisms. Further, the readers are requested to judge, on the authority of this account, the position of the modern preachers who claim for being perfectly established in the Basic Standard of these Moral Virtues such as Non-injury, Truthfulness and so forth.

though it be washed by earth and water, etc., desires to give up his own body. How can he mix with other bodies which are too impure ?[1]

सत्त्वशुद्धिसौमनस्यैकाग्र्येन्द्रियजयात्मदर्शनयोग्यत्वानि च ॥४१ ॥

The Purity of Essence, High-mindedness, One-pointedness, Sense-control and Fitness for self-observation (come in)—41

किंच? सत्त्वशुद्धिसौमनस्यैकाग्र्येन्द्रियजयात्मदर्शनयोग्यत्वानि च भवन्तीति वाक्यशेषः। शुचेः सत्त्वशुद्धिस्ततः सौमनस्यं तत एकाग्र्यं तत इन्द्रियजयस्ततश्चात्मदर्शनयोग्यत्वं बुद्धिसत्त्वस्य भवतीत्येतच्छौचस्थैर्यादधिगम्यत इति ॥ ४१ ॥

What more ? Purity of the (intellective) Essence, high-mindedness, one-pointedness, sense-control and fitness for self-observation appear. (The word) "appear" is the completion of the sentence. From purification comes the purity of the (mental) Essence, thence high-mindedness, therefrom one-pointedness, thence sense-control and thence fitness for self-observation comes to the Intellective Essence. All these are attained from the firmness of purification.

संतोषादनुत्तमः सुखलाभः ॥ ४२ ॥

From contentment comes the attainment of the highest happiness—42

संतोषादनुत्तमः सुखलाभः। तथा चोक्तम्—यच्च कामसुखं लोके यच्च दिव्यं महत्सुखम्। तृष्णाक्षयसुखस्यैते नार्हतः षोडशीं कलाम्॥ इति॥ ४२ ॥

So also it has been said :—"Whatever sensual pleasure is there in this world and whatever great pleasure is there in heaven, these cannot be equal to the sixteenth part of the happiness derived from the cessation of desires." (*Mahābhārata*).

कायेन्द्रियसिद्धिरशुद्धिक्षयात्तपसः ॥ ४३ ॥

From penance comes destruction of impurities, thence the perfection of the body and the senses—43

कायेन्द्रियसिद्धिरशुद्धिक्षयात्तपसः। निर्वर्त्यमानमेव तपो हिनस्त्यशुद्ध्यावरणमलं, तदावरणमलापगमात्कायसिद्धिरणिमाद्या। तथेन्द्रियसिद्धिर्दूराच्छ्रवणमननाद्येति ॥ ४३ ॥

The penance alone, being accomplished, destroys the dirt of the veil of impurities. From the cessation of that veil of dirt, come the physical perfections Aṇimā, etc.,[2] Similarly the perfections of the senses such as power of hearing from a distance, thought-reading, etc., (appear).

स्वाध्यायादिष्टदेवतासंप्रयोगः ॥ ४४ ॥

From study, comes communion with desired deity—44

स्वाध्यायादिष्टदेवतासंप्रयोगः। देवा ऋषयः सिद्धाश्च स्वाध्यायशीलस्य दर्शनं गच्छन्ति कार्ये चास्य वर्तन्त इति ॥ ४४ ॥

The gods, the Ṛṣis (Great Seers) and the Siddhas (Perfect Beings) come to the vision of the Yogi who is given to the Study; and they remain engaged in his work.[3]

समाधिसिद्धिरीश्वरप्रणिधानात् ॥ ४५ ॥

From the Profound Meditation upon Īśvara, the success in Spiritual Absorption—45

ईश्वरार्पितसर्वभावस्य समाधिसिद्धिः। यया सर्वमीप्सितमवितथं जानाति, देशान्तरे, देहान्तरे, कालान्तरे च ततोऽस्य प्रज्ञा यथाभूतं प्रजानातीति ॥ ४५ ॥

---

1. 'This Yogi' is not the stupid deceitful man who sees purity in the bodies of himself, his own wife, children, relatives, society and in the bodies of his own cats and dogs, and hates the bodies of the people of other classes and societies and also the images of gods in the temples of others.

The Yogi of the Great Vow is revered by all. He is quite aloof from the worldly noise and is solely devoted to the Yoga of Spiritual Action. When he is always ready to give up his own body on account of the defects and impurities of corporal nature, how can he mix even with his wife's body which is merely a store of flesh, blood, urine and excreta ? The following aphorism beautifully shows his character.

2. These will be described in the third chapter (*Y.S.* III-44).

3. This study is not mere vocal prayer but requires a great deal of effort in practice with a sincere heart.

The perfection of Spiritual Absorption comes to him whose full existence is dedicated to Īśvara. By this, he knows correctly all that he wants to know about objects in different places, in different bodies and at different times. Thence his Intellective Vision knows everything in reality.[1]

स्थिरसुखमासनम् ॥ ४६ ॥

Steady and comfortable is the Posture—46

उक्ताः सहसिद्धिभिर्यमनियमाः। आसनादीनि वक्ष्यामस्तत्र—स्थिरसुखमासनम्। तद्यथा पद्मासनं वीरासनं भद्रासनं स्वस्तिकं दण्डासनं सोपाश्रयं पर्यंकं क्रौञ्चनिषदनं हस्तिनिषदनमुष्ट्रनिषदनं समसंस्थानं स्थिरसुखं यथासुखं चेत्येवमादीनि ॥ ४६ ॥

The Restraints and Observances have been described with their perfections. (Now), we shall describe the postures and the rest (the other component parts of Yoga). There, the posture is steady and comfortable. These are as follows—*Padmāsana, Vīrāsana Bhadrāsana, Svastika, Daṇḍāsana, Sopāśraya, Paryaṅka, Krauñca-niṣadana, Hasti-niṣadana, Uṣṭra-niṣadana, Samasamsthāna, Sthira-sukha, Yathā-sukha,* etc.

प्रयत्नशैथिल्यानन्तसमापत्तिभ्याम् ॥ ४७ ॥

From the laxity in efforts and from the thought-transformation into infinity—47

प्रयत्नशैथिल्यानन्तसमापत्तिभ्याम्। भवतीति वाक्यशेषः। प्रयत्नोपरमात्सिध्यत्यासनं येन नाङ्गमेजयो भवति। अनन्ते वा समापन्नं चित्तमासनं निर्वर्तयतीति ॥ ४७ ॥

From the laxity in efforts and from the thought-transformation into infinity, the posture becomes steady and comfortable, such is the completion of the sentence. From the cessation of efforts, the posture gets perfected by which the body does not remain shaky[2]; or the mind being transformed into infinity, brings about the perfection of posture.[3]

ततो द्वन्द्वानभिघातः ॥ ४८ ॥

Thence, the cessation of disturbance from the pairs of opposites —48

ततो द्वन्द्वानभिघातः। शीतोष्णादिभिर्द्वन्द्वैरासनजयान्नाभिभूयते ॥ ४८ ॥

From the conquest of posture, the Yogi does not become overpowered by the pairs of opposites such as heat and cold, etc.

तस्मिन्त्सति श्वासप्रश्वासयोर्गतिविच्छेदः प्राणायामः ॥ ४९ ॥

On its achievement, comes Breath-control, the separation of the movement of inspiration and expiration—49

तस्मिन्त्सति श्वासप्रश्वासयोर्गतिविच्छेदः प्राणायामः। सत्यासनजये बाह्यस्य वायोराचमनं श्वासः कौष्ठ्यस्य वायोर्निस्सारणं तयोर्गतिविच्छेदे उभयाभावः प्राणायामः ॥ ४९

When the posture is achieved,[4] Breath-control (*Prāṇāyāma*), i.e., the separation of the movements of inspiration and expiration, takes place. Inspiration is the taking in of the external air; and expiration is the throwing out of the internal air of the lungs. In the separa-

---

1. The nature of the mind is to think again and again upon that object which it likes best. So a person to whom Īśvara (God) is the dearest of all, aspires after him and tries to hold communion with him. For this reason, the term "Īśvara-praṇidhāna" has been translated as full-aspiration-after-Īśvara, when it refers to the starting limit of Yoga; and the same term means "Profound meditation upon Īśvara" when it refers to the Finishing Limit of the same.

2. By this it is clear that the posture requires much effort and hard labour in the beginning. But when it is perfected, it becomes steady for all times without causing any trouble to the body.

3. This alternative is for him whose mind is already free from gross impurities. He stands in no need of the external component parts of Yoga; simply the internal parts of it viz,—the concentration, meditation and Spiritual Absorption (as have been described in the first chapter, and will also be described in the third) are suitable for him. But when he attains the third stage of Spiritual Absorption, he automatically obtains both the manifested and the unmanifested qualities, i.e., the results of the external and the internal component parts of Yoga.

4. By this, it is clear that without the acquisition of posture, the practice of Breath-control is not allowed. It is for this reason that he, who through ignorance of this rule, tries to control breath, gets many sorts of diseases; because the posture causes the purity of the nerve-system, so the Yogi never gets fat; his body remains bland like that of youth. He does not get any chronic disease (vide the *Śivasaṁhitā*).

tion of their movements, the cessation of them both is the *Prāṇāyāma* (breath-control).

बाह्याभ्यन्तरस्तम्भवृत्तिर्देशकालसंख्याभिः परिदृष्टो दीर्घसूक्ष्मः ॥ ५० ॥

The *Prāṇāyāma* having the external, the internal and the confining operations and being regulated by space, time and number, becomes long and subtle—50

स तु—बाह्याभ्यन्तरस्तम्भवृत्तिर्देशकालसङ्ख्याभिः परिदृष्टो दीर्घसूक्ष्मः। यत्र प्रश्वासपूर्वको गत्यभावः स बाह्यः। यत्र श्वासपूर्वको गत्यभावः स आभ्यन्तरः। तृतीयस्तम्भवृत्तिर्यत्रोभयाभावः सकृत्प्रयत्नाद्भवति।

That (breath-control) however becomes long and subtle. When its external, internal and confining operations are regulated by space, time and number. There, the external is that which is the cessation of movement after expiration ; the internal is the cessation of movement after inspiration ; the third is the confined operation where the cessation of both takes place by a single effort.

यथा तप्ते न्यस्तमुपले जलं सर्वतः संकोचमापद्यते तथा द्वयोर्युगपद्गत्यभाव इति। त्रयोऽप्येते देशेन परिदृष्टा इयानस्य विषयो देश इति, कालेन परिदृष्टाः क्षणानामियत्तावधारणेनावच्छिन्ना इत्यर्थः, सङ्ख्याभिः परिदृष्टा एतावद्भिः श्वासप्रश्वासैः प्रथम उद्घातस्तद्वन्निगृहीतस्यैतावद्भिर्द्वितीय उद्घात एवं तृतीयः। एवं मृदुरेवं मध्यः उद्घात एवं तीव्र इति सङ्ख्यापरिदृष्टः स खल्वयमेवमभ्यस्तो दीर्घसूक्ष्मः ॥ ५० ॥

As water thrown on a heated stone shrinks from all sides, so this is the simultaneous cessation of movement of both of them. Further, these three are regulated by space. "This much is its sphere" denotes space. They are regulated by time, i. e., limited by the ascertainment of duration of moments ; this is the meaning. They are regulated by number, i. e., "the first commencement is performed by so many inspirations and expirations"; similarly the second commencement of the regulated Prāṇāyāma is performed by so many and thus is the third. Thus it is mild, thus it is middle and thus it is intense. This *Prāṇāyāma* is indeed regulated by number and it being thus constantly practised, becomes long and subtle.

बाह्याभ्यन्तरविषयाक्षेपी चतुर्थः ॥ ५१ ॥

The fourth transcends the spheres of the external and the internal—51

बाह्याभ्यन्तरविषयाक्षेपी चतुर्थः। देशकालसङ्ख्याभिर्बाह्यविषयः परिदृष्ट आक्षिप्तः। तथाभ्यन्तरविषयः परिदृष्ट आक्षिप्तः। उभयथा दीर्घसूक्ष्मः। तत्पूर्वको भूमिजयात्क्रमेणोभयोर्गत्यभावश्चतुर्थः प्राणायामः।

The afore-said external sphere regulated by space, time and number, has been transcended, similarly the regulated internal sphere has been transcended. It is long and subtle in both ways. The fourth Prāṇāyāma (breath-control) is preceded by these two and is the gradual cessation of movement both by the conquest over the stages.

तृतीयस्तु विषयानालोचितो गत्यभावः सकृदारब्ध एव देशकालसङ्ख्याभिः परिदृष्टो दीर्घसूक्ष्मः।

The third, however, is the cessation of movement where the spheres are not considered, and which is commenced at once ; it, being regulated by space, time and number, becomes long and subtle.

चतुर्थस्तु श्वासप्रश्वासयोर्विषयावधारणात्क्रमेण भूमिजयादुभयाक्षेपपूर्वको गत्यभावश्चतुर्थः प्राणायाम इत्ययं विशेष इति ॥ ५१ ॥

The fourth however is the cessation of movement after passing over the both by gradual conquest of the stages through the determination of the spheres of inspiration and expiration. This is the distinctive fourth Prāṇāyāma.

ततः क्षीयते प्रकाशावरणम् ॥ ५२ ॥

Thence, the covering of the Effulgence is destroyed—52

ततः क्षीयते प्रकाशावरणम्। प्राणायामानभ्यस्यतोऽस्य योगिनः क्षीयते विवेकज्ञानावरणीयं कर्म यत्तदाचक्षते—महामोहमयेनेन्द्रियजालेन प्रकाशशीलं सत्त्वमावृत्य तदेवाकार्ये नियुङ्क्त इति। तदस्य प्रकाशावरणं कर्म संसारनिबन्धनं प्राणायामाभ्यासाद् दुर्बलं भवति प्रतिक्षणं च क्षीयते। तथा चोक्तम्—तपो न परं प्राणायामात्ततो विशुद्धिर्मलानां दीप्तिश्च ज्ञानस्येति ॥ ५२ ॥

Of the Yogi, who is given to the practice of breath-control, the action which covers the Intellective knowledge, is destroyed. This is what the wise say:—"The Effulgent Essence, being covered by the network of the senses full of extreme ignorance, is engaged by that action alone in vice." Of the Yogi, this action which is the covering of this luminosity and is the origin of re-birth, becomes feeble by the practice of breath-control and fades away every moment. So also it has been said:—"There is no other penance higher than breath-control, the dirts of impurities are purified and the brilliancy of knowledge is manifested thereby." (*Y. S.* 1-34).

धारणासु च योग्यता मनसः ॥ ५३ ॥*

And the capability of the mind for Concentration—53

किंच, धारणासु च योग्यता मनसः; प्राणायामाभ्यासादेव। प्रच्छर्दनविधारणाभ्यां वा प्राणस्येति वचनात् ॥ ५३ ॥

What more? And the capability of the mind for Concentration is indeed secured by the practice of breath-control on account of the authority of the aphorism "Or by the expulsion and retention of breath." (*Y. S.* 1-34).

स्वविषयासंप्रयोगे चित्तस्य स्वरूपानुकार इवेन्द्रियाणां प्रत्याहारः ॥ ५४ ॥

In the absence of union with their own objects, the function of the senses to follow, as it were, the nature of the mind, is Abstraction—54

अथ कः प्रत्याहारः? स्वविषयासंप्रोगे चित्तस्य स्वरूपानुकार इवेन्द्रियाणां प्रत्याहारः।

Now, what is Abstraction? In the absence of union with their own objects, the function of the senses to follow as it were the nature of the mind, is Abstraction.

स्वविषयसंप्रयोगाभावे चित्तस्वरूपानुकार इवेति। चित्तनिरोधे चित्तवन्निरुद्धानीन्द्रियाणि नेतरेन्द्रियजयवदुपायान्तरमपेक्षन्ते। यथा मधुकरराजानं मक्षिका उत्पतन्तमनूत्पतन्ति निविशमानमनुनिविशन्ते तथेन्द्रियाणि चित्तनिरोधे निरुद्धानीत्येष प्रत्याहारः ॥५४॥

In the absence of union with their own objects, the function of the senses becomes, as it were, the imitation of the nature of the mind. Further, on the subjugation of the mind, the senses being subjugated like the mind do not depend upon any other means like the conquest over the other organs. As the bees fly with the flying king and sit when he sits down, so the senses are subjugated by the subjugation of the mind. This is Abstraction.

ततः परमा वश्यतेन्द्रियाणाम् ॥५५॥

Thence, the highest subjugation of the senses—55

ततः परमा वश्यतेन्द्रियाणाम्। शब्दादिष्वव्यसनमिन्द्रियजय इति केचित्। सक्तिर्व्यसनं व्यस्यत्येनं श्रेयस इति।

Some one says that non-attachment towards sound, etc., is the conquest of the senses, because attachment is vice; it causes the Yogi to deviate from beatitude[1].

अविरुद्धप्रतिपत्तिर्न्याय्या। शब्दादिसंप्रयोगः स्वेच्छयेत्यन्ये।

Some others say that lawful enjoyment is proper; so the union with the sound,

---

* These aphorisms fully express that *Prāṇāyāma* is the best of all austerities and it makes the mind capable of concentration by removing its gross dirts. Hence, it is clear that *prāṇāyāma* itself is not Spiritual Absorption but is only the means of mental embellishment which makes the mind free from the heavy load of the senses.

1. This refers to the Agreeable End dealt with in the *Bhagavad Gītā*.

etc., of one's own desire, is the conquest[1].

रागद्वेषाभावे सुखदुःखशून्यं शब्दादिज्ञानमिन्द्रियजय इति केचित् ।

Others again say that in the absence of attraction and aversion, the sensation of sound, etc., devoid of pleasure and pain, is the conquest of the senses[2].

चित्तैकाग्र्यादप्रतिपत्तिरेवेति जैगीषव्यः । ततश्च परमा त्वियं वश्यता यच्चित्तनिरोधे निरुद्धानीन्द्रियाणि नेतरेन्द्रियजवत्प्रयत्नकृतमुपायान्तरमपेक्षन्ते इति ॥ ५५ ॥

But Jaigīṣavya says that it (the conquest of the senses) is only the absence of cognition due to the one-pointedness of the mind. Also for this reason, this is, indeed, the highest subjection which is the subjugation of the senses by the restraint of the mind[3]. The Yogis do not depend upon any other means caused by strong effort like the conquest of the other organs.

इति श्रीपातञ्जले सांख्यप्रवचने योगशास्त्रे साधननिर्देशो नाम द्वितीयः पादः समाप्तः ॥ २ ॥

1. This shows the Desirable End.

2. This is the same as the Finishing Limit of Action in the Sphere of the Cognitive-Spiritual Absorption.

3. This shows the Ultra-Cognitive-Spiritual-Absorption. Here the commentator strengthens his own conclusion on the authority of the revered Jaigīṣavya.

The author finishes here the subject of the external component parts of Yoga. The tendency of the mind is always to seek after peace which is its real nature. But it is bent down by the strong power of the senses. So these five external parts are necessary for washing out the gross dirt of the mind, i.e., for making the mind free from its subjection to the senses. The process of destroying the subtle dirts in the form of the habitual potencies has been described in the first chapter and will again be described in the third in connection with the internal component parts of Yoga.

Here ends the Second Chapter known as the Subject of Demonstrating the Means of Practice with regard to the Science of Yoga composed by Patañjali in the Excellent Teaching of the Sāṅkhya.

CHAPTER III

THE SUBJECT OF ACCOMPLISHMENTS (SIDDHIS)

देशबन्धश्चित्तस्य धारणा ॥ १ ॥

Concentration is the confinement of the mind in a place—1

उक्तानि पञ्च बहिरङ्गानि साधनानि । धारणा वक्तव्या—देशबन्धश्चित्तस्य धारणा । नाभिचक्रे हृदयपुण्डरीके मूर्धनि ज्योतिषि नासिकाग्रे जिह्वाग्र इत्येवमादिषु देशेषु बाह्ये वा विषये चित्तस्य वृत्तिमात्रेण बन्ध इति धारणा ॥ १ ॥

The five external component parts have been described. Now Concentration is to be considered. Concentration is the confinement of the mind in a place. The confinement of the mind by each operation, in such places as the navel-sphere, the lotus of the heart, the head, the shining part, the forepart of the nose, the forepart of the tongue, etc., or in any external object, is the Concentration[1].

तत्र प्रत्ययैकतानता ध्यानम् ॥ २ ॥

Meditation is the continuation of the cognition therein—2

तत्र प्रत्ययैकतानता ध्यानम् । तस्मिन्देशे ध्येयालम्बनस्य प्रत्ययस्यैकतानता सदृशः प्रवाहः प्रत्ययान्तरेणापरामृष्टो ध्यानम् ॥ २ ॥

Within that space of the designed object of meditation, the constant succession of the cognition, i.e., the uniform flow untouched by any other cognition, is Meditation.

तदेवार्थमात्रनिर्भासं स्वरूपशून्यमिव समाधिः ॥ ३ ॥

That Meditation itself, having the manifestation of truth alone as if devoid of its own form, is Spiritual Absorption—3

तदेवार्थमात्रनिर्भासं स्वरूपशून्यमिव समाधिः । ध्यानमेव ध्येयाकारनिर्भासं प्रत्ययात्मकेन स्वरूपेण शून्यमिव यदा भवति ध्येयस्वभावावेशात्तदा समाधिरित्युच्यते ॥ ३ ॥

---

1. Concentration is the first step for the achievement of Spiritual-Absorption. As the same earth, where a baby falls down, becomes also the only support for its rise, so this specific step of the Energies is the last limit where we have fallen down. By the help of this support alone we are to rise again.

There are many people who hate the worship of images which are the representations of God, by thinking it to be idolatory. But if we judge carefully, we can easily understand that this kind of worship alone is the only way to have a direct communion with God. The worshippers of trees and stones do not worship each and every one of their kind but they worship only the distinctive trees and stones on the idea of God. These worshippers are the true idealists; they alone can feel the omnipresence of God and become capable of reaching the highest stage of Spiritualism. The Scriptures confirm such form of worship.

On the contrary, it is admitted by all the philosophers in the world that the finite mind of a man cannot form an accurate conception of the Infinite or of anything Abstract. So one is at a loss to make out what the non-idolators think of at the time of their deepest devotion to God. Do they think of "airy nothings" ? If not, what they are thinking about at the time of their prayer ?

When the Meditation itself having the manifestation of designed form, becomes as if devoid of its cognitional character, due to the coming in of the real nature of the designed object, then it is called Spiritual Absorption[1].

त्रयमेकत्र संयमः ॥ ४ ॥

The three unified together is the Saṁyama—4

त्रयमेकत्र संयमः । तदेतद्धारणाध्यानसमाधि-त्रयमेकत्र संयमः । एकविषयाणि त्रीणि साधनानि संयम इत्युच्यते । तदस्य त्रयस्य तान्त्रिकी परिभाषा संयम इति ॥ ४ ॥

It is Saṁyama which is the union of those three—concentration, meditation and Spiritual Absorption. The three parts being engaged in one sphere are together called Saṁyama. This Saṁyama is the technical term of this trio.

तज्जयात्प्रज्ञालोकः ॥ ५ ॥

From its conquest, the Intellective-Vision (appears)—5

तज्जयात्प्रज्ञालोकः । तस्य संयमस्य जयात्समाधिप्रज्ञाया भवत्यालोको यथा यथा संयमः स्थिरपदो भवति तथा तथा समाधिप्रज्ञा विशारदीभवति ॥ ५ ॥

From the conquest of that Saṁyama, the Visibility of the Absorbent Cognition takes place. The more the Saṁyama becomes firm in position, the more brilliant becomes the Absorbent Cognition.

तस्य भूमिषु विनियोगः ॥६॥

Its application is by stages—6

तस्य भूमिषु विनियोगः । तस्य संयमस्य जितभूमेर्यानन्तरा भूमिस्तत्र विनियोगः । नह्यजिताधरभूमिरनन्तरभूमिं विलङ्घ्य प्रान्तभूमिषु संयमं लभते तदभावाच्च कुतस्तस्य प्रज्ञालोकः ?

The application of that Saṁyama should be in that stage which is the next to the conquered stage, because no body who has not conquered the lower stage, can achieve Saṁyama into the higher stage by jumping over the intermediate stage. So, by reason of its absence, whence can the visibility of his Intellective-Vision come in[2] ?

ईश्वरप्रणिधानाज्जितोत्तरभूमिकस्य च नाधरभूमिषु परचित्तज्ञानादिषु संयमो युक्तः । कस्मात्तदर्थस्यान्यथैवावगतत्वात् ।

Further the Saṁyama over the lower stages such as the knowledge of the minds of others, etc., is not necessary for him who is established in the higher stage by virtue of the profound-meditation upon Īśvara. Why ? On account of the achievement of that truth by other means[3].

भूमेरस्या इयमनन्तरा भूमिरित्यत्र योग एवोपाध्यायः कथम् ? एवं ह्युक्तम्—'योगेन योगो ज्ञातव्यो योगो योगात्प्रवर्तते । योऽप्रमत्तस्तु योगेन स योगे रमते चिरम्' इति ॥ ६ ॥

Here, the Yoga alone is the teacher to point out the stage next to that stage, etc., How ? Because it has been said thus :—"Yoga (Spiritual Absorption) is to be understood by the help of Yoga (the trio). Yoga (one-pointedness) comes up from Yoga (Spiritual Action); he who is assiduous in Yoga (Course of Action) rejoices in Yoga (union) for ever".

त्रयमन्तरङ्गं पूर्वेभ्यः ॥ ७ ॥

The trio is more internal than the preceding ones —7.

त्रयमन्तरङ्गं पूर्वेभ्यः । तदेतद्धारणाध्यानसमाधित्रयमन्तरङ्गं संप्रज्ञातस्य समाधेः पूर्वेभ्यो यमादिभ्यः पञ्चभ्यः साधनेभ्य इति ॥ ७ ॥

---

1. This subject has been described in the first chapter in connection with the Clear thought transformation (*Y.S.* 1-43).

2. By this the commentator confirms the necessity of cultivation for the achievement of the excellent fruit. He clearly affirms that without the regular course of procedure, nobody can ever hope for success. This aphorism refers to the successive steps of the Cognitive-Spiritual-Absorption stated in 1. 17.

3. Vāmadeva, Prahlāda, Śukadeva, Jaḍa Bharata, etc., are the illustrations to this rule; they observed no law or no process. They were established in the highest stage of Yoga with all powers and perfections (*vibhūtis and siddhis*) just from their very births by virtue of the profound meditation upon Īśvara. This is mere chance but not the means. Further, what we call "chance" is but the ready fruit of the hard labour done in previous births (*B.G.* VI 40-45).

That is this trio,—concentration, meditation and Spiritual Absorption,—which is more internal part of the Cognitive Spiritual Absorption than the preceding five component parts, the restraints etc.

तदपि बहिरङ्गं निर्बीजस्य ॥ ८ ॥

That also becomes the external part of the Seedless (Spiritual-Absorption).—8.

तदपि बहिरङ्गं निर्बीजस्य । तदप्यन्तरङ्गं साधनत्रयं निर्बीजस्य योगस्य बहिरंगं भवति । कस्मात्तदभावे भावादिति ॥ ८ ॥

That internal threefold part also becomes the external part of the Seedless Spiritual Absorption. Why ? On account of its appearance on the cessation of the trio[1].

व्युत्थाननिरोधसंस्कारयोरभिभवप्रादुर्भावौ निरोधक्षणचित्तान्वयो निरोधपरिणामः ॥ ९ ॥

The inhibitive-change connected with the mind of the inhibitive moments is the respective dissolution and evolution of the exhibitive and the inhibitive habits—9

अथ निरोधचित्तक्षणेषु चलं गुणवृत्तमिति कीदृशस्तदा चित्तपरिणामः? व्युत्थाननिरोधसंस्कारयोरभिभवप्रादुर्भावौ निरोधक्षणचित्तान्वयो निरोधपरिणामः ।

When the conduct of the Energies is ever changeful, what then is the nature of the mental change in the moments of the inhibitive mind ? The inhibitive change being connected with the mind of the inhibitive moments is the respective dissolution and evolution of the exhibitive and the inhibitive habits.

व्युत्थानसंस्काराश्चित्तधर्माः, न ते प्रत्ययात्मका इति प्रत्ययनिरोधे न निरुद्धाः । निरोधसंस्कारा अपि चित्तधर्मास्तयोरभिभवप्रादुर्भावौ व्युत्थानसंस्काराश्चित्तधर्मा हीयन्ते निरोधसंस्कारा आधीयन्ते ।

The exhibitive habits are the characteristics of the mind; they are not cognitional.[2] So they are not restrained by the suppression of the cognitions. The inhibitive habits are also the characteristics of the mind. "Their respective dissolution and evolution" means that the exhibitive habits of the mind are destroyed and the inhibitive habits are manifested.

निरोधक्षणं चित्तमन्वेति तदेकस्य चित्तस्य प्रतिक्षणमिदं संस्कारान्यथात्वं निरोधपरिणामस्तदा संस्कारशेषं चित्तमिति निरोधसमाधौ व्याख्यातम् ॥ ९ ॥

"That the inhibitive moment is connected with the mind" means that this alteration of the habits of the single mind in every moment is the inhibitive change. It has been described in connection with the inhibitive Spiritual Absorption that the mind then becomes possessed of the end of the habitual potencies.[3]

---

1. For example : The sleeping condition can never be achieved through personal effort, because it comes of its own accord after the cessation of all mental activities. But the preparatory arrangements are necessary for removing all obstacles to its approach. Similarly, the Cognitive-Spiritual-Absorption is the preparatory arrangement for the Seedless Spiritual Absorption; the latter appears on the cessation of the former. So the Vedānta Darśana holds that Brahma is self-manifested and not dependent upon any action.

2. Habit can only be destroyed by producing a counter-habit but not by mere want of cognition of the mind. The exhibitive habits begin from the Purposefulness of the Energies; so they are not cognitional. This Purposefulness is described to be the Intensive Cause in IV. 3. By this, the commentator means to say that the exhibitive habits of the mind cannot be destroyed by the laxity of the mind as in torpor but the inhibitive habit alone can destroy the exhibitive ones.

3. From this aphorism the author begins the description of the inhibitive mental change by many names which are the different modes of explaining the dissolutionary course of the mind. So there is no ground for us to think this Spiritual Absorption to be a senseless condition of the mind. When this mind becomes Spiritually Absorbed, it takes a reverse course for operation with each and every moment, i.e., it gives up the intellectual activities with the succession of moments and enters into the Intellective sphere according to the same degree of intensity. At last after destroying all the exhibitive habits by virtue of the inhibitive one, it ceases to exist just like quinine which passes away along with the malarial poison. This state is called the Ultra-Cognitive, the Seedless or the inhibitive Spiritual Absorption. The mind no more comes back (*Y.S.* I. 18, 51.). It is not at all the Spiritual-Absorption where there is no such successive change of the mind in its inhibitive course.

तस्य प्रशान्तवाहिता संस्कारात् ॥ १० ॥

Its Tranquil flow (comes) from the habitual potency—10

तस्य प्रशान्तवाहिता संस्कारात् । निरोधसंस्कारात् निरोधसंस्काराभ्यासपाटवापेक्षा प्रशान्तवाहिता चित्तस्य भवति । तत्संस्कारमान्द्ये व्युत्थानधर्मिणा संस्कारेण निरोधधर्मः संस्कारोऽभिभूयत इति ॥ १० ॥

The tranquil flow, depending upon skilfulness in practice of the inhibitive habitual potency, comes to the mind from the inhibitive habit. If there be any deficiency of that habit, then the inhibitive habitual potency is overpowered by the exhibitive habitual potency.

सर्वार्थतैकाग्रतयोः क्षयोदयौ चित्तस्य समाधिपरिणामः ॥ ११ ॥

The variation in the Spiritual Absorption of the mind is the respective fall and rise of all-pointedness and one-pointedness —11

सर्वार्थतैकाग्रतयोः क्षयोदयौ चित्तस्य समाधिपरिणामः । सर्वार्थता चित्तधर्मः । एकाग्रतापि चित्तधर्मः । सर्वार्थतायाः क्षयस्तिरोभाव इत्यर्थः । एकाग्रताया उदय आविर्भाव इत्यर्थः । तयोर्धर्मित्वेनानुगतं चित्तम् । तदिदं चित्तमपायोपजननयोः स्वात्मभूतयोर्धर्मयोरनुगतं समाधीयते स चित्तस्य समाधिपरिणामः ॥ ११ ॥

All-pointedness is the characteristic of the mind; and one-pointedness is also the characteristic of the mind. 'The fall of all-pointedness' means the disappearance thereof. 'The rise of one-pointedness' means the appearance thereof. The mind is followed by the state of being characterised by both of them. This is the same mind which, being followed by both these characteristics, i.e., fall and rise which are existent in its own nature, becomes Spiritually Absorbed. This is the change in the Spiritual Absorption of the mind.

ततः पुनः शान्तोदितौ तुल्यप्रत्ययौ चित्तस्यैकाग्रतापरिणामः ॥ १२ ॥*

Thence again the respective Disappearance and Appearance, having proportional dependence, become the transformation of one-pointedness of the mind—12

ततः पुनः शान्तोदितौ तुल्यप्रत्ययौ चित्तस्यैकाग्रतापरिणामः । समाहितचित्तस्य पूर्वप्रत्ययः शान्त उत्तरस्तत्सदृश उदितः । समाधिचित्तमुभयोरनुगतं पुनस्तथैवासमाधिभ्रेषादिति । स खल्वयं धर्मिणश्चित्तस्यैकाग्रतापरिणामः ॥ १२ ॥

The former dependence of the Spiritually Absorbed mind disappears and the latter appears in proportion to that (disappearance). The mind, pertaining to the Spiritual Absorption, is followed by both of them; it again moves in the same way upto the last extremity of the Spiritual Absorption (termed "Ultra-Cognitive"). That is, indeed, this transformation of one-pointedness of the characterized mind.

---

* Here I suggest some hints for the better understanding of the next aphorism.

With reference to a jar, earth is the characteristic (*Dharma*); the shape given to it is the symptom (*Lakṣaṇā*); oldness or newness is the condition (*Avasthā*); and the earth-atom is the Characterized matter (*Dharmi*). Similarly, with reference to the Creation, the Pradhāna is the Characterized Substance (*Dharmi*); the Energies are its Characteristics (*Dharma*) and the latter get changed into Symptom (*Lakṣaṇā*) known as the material growth or the phenomenal manifestation of the Pradhāna in the form of the mind (*citta*) after giving up its unmanifested state of being. And the condition (*Avasthā*) of the Symptom is that the exhibitive potency of the Energies becomes powerful from the loss of their inhibitive force. Thus the mind is fundamentally nothing but the Pradhāna in a developed form. So the mind is considered here as the Dharmi or the Characterized Matter, and the exhibitive and the inhibitive habits as its characteristics. Again at the time of its dissolutionary change, the inhibitive function in revealing its primitive state of being will be the Symptom of its inhibitive Characteristics. And that the inhibitive habits of the mind will get powerful by overpowering the exhibitive ones in the inhibitive change will be the condition of the inhibitive Symptoms. The following aphorism is the description of the dissolutionary change of the nineteenth aphorism in the second chapter. There, the mind has been said to be "omni-objective" or the fulfiller of all the Interests. In that case, its evolutionary change refers to the fulfilment of Experience (*Bhoga*) but here the dissolutionary change of the mind refers to the fulfilment of Emancipation.

एतेन भूतेन्द्रियेषु धर्मलक्षणावस्थापरिणामा व्याख्याताः ॥ १३ ॥

By this the changes of the Characteristics, Symptoms and Conditions in the elements and in the senses have been described — 13

एतेन भूतेन्द्रियेषु धर्मलक्षणावस्थापरिणामा व्याख्याताः । एतेन पूर्वोक्तेन चित्तपरिणामेन धर्मलक्षणावस्थारूपेण भूतेन्द्रियेषु धर्मपरिणामो लक्षणपरिणामोऽवस्थापरिणामश्चोक्तो वेदितव्यः ।

By the aforesaid mental change in the form of the characteristics, symptoms and conditions, it should be understood that the change of the characteristics, the change of the symptoms and the change of the conditions in the elements and in the senses have been described.

तत्र व्युत्थाननिरोधयोर्धर्मयोरभिभवप्रादुर्भावौ धर्मिणि धर्मपरिणामो लक्षणपरिणामश्च ।

There the respective dissolution and evolution of the exhibitive and the inhibitive habits is the change of the characteristics and the change of the symptoms in the characterized Substance.

निरोधस्त्रिलक्षणस्त्रिभिरध्वभिर्युक्तः । स खल्वनागतलक्षणमध्वानं प्रथमं हित्वा धर्मत्वमनतिक्रान्तो वर्तमानलक्षणं प्रतिपन्नः। यत्रास्य स्वरूपेणाभिव्यक्तिरेषोऽस्य द्वितीयोऽध्वा, न चातीतानागताभ्यां लक्षणाभ्यां विमुक्तः ।

The inhibitive habit, being possessed of three symptoms, is connected with three paths. It (the inhibitive habit) indeed, obtains the present symptom after giving up the first path which consists of the yet-unmanifested symptom and it does not transgress the reality of the characteristic. Here, it has its manifestation by its own real nature; this is its second path and is not devoid of the past and the yet unmanifested symptoms[1].

तथा व्युत्थानं त्रिलक्षणं त्रिभिरध्वभिर्युक्तं वर्तमानलक्षणं हित्वा धर्मत्वमनतिक्रान्तमतीतलक्षणं प्रतिपन्नमेषोऽस्य तृतीयोऽध्वा । न चानागतवर्तमानाभ्यां लक्षणाभ्यां विमुक्तम् ।

Similarly the exhibitive habit, being possessed of three Symptoms, is connected with three paths. It obtains the past Symptom after giving up the present Symptom and does not transgress the reality of the characteristic; this is its third path and it is not devoid of the yet-unmanifested and the present Symptoms.

एवं पुनर्व्युत्थानमुपसंपद्यमानमनागतलक्षणं हित्वा धर्मत्वमनतिक्रान्तं वर्तमानलक्षणं प्रतिपन्नं यत्रास्य स्वरूपाभिव्यक्तौ सत्यां व्यापार एषोऽस्य द्वितीयोऽध्वा । न चातीतानागताभ्यां लक्षणाभ्यां विमुक्तमित्येवं पुनर्निरोध एवं पुनर्व्युत्थानमिति ।

Thus again the inhibitive habit, being converted into the exhibitive habit, obtains the present Symptom after giving up the yet-unmanifested Symptom and does not transgress the reality of the characteristic. Here it (the inhibitive habit) has its operation for the manifestation of its own real nature. This is its second path and is not devoid of the past and the yet-unmanifested Symptoms. Thus again comes the inhibitive habit and thus again is the same transformed into exhibitive habit[2].

तथावस्थापरिणामः । निरोधक्षणेषु निरोधसंस्कारा बलवन्तो भवन्ति दुर्बला व्युत्थानसंस्कारा इति । एष धर्माणामवस्थापरिणामः ।

Similar is the change of condition. The inhibitive potencies become powerful and the exhibitive potencies become weak during the inhibitive moments.

1. The yet-unmanifested is the first path, the present is the second and the past is the third. The inhibitive habit of the mind always works with the present. So also the exhibitive habit works with the past, because it gives up its present habit every moment.

2. Suppose there are four successive gates of a palace. The first gate is internal with reference to a distant place. But when the first gate is reached, it becomes external with reference to the second inner gate. Again when the second is reached, it also becomes external regarding the third. Similarly, the Pradhāna is possessed of four steps. The mind runs through them all. This inhibitive habit of the mind becomes exhibitive with reference to the higher step. In this way the habit gradually goes on becoming exhibitive upto the end of its course till the mind, taking its last inhibitive habit, becomes dissolved into its own Cause known as the Pradhāna.

Such is the change of condition of the characteristics.

तत्र धर्मिणो धर्मैः परिणामो धर्माणां त्र्यध्वनां लक्षणैः परिणामो लक्षणानामप्यवस्थाभिः परिणाम इत्येवं धर्मलक्षणावस्थापरिणामैः शून्यं न क्षणमपि गुणवृत्तमवतिष्ठते । चलं च गुणवृत्तम् । गुणस्वाभाव्यं तु प्रवृत्तिकारणमुक्तं गुणानामिति ।

There the change of the Characterized Substance is caused by the characteristics; the change of the characteristics possessed of three paths is caused by the Symptoms and also the change of the Symptoms is caused by the conditions. Thus the function of the Energies does not stand even for a moment without the changes of the characteristics, symptoms and conditions. Further the function of the Energies is ever changeful, because it has been said that the cause of the rise of the Energies is the very essence of their nature.

एतेन भूतेन्द्रियेषु धर्मधर्मिभेदात्त्रिविधः परिणामो वेदितव्यः । परमार्थतस्त्वेक एव परिणामो धर्मिस्वरूपमात्रो हि धर्मो धर्मिविक्रियैवैषा धर्मद्वारा प्रपञ्च्यत इति । तत्र धर्मस्य धर्मिणि वर्तमानस्यैवाध्वस्वतीतानागतवर्तमानेषु भावान्यथात्वं भवति न तु द्रव्यान्यथात्वम् । यथा सुवर्णभाजनस्य भित्त्वान्यथा क्रियमाणस्य भावान्यथात्वं भवति न सुवर्णान्यथात्वमिति ।

By this, the threefold change in the elements and in the senses according to the difference of the characteristics and the Characterized Substance, is to be understood. However, in reality there is but one change, because the Characteristic is but the manifestation of the Characterized Substance; this modification of the Characterized Substance alone is amplified by the characteristic. There the alteration of state of the characteristic itself existent in the Characterized Substance, takes place in the past, the not-yet-come and the present paths, but there is no alteration of the Matter (dravya). As for example :—When the gold vessel is broken to be made into another form, it is the alteration of the state but not of the gold.

अपर आह—धर्मानभ्यधिको धर्मी पूर्वतत्त्वानतिक्रमात् । पूर्वापरावस्थाभेदमनुपतितः कौटस्थ्येनैव परिवर्तेत यद्यन्वयी स्यादिति ।

Others say that the Characterized Substance is nothing more than the characteristics, because the reality of the characteristics is not transgressed. If it (Characterized Substance) would be the relative cause, then it should vary through constant position (kūṭastha) after following the difference of the former and the latter conditions.[1]

अयमदोषः । कस्मात्? एकान्ततानभ्युपगमात्तदेतत्त्रैलोक्यं व्यक्तेरपैति नित्यत्वप्रतिषेधात् । अपेतमप्यस्ति विनाशप्रतिषेधात् । संसर्गाच्चास्य सौक्ष्म्यं सौक्ष्म्याच्चानुपलब्धिरिति ।

This is without any defect. Why ? Because the constancy is not found. It is this three-fold world which disappears from its manifestation, because its eternity is denied. Although it disappears, it still exists; because its destruction is denied. Its subtlety comes from commingled existence and the absence of perception is due to its subtlety.

लक्षणपरिणामो धर्मोऽध्वसु वर्तमानोऽतीतोऽतीतलक्षणयुक्तोऽनागतवर्तमानाभ्यां लक्षणाभ्यामविमुक्तः । तथा वर्तमानो वर्तमानलक्षणयुक्तोऽतीतानागताभ्यां लक्षणाभ्यामविमुक्त इति । तथानागतोऽनागतलक्षणयुक्तो वर्तमानातीताभ्यां लक्षणाभ्यामविमुक्त इति । यथा पुरुष एकस्यां स्त्रियां रक्तो न शेषासु विरक्तो भवतीति ।

The change of the Symptom is the characteristic present in the paths. It is the past (characteristic) which is connected with the past symptoms and is not devoid of the yet-unmanifested and pre-

1. Here the commentator refutes the theory of Nihilism and establishes his own theory of Theism, i.e; the real existence of the Substance termed "Pradhāna". He puts forward the objection of the opponents that as gold has its unchanging position, i.e., as it never gives up its real nature in spite of the various changes of forms; so if this creation were the consequence of some existing Reality, it also should have an unchanging position. Accordingly, as the world is perceived so the cause of it (known as Pradhāna) should also like-wise be perceived.

Now he replies that as gold, after giving up all its variations of forms, remains in its simple form, so this whole universe gives up the differentiations of the characteristics, symptoms and conditions. But in reality, it exists in its subtlety. Accordingly it is not perceived.

sent Symptoms. Similarly, it is the present which is connected with the present Symptom and is not devoid of the past and yet-unmanifested Symptoms. Similarly, the yet-unmanifested is connected with the yet-unmanifested Symptoms and is not devoid of the present and the past Symptoms. As for example :—A man, being attached to one woman, does not become averse to all other women.

अत्र लक्षणपरिणामे सर्वस्य सर्वलक्षणयोगादध्वसङ्करः प्राप्नोतीति परैर्दोषश्चोद्यत इति ।

Here an objection is raised by others that in the case of this change of the Symptoms, the confusion of the paths must come to all due to the intermixture of all Symptoms.

तस्य परिहारः । धर्माणां धर्मत्वमप्रसाध्यम् । सति च धर्मत्वे लक्षणभेदोऽपि वाच्यो न वर्तमानसमय एवास्य धर्मत्वम् । एवं हि न चित्तं रागधर्मकं स्यात् क्रोधकाले रागस्यासमुदाचारादिति । किंच? त्रयाणां लक्षणानां युगपदेकस्यां व्यक्तौ नास्ति सम्भवः । क्रमेण तु स्वव्यञ्जनस्य भावो भवेदिति । उक्तं च रूपातिशया वृत्त्यतिशयाश्च परस्परेण विरुध्यन्ते । सामान्यानि त्वतिशयैः सह प्रवर्तन्ते तस्मादसङ्करः । यथा रागस्यैव क्वचित्समुदाचार इति न तदानीमन्यत्राभावः किंतु केवलं सामान्येन समन्वागत इत्यस्ति तदा तत्र तस्य भावः ।

Its refutation is thus :—The essentiality of the characteristics requires no proof; where there is essentiality, the difference of the symptoms also must be considered; its essentiality is not for the present time only. If it be so, then the mind cannot have any impression of attachment on account of the absence of free action of the attachment at the time of anger. What more ? There can be no simultaneous occurrence of the three symptoms in one individual case of manifestation; the manifestation of their menifestative cause can only be by succession. Further, it has been said that the Energies, having predominance of forms and activities, become opposed to one another; the ordinary Energies however rise with the intense ones. Therefore there is no confusion (in the paths). As for example :—The attachment has its free action in some case, so it does not cease to exist at that time in another case but simply it becomes equally present in unity : so it has its existence therein.

तथा लक्षणस्येति । न धर्मी त्र्यध्वा । धर्मास्तु त्र्यध्वानस्ते लक्षिता अलक्षितास्तत्र लक्षितास्तां तामवस्थां प्राप्नुवन्तोऽन्यत्वेन प्रतिनिर्दिश्यन्ते अवस्थान्तरतो न द्रव्यान्तरतः । यथैका रेखा शतस्थाने शतं दशस्थाने दश, एका चैकस्थाने, यथा चैकत्वेऽपि स्त्री माता चोच्यते दुहिता च स्वसा चेति ।

Similar is the case with the Symptom. The Characterized Substance is not possessed of three paths. The characteristics however are possessed of the three paths; they may be visible or invisible. There, the visible characteristics get different conditions and are specified by the differentiation through the change of condition but not through the change of Matter (dravya). As the figure 1 is hundred in the place of hundred, ten in the place of ten and one in the place of one; in the same way a woman, even with her individuality remaining the same, is called wife, mother, daughter, sister and so on.

अवस्थापरिणामे कौटस्थ्यप्रसङ्गदोषः कैश्चिदुक्तः । कथम्? अध्वनो व्यापारेण व्यवहितत्वाद्यदा धर्मः स्वव्यापारं न करोति तदानागतो यदा करोति तदा वर्तमानो यदा कृत्वा निवृत्तास्तदातीत इत्येवं धर्मधर्मिणोर्लक्षणानामवस्थानां च कौटस्थ्यं प्राप्नोतीति परैर्दोष उच्यते ।

As regards the change of condition, the defect about the statement of Unchanging position is raised by some persons. How ? It is because of its being interposed by the operation of the paths. It is as follows :—It is the not-yet-come when the Characteristic does not perform its operation, (it is) the present when it performs its operation and (it is) the past when it ceases after performing the operation. Thus the Unchanging-position of the symptoms and the conditions of the characteristic and the Characterized substance comes in; this is the defect put forward by the opponents.[1]

1. This is the view of the opponents that when the Characterized Substance (Dharmi) is indestructible and has, in reality, its unchanging position, then the characteristics will also get unchanged by being obstructed by the paths. Accordingly the Symptoms and the conditions are also due to obtain the unchanging position.

नासौ दोषः । कस्मात्? गुणिनित्यत्वेऽपि गुणानां विमर्दवैचित्र्यात् । यथा संस्थानमादिमद्धर्ममात्रं शब्दादीनां गुणानां विनाश्यविनाशिनामेवं लिङ्गमादिमद्धर्ममात्रं सत्त्वादीनां गुणानां विनाश्यविनाशिनां तस्मिन्विकारसंज्ञेति । तत्रेदमुदाहरणम्, मृद्धर्मी पिण्डाकाराद्धर्माद्धर्मान्तरमुपसम्पद्यमानो धर्मतः परिणमते घटाकारमिति । घटाकारोऽनागतं लक्षणं हित्वा वर्तमानलक्षणं प्रतिपद्यत इति लक्षणतः परिणमते । घटो नवपुराणतां प्रतिक्षणमनुभवन्नवस्थापरिणामं प्रतिपद्यत इति । धर्मिणोऽपि धर्मान्तरमवस्था धर्मस्यापि लक्षणान्तरमवस्थेत्येक एव द्रव्यपरिणामो भेदेनोपदर्शित इति ।

It is not a defect. Why ? On account of the variegation in the interaction of the Energies even in spite of the eternity of the Substance possessed of the Energies. As the external world,—having only its beginning with the characteristic of sound, etc., which are born of the indestructible Energies,—is destructible; so the Traceable Step,—being possessed of only its beginning with the characteristic of Illumination (Sattva), etc., of the indestructible Energies,—is destructible; there (to the beginning with the characteristic) the term "Modification" (Vikāra) is applied. There is an example in this connection :—Earth is the characterized object; it acquires a different characteristic from the characteristic of the shape of a lump and is transformed into a jar by change of characteristic. The form of the jar, after giving up its yet-unmanifested symptom, obtains the present symptom; thus it (earth) is transformed by the change of symptom. The jar, experiencing newness and oldness every moment, obtains the change of condition. The change of the characteristic is also a condition of the characterized object and the change of the Symptom is also a condition of the characteristic; so the change of the Single Matter only is represented by differentiation[1].

एवं पदार्थान्तरेष्वपि योज्यमिति । त एते धर्मलक्षणावस्थापरिणामा धर्मिस्वरूपमनतिक्रान्ता इत्येक एव परिणामः सर्वानमून्विशेषानभिप्लवते ।

Thus it should be applied to other things also. These are the changes of the Characteristics, Symptoms and Conditions which do not transgress the real nature of the Characterized Substance; so it is but the single change which flows over all those Distinctive Steps.

अथ कोऽयं परिणामोऽवस्थितस्य द्रव्यस्य पूर्वधर्मनिवृत्तौ धर्मान्तरोत्पत्तिः परिणाम इति ॥ १३ ॥

Now what is this change ? This change is the rise of another characteristic on the cessation of the former characteristic of the Existing Matter.

शान्तोदिताव्यपदेश्यधर्मानुपाती धर्मी ॥ १४ ॥

The Characterized Substance follows the past, the present and the unpredicable characteristics—14

तत्र शान्तोदिताव्यपदेश्यधर्मानुपाती धर्मी । योग्यतावच्छिन्ना धर्मिणः शक्तिरेव धर्मः । स च फलप्रसवभेदानुमितसद्भाव एकस्यान्योऽन्यस्यान्यश्च परिदृष्टः । तत्र वर्तमानः स्वव्यापारमनुभवन्धर्मो धर्मान्तरेभ्यः शान्तेभ्यश्चाव्यपदेश्येभ्यश्च भिद्यते । यदा तु सामान्येन समन्वागतो भवति तदा धर्मिस्वरूपमात्रत्वात्कोऽसौ केन भिद्येत? तत्र ये खलु धर्मिणो धर्माः शान्ता उदिता अव्यपदेश्याश्चेति ।

1. The Object, having characteristics, is termed here "the Characterized Substance". By the illustration of "earth" the commentator means to say that in reality earth is not changed. Simply it seems to be changed owing to the variation of the characteristics, symptoms and conditions. Similarly, the Pradhāna itself is not changed in reality; simply its characteristics known as the functions of the Energies are changed into different symptoms and again the symptoms are changed into different conditions. Thus the whole change is supposed to be of that Single Substance termed "Pradhāna". Further, we are to note here the scientific difference between 'द्रव्य' (Matter) and 'वस्तु' (Substance). Matter is a thing which, according to Nyāya-Vaiśeṣika, begins from the Specific Step of the Energies. At last it then takes the name as Substance when it, being rectified and developed, reaches the Untraceable Step after passing through the higher successive steps in the Dissolutionary Change. In other words, a thing is called 'Matter' so long as it remains within the province of the Intellect, but the same Matter is termed 'Substance' when it reaches the state beyond the grasp of the Intellect.

There, the Characterized Substance follows the past, the present and the unpredicable characteristics. The characteristic, being differentiated by fitness, is merely the power of the Characterized Substance. Further it (the characteristic) is inferred to be existent according to the difference of the production of result which is seen to be of one sort in one (characteristic) and of another sort in another. There, the present characteristic knows its own operation and differs from the different characteristics, the past and the unpredicable. When however it becomes equally present in unity, then being the only manifestation of the Characterized Substance, what is it and by which can it be differentiated? There, those that are indeed the characteristics of the Characterized Substance come under the category of the past, the present and the unpredicable.

तत्र शान्ता ये कृत्वा व्यापारानुपरताः, सव्यापारा उदितास्ते चानागतस्य लक्षणस्य समनन्तराः । वर्तमानस्यानन्तरा अतीताः । किमर्थमतीतस्यानन्तरा न भवन्ति वर्तमानाः? पूर्वपश्चिमताया अभावात् ।

There, the past (characteristics) are those that have ceased after performing the operations; the present are those that are in operations. Further, they (the present ones) are the proximates of the yet-unmanifested symptoms. The past are the proximates of the present. Why are the present ones not the proximates of the past? On account of the absence of anteriority and posteriority.[1]

यथानागतवर्तमानयोः पूर्वपश्चिमता नैवमतीतस्य । तस्मान्नातीतस्यास्ति समनन्तरः । तस्मादनागत एव समनन्तरो भवति वर्तमानस्येति ।

As the relation of anteriority and posteriority exists between the not-yet-come and the present, it is not so in the case of the past. Therefore, there is no proximate of the past. Accordingly the not-yet-come alone is the proximate of the present.

अथाव्यपदेश्याः के? सर्वं सर्वात्मकमिति । यत्रोक्तम् --जलभूम्योः परिणामिकं रसादिवैश्वरूप्यं स्थावरेषु दृष्टम् । तथा स्थावराणां जङ्गमेषु जङ्गमानां स्थावरेष्वित्येवं जात्यनुच्छेदेन सर्वं सर्वात्मकमिति । देशकालाकारनिमित्तोपबन्धाद् न खलु समानकालमात्मनामभिव्यक्तिरिति ।

Now, what are the unpredicable (characteristics)? All have in them the nature of all. Here it has been said :—"The universal form of juice, etc., being the product of water and earth, is seen within the stationary beings (trees, plants etc.). Similarly that (form of juice, etc.) of the stationary ones is within the moving creatures, and that of the moving ones is within the stationary; thus all is of the nature of all without any exception of genus. But on account of the regulation of space, time, form and exciting cause[2], there is indeed no manifestation of all the varieties of nature at one and the same time".

य एतेष्वभिव्यक्तानभिव्यक्तेषु धर्मेष्वनुपाती सामान्यविशेषात्मा सोऽन्वयी धर्मी ।

What follows the generic and the specific nature within these manifested and unmanifested characteristics, is the Characterized Substance which is the Relative Cause.

यस्य तु धर्ममात्रमेवेदं निरन्वयं तस्य भोगाभावः । कस्मादन्येन विज्ञानेन कृतस्य कर्मणोऽन्यत्कथं भोक्तृ-

---

1. Suppose there is a constantly revolving wheel. If we want to determine its top, what are we to do ? We can only mark out a single point which separates the portion (of the wheel) not-yet-come from the portion which is past. Accordingly the point has its anteriority and posteriority.

Further, we can be aware of what is before us but not of what we have left behind. Similarly, regarding the revolving wheel of "Time", the present is a mere point, i.e., a moment only. The not-yet-come is its front, and the past is its back. So the not-yet-come and the present have their relation of anteriority and posteriority, i.e.. the not-yet-come is the anterior of the present, and the present is the posterior of the not-yet-come. The past is the posterior of the present, but the present cannot be the anterior of the past, because the past cannot be taken into account.

2. Here, the commentator describes the nature of the Objective Reality and also the interdependence of the whole creation. The "universal form of juice" denotes "universal food". According to the regulation of time, space, body and exciting cause, all is the food and support of all. But what is the means of ascertaining that regulation ? The Vedic Scriptures alone can supply proper answer on this point. The human mind can never ascertain the mutual relationship of the whole creation without the help of the Vedic Authority. The Manu-Smṛti can clear our doubts.

त्वेनाधिक्रियेत? तत्स्मृत्यभावश्च नान्यदृष्टस्य स्मरणमन्यस्यास्तीति । वस्तुप्रत्यभिज्ञानाच्च स्थितोऽन्वयी धर्मो यो धर्मान्यथात्वमभ्युपगतः प्रत्यभिज्ञायते तस्मान्नेदं धर्ममात्रं निरन्वयमिति ॥ १४ ॥

In the case of him, however, who thinks that this (perceivable) is simply the characteristic itself and it has no connection with the preceding cause, (for him) there must be the absence of Experience. Why? How can one cognition be charged with the duty of an enjoyer for the action performed by another (cognition)? Moreover, there would be the absence of remembrance, because no one can remember an object seen by another. Further, owing to the recognition of things, the Characterized Substance does exist as the Substratum which is recognized to have assumed the alteration of the characteristics. Therefore, this characteristic itself is not absolute.

क्रमान्यत्वं परिणामान्यत्वे हेतुः ॥ १५ ॥

The differentiation of succession is the cause for the differentiation of change—15

क्रमान्यत्वं परिणामान्यत्वे हेतुः । एकस्य धर्मिण एक एव परिणाम इति प्रसक्तेः क्रमान्यत्वं परिणामान्यत्वे हेतुर्भवतीति । तद्यथा चूर्णमृत्पिण्डमृद्घटमृत्कणमृदिति च क्रमः ।

By the application of the theory that it is but a single change of the single Characterized Substance, the differentiation of succession becomes the cause for the differentiation of the change. This is as follows :—The succession is the powdered earth, the lumped earth, the pot-shaped earth and the pot-sherd-earth.

यो यस्य धर्मस्य समनन्तरो धर्मः स तस्य क्रमः । पिण्डः प्रच्यवते घट उपजायत इति धर्मपरिणामक्रमः ।

The characteristic which is the immediate sequence of a characteristic, is the succession thereof. The lump disappears, the pot appears; this is the succession of the change of the characteristic[1].

लक्षणपरिणामक्रमो घटस्यानागतभावाद्वर्तमानभावः क्रमः । तथा पिण्डस्य वर्तमानभावादतीतभावः क्रमो नातीतस्यास्ति क्रमः । कस्मात्पूर्वपरतायां सत्यां समनन्तरत्वं सा तु नास्त्यतीतस्य तस्माद् द्वयोरेव लक्षणयोः क्रमः ।

The succession of the change of symptoms is the present manifestation of the pot out of the yet-unmanifested state. This is the succession. Similarly the past state of the lump out of the present state is the succession. There is no succession of the past. Why? Because the immediate sequentiality exists in relation to anteriority and posteriority, but there is no anteriority and posteriority in regard to the past. Therefore, only two symptoms have the succession.

तथावस्थापरिणामक्रमोऽपि घटस्याभिनवस्य प्रान्ते पुराणता दृश्यते । सा च क्षणपरम्परानुपातिना क्रमेणाभिव्यज्यमाना परां व्यक्तिमापद्यत इति । धर्मलक्षणाभ्यां च विशिष्टोऽयं तृतीयः परिणाम इति ।

Similar is also the succession of the change of condition. The oldness of a new pot is seen very near to its newness. This (oldness) also following the sequence of the moments and being manifested by succession, gets its highest manifestation. Further, this third change is distinguished from the characteristic and the symptom.

त एते क्रमा धर्मधर्मिभेदे सति प्रतिलब्धस्वरूपाः । धर्मोऽपि धर्मी भवत्यन्यधर्मस्वरूपापेक्षयेति । यदा तु परमार्थतो धर्मिणोऽभेदोपचारस्तद्द्वारेण स एवाभिधीयते धर्मस्तदायमेकत्वेनैव क्रमः प्रत्यवभासते ।

All these successions obtain their manifestations when there is a difference between the characteristic and the Characterized Substance. The characteristic also becomes the Characterized Substance with reference to the manifestation of another characteristic[2]. When however, in reality, the Characterized Substance has its application of identity

1. The power of the Substance is considered to be characteristic, and the manifestation of the latter is the symptom.

2. This refers to the exhibitive operation of the intellect where the characteristic becomes the characterized Matter in regard to its further lower change.

and it by itself is called the characteristic on the strength of that application, then this succession reappears only in unity[1].

चित्तस्य द्वये धर्माः परिदृष्टाश्चापरिदृष्टाश्च । तत्र प्रत्ययात्मकाः परिदृष्टा वस्तुमात्रात्मका अपरिदृष्टास्ते च सप्तैव भवन्त्यनुमानेन प्रापितवस्तुमात्रसद्भावाः । "निरोधधर्मसंस्काराः परिणामोऽथ जीवनम् । चेष्टाशक्तिश्च चित्तस्य धर्मा दर्शनवर्जिताः" इति ॥

There are two kinds of characteristics of the *mind*,—the visible (Paridṛṣṭa) and the invisible (Aparidṛṣṭa). There, the visible are those that are the cognitional ones and the invisible are those that are of the nature of the Substance itself. Further, they (the invisible ones) are only seven in number and by inference are proved to be existent in the Substance itself. Restraint, peculiarity, habit, change, life-force, activity and power are the invisible characteristics of the *mind*.

अतो योगिन उपात्तसर्वसाधनस्य बुभुत्सितार्थप्रतिपत्तये संयमस्य विषय उपक्षिप्यते ॥ १५ ॥

Henceforward, the subject of the Saṁyama is introduced for the attainment of the object wanted by the Yogi who has achieved all the component parts.

परिणामत्रयसंयमादतीतानागतज्ञानम् ॥ १६ ॥

From the Saṁyama over the three-fold-change, comes the knowledge of the past and the future—16

परिणामत्रयसंयमादतीतानागतज्ञानम् । धर्मलक्षणावस्थापरिणामेषु संयमाद्योगिनां भवत्यतीतानागतज्ञानम् । धारणाध्यानसमाधित्रयमेकत्र संयम उक्तस्तेन परिणामत्रयं साक्षात्क्रियमाणमतीतानागतज्ञानं तेषु सम्पादयति ॥ १६ ॥

From the Saṁyama over the changes of the characteristic, symptom and condition, the knowledge of the past and the future comes to the Yogis. It has been said that the trio,—concentration, meditation and Spiritual Absorption together, is called Saṁyama. Thereby the three-fold change being observed brings about the knowledge of the past and the future in them (Yogis).

शब्दार्थप्रत्ययानामितरेतराध्यासात्सङ्करस्तत्प्रविभागसंयमात्सर्वभूतरुतज्ञानम् ॥ १७ ॥

The confusion of word, object and idea ensues, because each resides with the other; from the Saṁyama over their divisions comes the knowledge of the cry of all living beings—17

शब्दार्थप्रत्ययानामितरेतराध्यासात्सङ्करस्तत्प्रविभागसंयमात्सर्वभूतरुतज्ञानम् । तत्र वाग्वर्णेष्वेवार्थवती । श्रोत्रं च ध्वनिपरिणाममात्रविषयम् । पदं पुनर्नादानुसंहारबुद्धिनिर्ग्राह्यमिति । वर्णा एकसमयासम्भवित्वात्परनिरनुग्रहात्मानस्ते पदमसंस्पृश्यानुपस्थाप्याविर्भूतास्तिरोभूताश्चेति प्रत्येकमपदस्वरूपा उच्यन्ते ।

There, the speech is effective in letters and the sense of hearing has the sphere of the change of sound only. The word again is determined by the intellect at the end of the literal sound. The alphabets, owing to the impossibility of being expressed simultaneously, are possessed of the nature of not-giving support to one another; they appear and disappear without touching the word and without bringing it (to the intellect). So they individually are not said to be the word.

वर्णः पुनरेकैकः पदात्मा सर्वाभिधानशक्तिप्रचितः सहकारिवर्णान्तरप्रतियोगित्वाद्वैश्वरूप्यमिवापन्नः । पूर्वश्चोत्तरेणोत्तरश्च पूर्वेण विशेषेऽवस्थापित इत्येवं बहवो वर्णाः क्रमानुरोधिनोऽर्थसङ्केतेनावच्छिन्नाः ।

The letter again, being individually possessed of the nature of the word and being supplied with the power of signifying all appears as if it has got the reality of the universal form on account of being helpful to one and adverse to another (letter). The former is placed with the latter and the latter with the former in a special arrangement; thus

1. This refers to the inhibitive operation of the intellect where the Characterized Matter becomes the characteristic by being related to some higher truth. Here the commentator leaves this subject for the Vedānta Darśana by establishing that the Characterized Substance (*Pradhāna*) becomes the characteristic only at the end of succession. It has already been said that this is but the description of the Dissolutionary Change for the attainment of Emancipation.

many letters are limited by the conventional meaning according to the order of their position.

इयन्त एते सर्वाभिधानशक्तिपरिवृत्ता गकारौकारविसर्जनीयाः सास्नादिमन्तमर्थं द्योतयन्तीति। तदेतेषामर्थसङ्केतेनावच्छिन्नानामुपसंहृतध्वनिक्रमाणां य एको बुद्धिनिर्भासस्तत्पदं वाचकं वाच्यस्य सङ्केत्यते । तदेकं पदमेकबुद्धिविषयमेकप्रयत्नाक्षिप्तमभागमक्रममवर्णं बौद्धमन्त्यवर्णप्रत्ययव्यापारोपस्थापितं परत्र प्रतिपिपादयिषया वर्णैरेवाभिधीयमानैरुच्चार्यमाणैः श्रूयमाणैश्च श्रोतृभिरनादिवाग्व्यवहारवासनानुविद्धया लोकबुद्ध्या सिद्धवत्संप्रतिपत्त्या प्रतीयते। तस्य सङ्केतः बुद्धितः प्रविभागः। एतावतामेवंजातीयकोऽनुसंहार एतस्यार्थस्य वाचक इति ।

So many letters which are invested with the power of supplying name for all such as "g, a, uḥ" (cow) denote the animal possessed of dew-lap, etc. That which is the single intellectual representation of those (letters) that are limited by the conventional meaning and whose succession of the literal sounds are drawn in, is the word, i.e., the signifying word becomes the convention of the signified. That single word is of the single intellectual sphere and is thrown away by a single effort. It is neither a part, nor a succession, nor a letter but intellectual; it is brought in by the function of the idea derived from the last letter; it has the sphere for the purpose of establishing truth elsewhere. It (the word) being named, uttered and heard by the help of letters alone, is ascertained by the hearers through the worldly intellect which, being intermixed with the beginningless habit of verbal discussion, is understood to be accomplished as a single whole (word, object and idea). Its convention is possessed of divisions from the intellect. "So and so," being of such and such class and having so and so ending, becomes the significant of such and such object.

सङ्केतस्तु पदपदार्थयोरितरेतराध्यासरूपः स्मृत्यात्मकः । योऽयं शब्दः सोऽयमर्थो योऽयमर्थः सोऽयं शब्द इत्येवमितरेतराध्यासरूपः संकेतो भवतीति। एवमेते शब्दार्थप्रत्यया इतरेतराध्यासात्सङ्कीर्णाः। तद्यथा गौरितिशब्दो गौरित्यर्थो गौरिति ज्ञानं य एषां प्रविभागज्ञः स सर्ववित् ।

The convention, however, is of the nature of memory in the form of the mutual abode of word and object (meaning). "That which is this word, is this object; what is this object, is this word", thus the convention assumes the shape of their mutual abode. Similarly the word, the object and the idea are mixed up, because each resides with the other. This is as follows :—The cow is a word; the cow is an object and the cow is an idea. He who is the knower of these divisions, is all-knowing.

सर्वपदेषु चास्ति वाक्यशक्तिर्वृक्ष इत्युक्तेऽस्तीति गम्यते न सत्तां पदार्थो व्यभिचरतीति । तथा नह्यसाधना क्रियास्तीति । तथा च पचतीत्युक्ते सर्वकारकाणामाक्षेपो नियमार्थोऽनुवादः कर्तृकरणकर्मणां चैत्राग्नितण्डुलानामिति ।

Further, the power of a sentence exists in all words. When the word "tree" is mentioned, the verb "is" also is understood there. An existing thing can never go away from its being. Similarly, there can be no action without process. So when the term "cooks" is mentioned, the hint of all active causes is also mentioned for necessary things viz : the subject, the instrument and the object, i.e., Caitra (a person), fire and rice.

दृष्टं च वाक्यार्थे पदरचनं श्रोत्रियश्छन्दोऽधीते जीवति प्राणान्धारयति । तत्र वाक्ये पदपदार्थाभिव्यक्तिस्ततः पदं प्रविभज्य व्याकरणीयं क्रियावाचकं वा कारकवाचकं वा अन्यथा भवत्यश्वोऽजापय इत्येवमादिषु नामाख्यातसारूप्यादनिर्ज्ञातं कथं क्रियायां कारके वा व्याक्रियेतेति ।

The composition of words is also seen for the meaning of a sentence. "The Vedic student reads the hymns, lives and maintains life"; here there is a full expression of the words and their meaning in the sentence. Therefore, the word should be analysed separately as signifying the predicate and signifying the subject. Otherwise, regarding the words "Bhavati", "Aśva", "Ajāpayas", etc.[1] on

1. As a subject *Bhavati* signifies "your ladyship", and as a predicate it denotes "is or exists." Similarly *Aśva* denotes a horse (noun) and to appease (verb); *Ajāpaya* means goatmilk (noun) and to overpower (verb).

account of the similarity of their noun and verb forms,—how can they, being unknown, be analysed into predicate and subject ?

तेषां शब्दार्थप्रत्ययानां प्रविभागः । तद्यथा श्वेतते प्रासाद इति क्रियार्थः, श्वेतः प्रासाद इति कारकार्थः ।

Here is the classification of these, the word, the object and the idea. It is as follows :—Śvetate prāsādaḥ (the palace shines white) ; here "śveta" is used as a predicate; "śvetaḥ prāsādaḥ" (white palace) ; here "Śveta" is used as a subject.

शब्दः क्रियाकारकात्मा तदर्थः प्रत्ययश्च । कस्मात्? सोऽयमित्यभिसंबन्धादेकाकार एव प्रत्ययः संकेत इति । यस्तु श्वेतोऽर्थः स शब्दप्रत्यययोरालम्बनीभूतः स हि स्वाभिरवस्थाभिर्विक्रियमाणो न शब्दसहगतो न बुद्धिसहगतः ।

The word is possessed of the nature of predicate and subject, (and also possessed of) that of object and idea. Why ? On account of the correlation such as "this is he," here the notion of "one appearance" only is the convention. That however, which is the "white" object, is the support for both the word and the idea. In fact it, being changed by its own conditions, neither goes along with the word, nor with the intellect (idea).

एवं शब्द एवं प्रत्ययो नेतरेतरसहगत इत्यन्यथार्थोऽन्यथाशब्दोऽन्यथाप्रत्यय इति विभागः । एवं तत्प्रविभागसंयमाद्योगिनः सर्वभूतरुतज्ञानं सम्पद्यत इति ॥ १७ ॥

Such is the word, such is the idea; they do not go with each other. The object is different, the word is different and the idea is different; this is their division. Thus, by Saṁyama over their division, the Yogi attains the knowledge of the cry of all living beings.

संस्कारसाक्षात्करणात्पूर्वजातिज्ञानम् ॥ १८ ॥

From the direct observation of the habitual potencies, the knowledge of the previous births—18

संस्कारसाक्षात्करणात्पूर्वजातिज्ञानम् । द्वये खल्वमी संस्काराः । स्मृतिक्लेशहेतवो वासनारूपाः, विपाकहेतवो धर्माधर्मरूपास्ते पूर्वभवाभिसंस्कृताः । परिणामचेष्टानिरोधशक्तिजीवनधर्मवदपरिदृष्टाश्चित्तधर्मास्तेषु संयमः संस्कारसाक्षात्क्रियायै समर्थः । न च देशकालनिमित्तानुभवैर्विना तेषामस्ति साक्षात्करणम् ।

Of two kinds indeed are the habitual potencies.—"the origins of memory and affliction in the shape of residua[1]" and "the origins of fruition in the shape of virtue and vice"[2]; they are accurately formed by the former births. They are the unseen characteristics of the mind like change, activity, restraint, power, life-force and peculiarity (*Y.S.* III 15). The Saṁyama over them is able to have the direct observation of the habitual potencies. Further, there can be no direct observation of them without the understanding of space, time and exciting cause.

तदित्थं संस्कारसाक्षात्करणात्पूर्वजातिज्ञानमुत्पद्यते योगिनः । परत्राप्येवमेव संस्कारसाक्षात्करणात्परजातिसंवेदनम् । अत्रेदमाख्यानं श्रूयते । भगवतो जैगीषव्यस्य संस्कारसाक्षात्करणाद्दशसु महासर्गेषु जन्मपरिणामक्रममनुपश्यतो विवेकजं ज्ञानं प्रादुरभूत् ।

It is from this direct observation of the habitual potencies that the knowledge of the previous births is born to the Yogi. Also thus in other cases, simply from the direct observation of the habitual potencies, the knowledge of other births appears. Here this story is heard:—From the direct observation of the habitual potencies the Intellect-born-knowledge (*Vivekaja-jñāna*) was born to the Lord Jaigīṣavya who had been seeing the succession of life-change in ten great creations (*mahā-sarga*).

अथ भगवानावट्यस्तनुधरस्तमुवाच—दशसु महासर्गेषु भव्यत्वादनभिभूतबुद्धिसत्त्वेन त्वया नरकतिर्यग्गर्भसंभवं दुःखं संपश्यता देवमनुष्येषु पुनः पुनरुत्पद्यमानेन सुखदुःखयोः किमधिकमुपलब्धमिति?

The Holy Āvaṭya, assuming a human form, said to him,—"On account of your presence in ten great creations you had been fully seeing, with your undefeated Intellective Essence, the pain born of the wombs in hellish and animal lives

1. This refers to the actions remaining in the store (*Sañcita Karma*) of the habitual residua.
2. This refers to the Regulated fruitive actions (*Prārabdha Karma*).

and you had been born again and again among gods and men. Thereby, of pleasure and pain, what has been experienced by you in excess ?''

भगवन्तमावटच्यं जैगीषव्य उवाच—दशसु महासर्गेषु भव्यत्वादनभिभूतबुद्धिसत्त्वेन मया नरकतिर्यग्गर्भसंभवं दुःखं संपश्यता देवमनुष्येषु पुनः पुनरुत्पद्यमानेन यत्किंचिदनुभूतं तत्सर्वं दुःखमेव प्रत्यवैमि ।

Lord Jaigīṣavya replied to the Holy Āvaṭya :—"Due to my presence in the ten great creations and by virtue of my undefeated Intellective Essence, I had been fully seeing the pain born of the wombs in hellish and animal lives. I had been born again and again among gods and men. Whatever had been experienced by me thereby, I consider all that to be pain only.''

भगवानावटच्य उवाच—यदिदमायुष्मतः प्रधानवशित्वमनुत्तमं च संतोषसुखं किमिदमपि दुःखपक्षे निःक्षिप्तमिति?

The Holy Āvaṭya said :—"Has this mastery of your Long-lived Self over the Pradhāna (the Principal Cause) and the highest pleasure of contentment of yours too, been placed in the category of pain ?''

भगवान् जैगीषव्य उवाच—विषयसुखापेक्षयैवेदमनुत्तमं संतोषसुखमुक्तम् । कैवल्यसुखापेक्षया दुःखमेव ।

Lord Jaigīṣavya replied :—"This pleasure of contentment is the highest in comparison with the sensual pleasure, but in comparison with the happiness derived from Absoluteness, it is nothing but pain.''[1]

बुद्धिसत्त्वस्यायं धर्मस्त्रिगुणस्त्रिगुणश्च प्रत्ययो हेयपक्षे न्यस्त इति दुःखरूपस्तृष्णातन्तुः तृष्णादुःखसन्तापापगमात्तु प्रसन्नमबाधं सर्वानुकूलं सुखमिदमुक्तमिति ॥ १८ ॥

This virtue of the Intellective Essence is possessed of the three Energies. Further, whatever depends upon the three Energies is placed in the category of the Avoidable. So it has been said :—"The chain of desire is pain itself; simply from the disappearance of the heat of affliction caused by desire, appears this gracious, undefeated and all-beneficial happiness.

प्रत्ययस्य परचित्तज्ञानम् ॥ १९ ॥

Of the notions, the knowledge of other minds—19

प्रत्ययस्य परचित्तज्ञानम् । प्रत्यये संयमात्प्रत्ययस्य साक्षात्करणात्ततः परचित्तज्ञानम् । न च तत्सालम्बनं तस्याविषयीभूतत्वात् । रक्तं प्रत्ययं जानात्यमुष्मिन्नालम्बने रक्तमिति न जानाति । परचित्तस्य प्रत्ययस्य यदालम्बनं तद्योगिचित्तेन नालम्बनीकृतं परप्रत्ययमात्रं तु योगिचित्तस्यालम्बनीभूतमिति ॥ १९ ॥

From the Saṁyama over the notions and from the direct observations of the notions, comes the knowledge of other minds, but not the support (object) thereof; because that is not the sphere of his mind. He knows the longing notion but does not know the object for which it longs. That which is the object of the mental notion of another, is not grasped by the Yogi's mind; but simply the notion of another's mind can be brought within the grasp of the Yogi's mind.

कायरूपसंयमात्तद्ग्राह्यशक्तिस्तम्भे चक्षुःप्रकाशासंप्रयोगेऽन्तर्धानम् ॥ २० ॥

From the Saṁyama over the figure of his body, on the stoppage of the receivable power and for want of contact with the light of the eye, comes the sudden disappearance—20

कायरूपसंयमात्तद्ग्राह्यशक्तिस्तम्भे चक्षुःप्रकाशासंप्रयोगेऽन्तर्धानम् । कायस्य रूपे संयमाद्रूपस्य या ग्राह्या शक्तिस्तां प्रतिष्टभ्नाति । ग्राह्यशक्तिस्तम्भे सति चक्षुःप्रकाशासंप्रयोगेऽन्तर्धानमुत्पद्यते योगिनः । एतेन शब्दाद्यन्तर्धानमुक्तं वेदितव्यम् ॥ २० ॥

From the Saṁyama upon the figure of his body, he checks the receivable power of his figure. When the stoppage of that receivable power is performed, then for want of contact with the light of the eye, the sudden disappearance

1. Now on the authority of this commentary, let us determine the true nature of Emancipation which has been put into many ambiguous theories by the sectarians by means of representing their own fabricated regions together with the varieties of happiness.

is born to the Yogi. By this it should be understood that the sudden disappearance of sound, etc., has been mentioned.

सोपक्रमं निरुपक्रमं च कर्म तत्संयमादपरान्तज्ञानमरिष्टेभ्यो वा ॥ २१ ॥

The action is quickly fruitive and slowly fruitive; from the saṁyama thereupon comes the knowledge of death, or from the symptoms of approaching evil—21

सोपक्रमं निरुपक्रमं च कर्म तत्संयमादपरान्तज्ञानमरिष्टेभ्यो वा। आयुर्विपाकं कर्म द्विविधं सोपक्रमं निरुपक्रमं च। तत्र यथार्द्रं वस्त्रं वितानितं ह्रसीयसा कालेन शुष्येत्तथा सोपक्रमम्। यथा च तदेव सम्पिण्डितं चिरेण संशुष्येदेवं निरुपक्रमम्।

The action whose fruition is the life-period, is of two descriptions. One gives the fruit quickly and the other slowly. As a wet cloth, being expanded, dries within a short time, so is the quickly fruitive action. Further, as the same cloth, when furled up, takes a long time to dry, so is the slowly fruitive action.

यथा वाग्निः शुष्के कक्षे मुक्तो वातेन समन्ततो युक्तः क्षेपीयसा कालेन दहेत्तथा सोपक्रमम्। यथा वा स एवाग्निस्तृणराशौ क्रमशोऽवयवेषु न्यस्तश्चिरेण दहेत्तथा निरुपक्रमम्।

Or as fire, being set to the dry hay and being blown up by wind from all sides, burns it within a short time, so is the quickly fruitive action. Again as the same fire, being set to pieces of straw spread gradually out of a heap, takes a long time to burn it (the heap), so is the slowly fruitive action.

तदेकभविकमायुष्करं कर्म द्विविधं सोपक्रमं निरुपक्रमं च। तत्संयमादपरान्तस्य प्रायणस्य ज्ञानम्।

Thus, the action which is productive of single-life and is fruitive of the life-period is two-fold,—quickly fruitive and slowly fruitive. From the Saṁyama, comes the knowledge of death, i.e., the end of the life-period.

अरिष्टेभ्यो वेति त्रिविधमरिष्टमाध्यात्मिकमाधिभौतिकमाधिदैविकं च। तत्राध्यात्मिकं घोषं स्वदेहे पिहितकर्णो न शृणोति ज्योतिर्वा नेत्रेऽवष्टब्धे न पश्यति। तथाधिभौतिकं यमपुरुषान्पश्यति पितॄनतीतानागतानकस्मात्पश्यति। तथाधिदैविकं स्वर्गमकस्मात्सिद्धान्वा पश्यति। विपरीतं वा सर्वमित्यनेन वा जानात्यपरान्तमुपस्थितमिति ॥ २१ ॥

Or from the symptom of approaching evil :—the symptom thereof is three-fold,—relating to body and mind (Ādhyātmika), caused by other beings (Ādhibhautika) and coming from gods (Ādhidaivika). There regarding the evil omens pertaining to body and mind he does not hear sound in his own body after stopping his ears, or does not see light after closing his eyes. Similarly, regarding the evil omens caused by other beings, he sees the officers of Yama (the Controller of death), and all of a sudden he sees his past ancestors to be present. Similarly, concerning the portents coming from gods, he suddenly sees the heaven or the perfect ones (*Siddhas*); or he sees every thing opposite. By this too, he knows death to be nearing.

मैत्र्यादिषु बलानि ॥ २२ ॥

On Friendship, etc., the powers—22

मैत्र्यादिषु बलानि। मैत्रीकरुणामुदितेति तिस्रो भावनास्तत्र भूतेषु सुखितेषु मैत्रीं भावयित्वा मैत्रीबलं लभते। दुःखितेषु करुणां भावयित्वा करुणाबलं लभते। पुण्यशीलेषु मुदितां भावयित्वा मुदिताबलं लभते। भावनातः समाधिर्यः स संयमस्ततो बलान्यवन्ध्यवीर्याणि जायन्ते। पापशीलेषूपेक्षा न तु भावना। ततश्च तस्यां नास्ति समाधिरित्यतो न बलमुपेक्षातस्तत्र संयमाभावादिति ॥ २२ ॥

Friendship, compassion and joy are the three powers to be developed. There, by developing friendship towards the happy beings, he attains the power of friendship; by developing compassion towards the sufferers, he attains the power of compassion; and by developing joy towards the virtuous ones, he attains the power of joy. The Absorption which comes from the development (of these) is the Saṁyama itself. The powers, full of irresistible force of action, are born thereform. There is the neutrality (cessation) towards the vicious, but it is not a development (causation); also for this reason, there is no Absorption therein. Hence, there is no power from neutrality on account of the absence of Saṁyama therein.

बलेषु हस्तिबलादीनि ॥ २३ ॥

Upon the powers, the powers of elephant, etc—23

बलेषु हस्तिबलादीनि । हस्तिबले संयमाद्धस्तिबलो भवति । वैनतेयबले संयमाद्वैनतेयबलो भवति । वायुबले संयमाद्वायुबलो भवतीत्येवमादि ॥२३ ॥

From Saṁyama upon the power of the elephant, he becomes possessed of the elephantine power, from the Saṁyama over the strength of Garuḍa (the conveyance of the Lord Viṣṇu), he becomes possessed of the power of Garuḍa; from the Saṁyama upon the power of Air he becomes possessed of the power of Air and so on.

प्रवृत्त्यालोकन्यासात्सूक्ष्मव्यवहितविप्रकृष्टज्ञानम् ॥ २४ ॥

Through the application of the sense-objective manifestation, the knowledge of the subtle, the obstructed and the distant—24

प्रवृत्त्यालोकन्यासात्सूक्ष्मव्यवहितविप्रकृष्टज्ञानम् । ज्योतिष्मती प्रवृत्तिरुक्ता मनसस्तस्यां य आलोकस्तं योगी सूक्ष्मे वा व्यवहिते वा विप्रकृष्टे वार्थे विन्यस्य तमर्थमधिगच्छति ॥ २४ ॥

The effulgent manifestation of the mind has been described (*Y.S.* I-35). The Yogi, by applying the light which exists therein, to the subtle, the obstructed or to the distant object, understands the truth thereof.

भुवनज्ञानं सूर्ये संयमात् ॥ २५ ॥

The knowledge of the universe comes from the Saṁyama upon the sun—25

भुवनज्ञानं सूर्ये संयमात् । तत्प्रस्तारः सप्तलोकास्तत्रावीचेः प्रभृति मेरुपृष्ठं यावदित्येवं भूर्लोकः । मेरुपृष्ठादारभ्य आध्रुवाद् ग्रहनक्षत्रताराविचित्रोऽन्तरिक्षलोकः । ततः परः स्वर्लोकः पञ्चविधो माहेन्द्रस्तृतीयो लोकः । चतुर्थः प्राजापत्यो महर्लोकस्त्रिविधो ब्राह्मः । तद्यथा जनलोकस्तपोलोकः सत्यलोक इति । "ब्राह्मस्त्रिभूमिको लोकः प्राजापत्यस्ततो महान् । माहेन्द्रश्च स्वरित्युक्तो दिवि तारा भुवि प्रजा" इति संग्रहश्लोकः ।

Its (of the universe) expansion covers seven regions. There the region beginning from hell upto the back of the Meru, is the Bhū-Loka. The aerial region, beginning from the back of the Meru upto the pole-star and decorated with planets, asterisms and stars, is the Antarīkṣa (or the Bhuva Loka). Above that, the divine region is five-fold. The region of Mahendra is the third; the fourth is the Maharloka belonging to the Creator. The region of Brahmā is threefold; these are as follows :—The Janaloka, the Tapoloka and the Satyaloka. "The region of Brahmā is concerned with three regions, then comes the Maharloka of the Creator; the region of Mahendra is called the Svaḥ and in the sky are the stars; on the earth are the creatures",—this is the compiled verse.

तत्रावीचेरुपर्युपरि निविष्टाः षण्महानरकभूमयो घनसलिलानलानिलाकाशतमःप्रतिष्ठा महाकालाम्बरीषरौरवमहारौरवकालसूत्रान्धतामिस्राः । यत्र स्वकर्मोपार्जितदुःखवेदनाः प्राणिनः कष्टमायुर्दीर्घकालमाक्षिप्य जायन्ते ।

In the hellish world, there are the six great hells one above the other, they have firm foundation in earth, water, fire, air, ether and darkness respectively; these are Mahākāla, Ambarīṣa, Raurava, Mahā-raurava, Kālasūtra and Andhatāmisra—where the beings who are to suffer pain earned by their own actions, are born after having taken to themselves the long life of pain.

ततो महातलरसातलातलसुतलवितलतलातलपातालाख्यानि सप्त पातालानि ।

Beneath them are the seven Pātālas (nether lands) such as Mahātala, Rasātala, Atala, Sutala, Vitala, Talātala and Pātāla.

भूमिरियमष्टमी सप्तद्वीपा वसुमती यस्याः सुमेरुर्मध्ये पर्वतराजः काञ्चनस्तस्य रजतवैदूर्यस्फटिकहेममणिमयानि शृङ्गाणि । तत्र वैदूर्यप्रभानुरागान्नीलोत्पलपत्रश्यामो नभसो दक्षिणभागः श्वेतः पूर्वः स्वच्छः पश्चिमः कुरण्टकाभ उत्तरः ।

The eighth is this earth possessed of seven islands and known as Vasumatī, in the middle of which is the golden Sumeru, the king of mountains; its peaks are of silver, coral, crystal, gold and jewels. There the Southern portion of the sky being coloured by the radiance of emerald, is blue like the leaf of blue-lotus; the Eastern is white; the Western is bright and the Northern is yellow.

दक्षिणपार्श्वे चास्य जम्बूर्यतोऽयं जम्बूद्वीपस्तस्य सूर्यप्रचाराद्रात्रिदिवं लग्नमिव वर्तते । तस्य नीलश्वेतशृङ्गवन्त उदीचीनास्त्रयः पर्वता द्विसहस्रायामास्तदन्तरेषु त्रीणि वर्षाणि नवनवयोजनसाहस्राणि रमणकं हिरण्मयमुत्तराः कुरव इति ।

Further, on its Southern side, there is the Jambū (tree). So it is known as the Jambū-dvīpa (island); its night and day exist as if held by the movement of the sun. It has three Northern mountains which are possessed of blue and white peaks and are two thousand yojanas in extent. Surrounded by them, are three continents each of which is of nine-thousand yojanas. They are the Ramaṇaka, the Hiraṇmaya and the Uttarakuru.

निषधहेमकूटहिमशैला दक्षिणतो द्विसाहस्रायामास्तदन्तरेषु त्रीणि वर्षाणि नवनवयोजनसाहस्राणि हरिवर्षं किंपुरुषं भारतमिति ।

To the South, are three mountains—the Niṣadha, the Hemakūṭa and the Himaśṛṅga, which are of two thousand yojanas in extent each. Within these, are three continents; each of them is of nine-thousand-yojanas. These are Harivarṣa, Kimpuruṣa and Bhārata.

प्राचीना भद्राश्वमाल्यवत्सीमानः प्रतीचीनाः केतुमालगन्धमादनसीमानः मध्ये वर्षमिलावृतम् ।

The Eastern boundary is formed by the Bhadrāśva and the Mālyavat. The West is bounded by the Ketumāla and the Gandhamādana. In the middle is the continent Ilāvṛta.

तदेतद्योजनशतसाहस्रं सुमेरोर्दिशि दिशि तदर्धेन व्यूढम् । स खल्वयं शतसाहस्रायामो जम्बूद्वीपस्ततो द्विगुणेन लवणोदधिना वलयाकृतिना वेष्टितः ।

All this (Jambū dvīpa) is of one hundred-thousand-yojanas. From the Sumeru each side is arranged by half of that extent. It is indeed this Jambu dvīpa which is of one-hundred thousand yojanas in extent. It is encircled by the salt ocean twice of that extent in the form of a bracelet.

ततश्च द्विगुणा द्विगुणाः शाककुशक्रौञ्चशाल्मलगोमेधपुष्करद्वीपाः सप्त समुद्राश्च सर्षपराशिकल्पाः सविचित्रशैलावतंसा इक्षुरससुरासर्पिर्दधिमण्डक्षीरस्वादूदकसप्तसमुद्रपरिवेष्टिता वलयाकृतयो लोकालोकपर्वतपरिवाराः पञ्चशद्योजनकोटिपरिसङ्ख्याताः ।

Further, each being double of the preceding ene, the other islands are Śāka, Kuśa, Krauñca, Śālmala, Gomedha (or Plakṣa) and Puṣkara. And also there are the seven oceans. They (islands) are decorated with various beautiful mountains which look like the heap of mustard seed. They, being formed like bracelet,[1] are encircled by seven oceans; the waters of which taste as sugar-cane-juice, wine, butter, curd, gruel and milk respectively. They are furnished with the natural and divine mountains. They measure five hundred crores of yojanas.

तदेतत्सर्वं सुप्रतिष्ठितसंस्थानमण्डमध्ये व्यूढम् । अण्डं च प्रधानस्याणुरवयवो यथाकाशे खद्योत इति ।

All this is placed in order on the well-established surface of this universe. Further, this universe is of the form of the minutest particle of the Pradhāna (the Principal Cause) as the fire-fly in the sky.

1. As for example : Suppose a rosary is made up of the big beads of Rudrākṣa. If an ant takes a round upon the surface of a bead, it will reach the same place from which it started, without changing any direction. It cannot go from one surface to another. But if the ant can pass through the string, i.e., through the centre of the beads, it can see all the beads one after the other. Similarly, the Geographer says that the earth is round. Why ? Because a man arrives at the same place from which he starts after taking a round from East to the West without changing his direction. But a man can never take a course from the South to the North. If he can pass through the North pole to the South pole, then he is able to see the other six islands of this earth, surrounded by other six oceans of various tastes as have been described in the commentary. Further, the Sumeru, the golden King of mountains, is situated in the middle position encircled by those seven islands having been surrounded by seven separate oceans of different tastes. Accordingly the Sumeru is not visible from this Jambū Dvīpa.

तत्र पाताले जलधौ पर्वतेष्वेतेषु देवनिकाया असुरगन्धर्वकिन्नरकिंपुरुषयक्षराक्षसभूतप्रेतपिशाचापस्मारकाप्सरोब्रह्मराक्षसकूष्माण्डविनायकाः प्रतिवसन्ति ।

There in the nether lands, in the oceans and in these mountains, live the semi-divine beings namely the Asuras, the Gandharvas, the Kinnaras, the Kimpuruṣas, the Yakṣas, the Rākṣasas, the Bhūtas, the Pretas, the Piśācas, the Apasmārakas, the Apsarās, the Brahmarākṣasas, the Kūṣmāṇḍas and the Vināyakas.

सर्वेषु द्वीपेषु पुण्यात्मानो देवमनुष्याः । सुमेरुस्त्रिदशानामुद्यानभूमिः । तत्र मिश्रवनं नन्दनं चैत्ररथं सुमानसमित्युद्यानानि । सुधर्मा देवसभा । सुदर्शनं पुरम् । वैजयन्तः प्रासादः ।

In all these islands live the virtuous men and gods. The Sumeru is the gardening land of the gods; there the Miśravana, the Nandana, the Caitra-ratha and the Sumānasa are the gardens. Sudharmā is the council of the gods; the Sudarśana is the city and Vaijayanta the palace.

ग्रहनक्षत्रतारकास्तु ध्रुवे निबद्धाः । वायुविक्षेपनियमेनोपलक्षितप्रचाराः। सुमेरोरुपर्युपरिसन्निविष्टा दिवि विपरिवर्तन्ते ।

The planets, the asterisms and the stars however are fixed in the pole-star. They are observed to move by the regulation of the force of the airs[1]. Above the Sumeru, they, being placed one above the other, are turning about their course in the sky.

माहेन्द्रनिवासिनः षडेव देवनिकायाः । त्रिदशा अग्निष्वात्तायामास्तुषिता अपरिनिर्मितवशवर्तिनः परिनिर्मितवशवर्तिनश्चेति । ते सर्वे सङ्कल्पसिद्धाः । अणिमाद्यैश्वर्योपपन्नाः कल्पायुषो वृन्दारकाः कामभोगिन औपपादिकदेहा उत्तमानुकूलाभिरप्सरोभिः कृतपरिचाराः ।

The inhabitants of the Mahendraloka are the divine beings of six classes only—the Tridaśas, the Agniṣvāttas, the Yāmas, and the Tuṣitas, the Aparinirmita-vaśavartins and the Parinirmita-vaśavartins. They are all possessed of the perfection of the will-power and have the attainments known as Aṇimā, etc. They have their life-periods of one Kalpa (creation) and are very beautiful; they enjoy the fruits of their Actions for Desirable End. They have their bodies born of their own actions (not from their parents). They are served by good and obedient nymphs.

महति लोके प्राजापत्ये पञ्चविधा देवनिकायाः कुमुदा ऋभवः प्रतर्दना अञ्चनाभाः प्रचित्ताभाः इत्येते महाभूतवशिनो ध्यानाहाराः कल्पसहस्रायुषः ।

In the Maharloka, the region of the Creator, live the divine beings of five descriptions,—the Kumudas, the Ṛbhus, the Pratardanas, the Añcanābhas and the Pracittābhas. They all have the mastery over the gross elements. They live upon meditation and they have the life-period of one thousand kalpas.

प्रथमे ब्रह्मणो जनलोके चतुर्विधा देवनिकाया ब्रह्मपुरोहिता ब्रह्मकायिका ब्रह्ममहाकायिका अमरा इति । ते भूतेन्द्रियवशिनो द्विगुणद्विगुणोत्तरायुषः ।

In the Janaloka, the first region of Brahmā, live four kinds of divine beings,—the Brahma-purohitas, the Brahma-kāyikas, the Brahma-mahākāyikas and the Amaras. They have mastery over the elements and the senses. Each of these classes has the life-period twice that of the preceding ones.

द्वितीये तपसि लोके त्रिविधा देवनिकाया आभास्वरा महाभास्वराः सत्यमहाभास्वरा इति । ते भूतेन्द्रियप्रकृतिवशिनो द्विगुणद्विगुणोत्तरायुषः सर्वे ध्यानाहारा ऊर्ध्वरेतस ऊर्ध्वमप्रतिहतज्ञाना अधरभूमिष्वनावृतज्ञानविषयाः ।

In the Tapoloka, the second region of Brahmā, live three kinds of divine beings,—the Ābhāsvaras, the Mahābhāsvaras and the Satya-mahā-bhāsvaras. They have mastery over the elements, the senses and the creative causes. Each of these classes has the life-period twice that of the preceding ones and they all live upon meditation. They live in their perpetual continence. They have the unchecked knowledge for the above regions and have the sphere of clear knowledge about the lower stages.

तृतीये ब्रह्मणः सत्यलोके चत्वारो देवनिकाया अच्युताः शुद्धनिवासाः सत्याभाः संज्ञासंज्ञिनश्चेति ।

1. The Vedic Scriptures hold that the airs are forty-nine in number.

ऽकृतभवन्यासाः स्वप्रतिष्ठा उपर्युपरिस्थिताः प्रधानवशिनो यावत्सर्गायुषः । तत्राच्युताः सवितर्कध्यानसुखाः शुद्धनिवासाः सविचारध्यानसुखाः सत्याभा आनन्दमात्रध्यानसुखाः संज्ञासंज्ञिनश्चास्मितामात्रध्यानसुखास्तेऽपि त्रैलोक्यमध्ये प्रतिष्ठन्ते ।

In the Satya-loka, the third region of Brahmā, live four kinds of divine beings, —the Acyutas, the Śuddhanivāsas, the Satyābhas and the Sañjñā-sañjñins. They live in the unbuilt existence and are established in themselves. Each of these classes is placed one above the other. They have mastery over the Pradhāna and have the life-period until the end of the creation There the Acyutas have the pleasure of the Suppositional thought transformation. The Śuddha-nivāsas have the pleasure of the Clear thought-transformation. The Satyābhas have the pleasure of the purely Joyful thought-transformation and the Sañjñā-sañjñins have the pleasure of the purely Egoistic thought-transformation. They also are established in the three-fold world.

त एते सप्तलोकाः सर्वे सब्रह्मकाः । विदेहप्रकृतिलयास्तु मोक्षपदे वर्तन्ते इति न लोकमध्ये न्यस्ताः ।

These all are seven regions including the regions of Brahmā. The Videhas and the Prakṛtilayas however stand in the rank of liberation; therefore they are not placed in the regions.

इत्येतद्योगिना साक्षात्करणीयम् । सूर्यद्वारे संयमं कृत्वा ततोऽन्यत्रापि एवं तावदभ्यसेद्यावदिदं सर्वं दृष्टमिति ॥ २५ ॥

Hence all this must be seen by the Yogi. After performing Saṁyama upon the solar entrance and thence also over the other parts, he should practise thus until all this is seen.

चन्द्रे ताराव्यूहज्ञानम् ॥ २६ ॥

Upon the moon, the knowledge of the arrangement of the stars —26

चन्द्रे ताराव्यूहज्ञानम् । चन्द्रे संयमं कृत्वा ताराणां व्यूहं विजानीयात् ॥ २६ ॥

After performing Saṁyama upon the moon, he should have the knowledge of the arrangements of the stars.

ध्रुवे तद्गतिज्ञानम् ॥२७॥

Upon the pole star, the knowledge of their movement—27

ध्रुवे तद्गतिज्ञानम् । ततो ध्रुवे संयमं कृत्वा ताराणां गतिं विजानीयात् । ऊर्ध्वविमानेषु संयमं कृत्वा तानि विजानीयात् ॥२७॥

Thence after performing Saṁyama upon the pole-star, he should know the movement of the stars. After performing Saṁyama over the higher planes, he should know them.

नाभिचक्रे कायव्यूहज्ञानम् ॥२८॥

Upon the navel circle, the knowledge of the bodily system —28

नाभिचक्रे कायव्यूहज्ञानम् । नाभिचक्रे संयमं कृत्वा कायव्यूहं विजानीयात् । वातपित्तश्लेष्माणस्त्रयो दोषाः । धातवः सप्त त्वग्लोहितमांसस्नाय्वस्थिमज्जाशुक्राणि । पूर्वं पूर्वमेषां बाह्यमित्येष विन्यासः ॥२८॥

After performing Saṁyama upon the navel circle, he should know the bodily system. The gas, the bile and the phlegm (vāta, pitta, śleṣma) are the three humours. The materials are seven: skin, blood, flesh, nerve, bone, majjā (marrow) and semen; the respective former ones are external with regard to the respective latter ones. Such is their arrangement.

कण्ठकूपे क्षुत्पिपासानिवृत्तिः ॥ २९ ॥

Upon the pit of the throat, the suppression of hunger and thirst —29

कण्ठकूपे क्षुत्पिपासानिवृत्तिः । जिह्वाया अधस्तात्तन्तुस्ततोऽधस्तात्कण्ठस्ततोऽधस्तात्कूपस्तत्र संयमात्क्षुत्पिपासे न बाधेते ॥ २९ ॥

Below the tongue is the tonsil: below that is the throat and beneath that is the pit. From the Saṁyama thereupon, hunger and thirst do not afflict (the Yogi).

कूर्मनाड्यां स्थैर्यम् ॥ ३० ॥

Upon the Kūrmanāḍi (tortoise-tube), firmness—30

कूर्मनाड्यां स्थैर्यम् । कूपादध उरसि कूर्माकारा नाडी तस्यां कृतसंयमः स्थिरपदं लभते । यथा सर्पा गोधा चेति ॥ ३० ॥

Below the pit is the pipe in the form of a tortoise. The performer of Saṁyama thereupon attains the firm opposition like the serpent, the iguana, etc.. (the hibernant state).

मूर्धज्योतिषि सिद्धदर्शनम् ॥ ३१ ॥

Upon the cerebral light, the vision of the Siddhas (the Perfect ones)—31

मूर्धज्योतिषि सिद्धदर्शनम् । शिरःकपालेऽन्तश्छिद्रं प्रभास्वरं ज्योतिस्तत्र संयमं कृत्वा सिद्धानां द्यावापृथिव्योरन्तरालचारिणां दर्शनम् ॥ ३१ ॥

There is a shining light in the hole which is within the skull. From the performance of Saṁyama thereupon comes the vision of the Siddhas who move through the ethereal space between the earth and the sky.

प्रातिभाद्वा सर्वम् ॥ ३२ ॥

And from the Truth born of genius, all (is known)—32

प्रातिभाद्वा सर्वम् । प्रातिभं नाम तारकं तद्विवेकजस्य ज्ञानस्य पूर्वरूपम् । यथोदये प्रभा भास्करस्य तेन वा सर्वमेव जानाति योगी प्रातिभस्य ज्ञानस्योत्पत्ताविति ॥३२॥

The Truth born of genius (Pratibhā) is indeed the rescuer (Tāraka). It is the preceding form of the Intellect-born-knowledge just like the luminosity at the rise of the sun. And by this, the Yogi positively knows all on the rise of the knowlenge which is the Truth born of his own genius.

हृदये चित्तसंवित् ॥ ३३ ॥

Upon the heart, the knowledge of the mind—33

हृदये चित्तसंवित् । यदिदमस्मिन्ब्रह्मपुरे दहरं पुण्डरीकं वेश्म तत्र विज्ञानं तस्मिन्संयमाच्चित्तसंवित् ॥ ३३ ॥

The intelligence lives in that hollow which is the shrine in the form of a lotus within this city of Brahma. From the Saṁyama thereupon comes the knowledge of the *mind*.

सत्त्वपुरुषयोरत्यन्तासङ्कीर्णयोः प्रत्ययाविशेषो भोगः परार्थत्वात्स्वार्थसंयमात्पुरुषज्ञानम् ॥ ३४ ॥

The Intellective Essence and the Puruṣa are extremely different; the inseparate cognition of these two is the Experience on account of its (of the Essence) Existence for another's interest; from the Saṁyama over the self-interest, comes the knowledge of the Puruṣa—34

सत्त्वपुरुषयोरत्यन्तासंकीर्णयोः प्रत्ययाविशेषो भोगः परार्थत्वात्स्वार्थसंयमात्पुरुषज्ञानम् । बुद्धिसत्त्वं प्रख्याशीलम् । समानसत्त्वोपनिबन्धने रजस्तमसी वशीकृत्य सत्त्वपुरुषान्यताप्रत्ययेन परिणतम् । तस्माच्च सत्त्वात्परिणामिनोऽत्यन्तविधर्मा विशुद्धोऽन्यश्चितिमात्ररूपः पुरुषस्तयोरत्यन्तासंकीर्णयोः प्रत्ययाविशेषो भोगः पुरुषस्य दर्शितविषयत्वात् । स भोगप्रत्ययः सत्त्वस्य, परार्थत्वाद् दृश्यः ।

The Intellective Essence shining with illumination becomes changed into the cognition of the distinction between the Essence and the Puruṣa after overpowering the active and the inert Energies which are dependent upon the same Essence. Further, the Puruṣa who is the external form of the Con-Science itself, is pure and extremely opposite to that changing Essence; the inseparate cognition of these two which are extremely different, is the Experience of the Puruṣa because of the fact that objects are presented to Him. This cognition of Experience belongs to the Essence, because the Perceivable exists for another's interest.

यस्तु तस्माद्विशिष्टश्चितिमात्ररूपोऽन्यः पौरुषेयः प्रत्ययस्तत्र संयमात्पुरुषविषया प्रज्ञा जायते ।

That however, which is distinguished from this Essence and is the external form of the Con-Science itself, is the other Cognition pertaining to the Puruṣa. From the Saṁyama over this cognition, the (Intellective) Vision being possessed of the sphere of the Puruṣa, is born.

न च पुरुषप्रत्ययेन बुद्धिसत्त्वात्मना पुरुषो दृश्यते। पुरुष एव तं प्रत्ययं स्वात्मावलम्बनं पश्यति । तथा ह्युक्तम्—विज्ञातारमरे केन विजानीयादिति ॥ ३४ ॥

Further, the Puruṣa is not seen by that Puruṣa's cognition which is the self-same as the intellectual Essence. The Puruṣa himself sees that cognition to be the support of Himself. So it has been said :—"Oh ! By what is the knower to be known ?"

ततः प्रातिभश्रावणवेदनादर्शास्वादवार्ता जायन्ते ॥ ३५ ॥*

Therefrom arise the Truth born of genius, the higher hearing, the higher touching, the higher seeing, the higher tasting and the higher smelling—35

ततः प्रातिभश्रावणवेदनादर्शास्वादवार्ता जायन्ते । प्रातिभात्सूक्ष्मव्यवहितविप्रकृष्टातीतानागतज्ञानम् । श्रावणाद्दिव्यशब्दश्रवणम् । वेदनाद्दिव्यस्पर्शाधिगमः। आदर्शाद्दिव्यरूपसंवित् । आस्वादाद्दिव्यरससंवित् । वार्तातो दिव्यगन्धविज्ञानमित्येतानि नित्यं जायन्ते ॥ ३५ ॥

From the Truth born of genius comes the knowledge of the subtle, the obstructed, the distant, the past and the not-yet-come. From the higher hearing comes the power of hearing the divine sound ; from the higher touching comes the attainment of the divine touch; from the higher seeing comes the understanding of the divine colour; from the higher tasting comes the knowledge of the divine taste and from the higher smelling comes the cognition of the divine smell. So these are positively born.

ते समाधावुपसर्गा व्युत्थाने सिद्धयः ॥ ३६ ॥

They are the obstacles to the Spiritual Absorption and are the accomplishments of the exhibitive mind—36

ते समाधावुपसर्गा व्युत्थाने सिद्धयः । ते प्रातिभादयः समाहितचित्तस्योत्पद्यमाना उपसर्गास्तद्दर्शनप्रत्यनीकत्वात् । व्युत्थितचित्तस्योत्पद्यमानाः सिद्धयः ॥ ३६ ॥

They, i.e., the Truth born of genius, etc., when produced of a Spiritually Absorbed mind, become the obstacles on account of their opposition to the Observation. When they are produced of an exhibitive mind, they become the accomplishments.

बन्धकारणशैथिल्यात्प्रचारसंवेदनाच्च चित्तस्य परशरीरावेशः ॥ ३७ ॥

From the relaxation of the cause of bondage and by the perfect knowledge of the movement of the mind (comes the power of) entering into another body —37

बन्धकारणशैथिल्यात्प्रचारसंवेदनाच्च चित्तस्य परशरीरावेशः । लोलीभूतस्य मनसोऽप्रतिष्ठस्य शरीरे कर्माशयवशाद् बन्धः प्रतिष्ठेत्यर्थः । तस्य कर्मणो बन्धकारणस्य शैथिल्यं समाधिबलाद्भवति । प्रचारसंवेदनं च चित्तस्य समाधिजमेव, कर्मबन्धक्षयात्स्वचित्तस्य प्रचारसंवेदनाच्च योगी चित्तं स्वशरीरान्निष्कृष्य शरीरान्तरेषु निःक्षिपति, निःक्षिप्तं चित्तं चेन्द्रियाण्यनुपतन्ति । यथा मधुकरराजानं मक्षिका उत्पतन्तमनूत्पतन्ति निविशमानमनुनिविशन्ति तथेन्द्रियाणि परशरीरावेशे चित्तमनुविधीयन्त इति ॥ ३७ ॥

The confinement of the fickle mind, which is ever restless, in a body in obedience to the vehicle of action, is its settlement; this is the meaning. The relaxation of that action which is the cause of bondage, comes from the force of the Spiritual Absorption; also the perfect knowledge of the movement of the mind is born of the Spiritual Absorption alone. From the destruction of the bondage of action and from the perfect knowledge of the movement of his own mind, the Yogi takes out the mind from his own body and then throws it into another body; then the senses follow the thrown-out mind. As the bees fly with the flying king and sit down when he sits, so do the senses follow the mind in entering into another body.

उदानजयाज्जलपङ्ककण्टकादिष्वसङ्ग उत्क्रान्तिश्च ॥ ३८ ॥

* It should be understood here that other accomplishments appear from the respective Saṁyama upon those respective items. But these accomplishments must appear from the very Spiritual Absorption. So in the following aphorism the commentator warns us against our being proud of those accomplishments and also against our engaging them in earning name and fame.

From the conquest of the Udāna, Non-contact with water, mud, thorn, etc., and Ascension (passing out of the body)—38

उदानजयाज्जलपङ्ककण्टकादिष्वसङ्ग उत्क्रान्तिश्च । समस्तेन्द्रियवृत्तिः प्राणादिलक्षणा जीवनं तस्य क्रिया पञ्चतयी । प्राणो मुखनासिकागतिराहृदयवृत्तिः । समं नयनात्समानश्चानाभिवृत्तिः । अपनयनादपान आपादतलवृत्तिः । उन्नयनादुदान आशिरोवृत्तिः व्यापी व्यान इति । एषां प्रधानं प्राणः । उदानजयाज्जलपङ्ककण्टकादिष्वसङ्ग उत्क्रान्तिश्च प्रयाणकाले भवति तां वशित्वेन प्रतिपद्यते ॥ ३८ ॥

The function of all the senses as indicated by the movement of the Prāṇa (the breathing force), etc., is "life". It has five-fold action :—The Prāṇa is the operation which, rising from the chest, moves through the mouth and the nose. The Samāna is the operation which moves down to the navel sphere on account of its equal conveyance. The Apāna is the operation moving down to the soles of the feet on account of its removing action. The Udāna is the operation moving up to the head on account of its upward conveyance, and the Vyāna pervades the whole body. The Prāṇa is the chief of them. From the conquest of the Udāna, Non-contact with water, mud, thorn, etc., appears, and also Ascension comes at the time of death. These are achieved by the Mastery over the Udāna.

समानजयाज्ज्वलनम् ॥ ३९ ॥

From the conquest of the Samāna, comes Effulgence—39

समानजयाज्ज्वलनम् । जितसमानस्तेजस उपध्मानं कृत्वा ज्वलयति ॥ ३९ ॥

The conqueror of the Samāna, blows upon his splendour and thus shines.

श्रोत्राकाशयोः संबन्धसंयमाद्दिव्यं श्रोत्रम् ॥ ४० ॥

From the Saṁyama upon the relation between the sense of hearing and the ether, (comes) the divine power of hearing—40

श्रोत्राकाशयोः संबन्धसंयमाद्दिव्यं श्रोत्रम् । सर्वश्रोत्राणामाकाशं प्रतिष्ठा सर्वशब्दानां च । यथोक्तम्—तुल्यदेशश्रवणानामेकदेशश्रुतित्वं सर्वेषां भवतीति । तच्च तदाकाशस्य लिङ्गम् । अनावरणं चोक्तम् । तथामूर्तस्याप्यन्यत्रानावरणदर्शनाद्विभुत्वमपि प्रख्यातमाकाशस्य । शब्दग्रहणनिमित्तं श्रोत्रम् । बधिराबधिरयोरेकः शब्दं गृह्णात्यपरो न गृह्णातीति तस्माच्छ्रोत्रमेव शब्दविषयम् । श्रोत्राकाशयोः संबन्धे कृतसंयमस्य योगिनो दिव्यं श्रोत्रं प्रवर्तते ॥ ४० ॥

The ether is the foundation of all the senses of hearing and also of all sounds. As it is said:—"Of all persons whose senses of hearing are placed in the same space, the action of hearing becomes similar". Further, this is the mark of the ether and it is said to be coverless. Similarly, omni-presence of the ether has also been affirmed, because coverlessness even of a formless object is seen elsewhere. The sense of hearing is the instrument of receiving the sound. Between the deaf and the not deaf, one receives the sound and the other does not. Therefore the sense of hearing alone is possessed of the sphere of sound. In the Yogi who performs Saṁyama upon the relation between the sense of hearing and the ether, the divine power of hearing arises.

कायाकाशयोः संबन्धसंयमाल्लघुतूलसमापत्तेश्चाकाशगमनम् ॥ ४१ ॥

From the Saṁyama upon the relation between the body and the ether, and from the attainment of the lightness of cotton, comes the passage through the sky—41

कायाकाशयोः संबन्धसंयमाल्लघुतूलसमापत्तेश्चाकाशगमनम् । यत्र कायस्तत्राकाशं तस्यावकाशदानात्कायस्य तेन संबन्धावाप्तिस्तत्र कृतसंयमो जित्वा तत्संबन्धं लघुषु तूलादिष्वापरमाणुसमापत्तिं लब्ध्वा जितसंबन्धो लघुर्भवति, लघुत्वाच्च जले पादाभ्यां विहरति, ततस्तूर्णनाभितन्तुमात्रे विहृत्य रश्मिषु विहरति ततो यथेष्टमाकाशगतिरस्य भवतीति ॥ ४१ ॥

Where there is body there is the ether, because it gives space to the body; the relation is obtained thereby. After conquering that relation by the performance of Saṁyama thereupon and by obtaining the transformation into light things such as cotton, etc., down to an atom, the conqueror of the relation becomes light. On account of that lightness he walks over water, then walking on each line of the spider's web (he) walks over the rays, then he moves through the sky at will.

बहिरकल्पिता वृत्तिर्महाविदेहा ततः प्रकाशावरणक्षयः ॥ ४२ ॥

The unformed external activity is the Great Excorporeal; thence (comes) the destruction of the covering of the light—42

बहिरकल्पिता वृत्तिर्महाविदेहा ततः प्रकाशावरणक्षयः । शरीराद् बहिर्मनसो वृत्तिलाभो विदेहा नाम धारणा सा यदि शरीरप्रतिष्ठस्य मनसो बहिर्वृत्तिमात्रेण भवति सा कल्पितेत्युच्यते ।

The acquisition of mental activity outside the body is indeed the excorporeal steadiness. If it takes place by each external function of the mind resting in the body, it is called the Formed-Excorporeal.

या तु शरीरनिरपेक्षा बहिर्भूतस्यैव मनसो बहिर्वृत्तिः सा खल्वकल्पिता ।

When however, the external activity of the mind that has come out of the body and the activity itself is not dependent upon the body, it is in fact the Unformed Excorporeal.

तत्र कल्पितया साधयन्त्यकल्पितां महाविदेहामिति । यया परशरीराण्याविशन्ति योगिनः । ततश्च धारणातः प्रकाशात्मनो बुद्धिसत्त्वस्य यदावरणं क्लेशकर्मविपाकत्रयं रजस्तमोमूलं तस्य च क्षयो भवति ॥ ४२ ॥

There the Yogis accomplish the unformed Great-Excorporeal by the help of the formed-excorporeal[1]. By this (Great Excorporeal), the Yogis enter into other bodies. Further, affliction, action and the threefold fruition which have their root in the active and the inert Energies and which are the covering of the luminous Intellective Essence, are destroyed by that steadiness.

स्थूलस्वरूपसूक्ष्मान्वयार्थवत्त्वसंयमाद् भूतजयः ॥ ४३ ॥

From the Saṁyama upon the gross, the manifestative, the subtle, the correlative and the purposive, (comes) the mastery over the elements—43

स्थूलस्वरूपसूक्ष्मान्वयार्थवत्त्वसंयमाद् भूतजयः । तत्र पार्थिवाद्याः शब्दादयो विशेषाः सहकारादिभिर्धर्मैः स्थूलशब्देन परिभाषिताः । एतद्भूतानां प्रथमं रूपम् ।

There, the specific sound, etc., pertaining to earth, etc., with their mutual helpful characteristics are technically named by the word "gross". This is the first appearance of the elements.[2]

द्वितीयं रूपं स्वसामान्यम् मूर्तिर्भूमिः स्नेहो जलं वह्निरुष्णता वायुः प्रणामी सर्वतो गतिराकाश इत्येतत्स्वरूपशब्देनोच्यते । अस्य सामान्यस्य शब्दादयो विशेषाः । तथा चोक्तम् एकजातिसमन्वितानामेषां धर्ममात्रव्यावृत्तिरिति ।

The second appearance is generic to itself. Earth has hardness, water has stickiness, the fire has heat, the air has motivity and the ether pervades them all. These are called by the word "manifestative." The (sense-object) sound, etc., are the specific appearances of this generic property. So also it has been said:—thus comes the differentiation of the pure characteristic of those that are correlated with one class.

सामान्यविशेषसमुदायोऽत्र द्रव्यं द्रष्टव्यम् । द्विष्ठो हि समूहः प्रत्यस्तमितभेदावयवानुगतः शरीरं वृक्षः, यूथं वनमितिशब्देनोपात्तभेदावयवानुगतः समूहः । उभये देवमनुष्याः—समूहस्य देवा एव एको

---

1. This formed excorporeal activity is the instrumental manifestation of the Cognitive-Spiritual Absorption (*Y.S.* 1-44). It is clear from the commentary that the higher end can never be achieved without performing the ground work.

2. Here the specific sound, etc. are the sense-objects and are the elemental changes which fall under the head of the 'Specific Step of the Energies.' Further, this Specific stage has been established as the "Matter" by the Nyāya-Vaiśeṣika. The commentator accepts this theory as the primary truth of his own conclusion.

भागो मनुष्याः द्वितीयो भागस्ताभ्यामेवाभिधीयते समूहः ।

Here, the collection of the generic and the specific properties is understood as Matter (*Dravya*). The collection is in fact of two kinds:—A person or a tree is followed by the body of the absent-disunion, and by the word "herd" or "forest" the collection is followed by the body of the present-disunion. In the herd signifying "both gods and men" one part of the collection is the "Gods" alone and the other part is the "Men"; the collection is signified by them both.

स च भेदाभेदविवक्षितः । आम्राणां वनं ब्राह्मणानां सङ्घ इति । आम्रवनं ब्राह्मणसङ्घ इति । स पुनर्द्विविधो युतसिद्धावयवोऽयुतसिद्धावयवश्च । युतसिद्धावयवः समूहो वनं सङ्घ इति । अयुतसिद्धावयवः सङ्घातः शरीरं वृक्षः परमाणुरिति । अयुतसिद्धावयवभेदानुगतः समूहो द्रव्यमिति पतञ्जलिः । एतत्स्वरूपमित्युक्तम् ।

Further, it (the collection) is meant to be spoken of either with disunion or without disunion such as the grove of mangoes, the group of Brāhmins; or the mango-grove, the Brāhmin-group. Again it is of two descriptions :—The separable-accomplished-body and the inseparable-accomplished-body. The separable-accomplished-body is the collection such as a forest, a group; and the inseparable-accomplished-body is the collection such as a person, a tree, an atom. According to the theory of Patañjali, the Matter is the collection followed by the difference of the inseparable-accomplished-body. It is said to be the "manifestative".

अथ किमेषां सूक्ष्मरूपम् ? तन्मात्रं भूतकारणं तस्यैकोऽवयवः परमाणुः सामान्यविशेषात्मा अयुतसिद्धावयवभेदानुगतः समुदाय इत्येवं सर्वतन्मात्राण्येतत्तृतीयम् ।

Now, what is their (of the elements) subtle appearance? It is the pure Ultimate Atom[1] which is the origin of the elements. Its single body is the Atom possessed of the generic and the specific properties and is the collection followed by the difference of the inseparable-accomplished-body. Thus all the subtile rudiments are of this third appearance.

अथ भूतानां चतुर्थं रूपं ख्यातिक्रियास्थितिशीला गुणाः कार्यस्वभावानुपातिनोऽन्वयशब्देनोक्ताः ।

Now the fourth appearance of the elements is called by the word "correlative"; it is the Energies possessed of illumination, activity and inertia which follow the nature of their actions.

अथैषां पञ्चमं रूपमर्थवत्त्वं भोगापवर्गार्थता गुणेष्वेवान्वयिनी । गुणास्तन्मात्रभूतभौतिकेष्विति सर्वमर्थवत् ।

Now their fifth appearance is the purposefulness which is correlated with the Energies possessed of the purpose of Experience and Emancipation. The Energies remain in these subtile rudiments, the elements and in the elemental products; so all this is purposive.

तेष्विदानीं भूतेषु पञ्चसु पञ्चरूपेषु रूपे संयमात्तस्य तस्य रूपस्य स्वरूपदर्शनं जयश्च प्रादुर्भवति । तत्र पञ्चभूतस्य रूपाणि जित्वा भूतजयी भवति । तज्जयाद्वत्सानुसारिण्य इव गावोऽस्य सङ्कल्पानुविधायिन्यो भूतप्रकृतयो भवन्ति ॥ ४३ ॥

Now from the Saṁyama upon the appearance which exists in these five elements in their five respective appearances, the visibility of the manifestation of those appearances and also the mastery over them appear. There the Yogi, after conquering the appearances of the five elements, becomes the Master of the elements[2]. On account of that mastery, the elemental powers become subordinate to his will like the cows following their own calves.

ततोऽणिमादिप्रादुर्भावः कायसम्पत्तद्धर्मानभिघातश्च ॥ ४४ ॥

Thence (come) the rising of Attenuation, etc., the perfections of the body and also the non-resistance of its characteristics—44

ततोऽणिमादिप्रादुर्भावः कायसम्पत्तद्धर्मानभिघातश्च । तत्राणिमा भवत्यणुः । लघिमा लघुर्भवति ।

1. Now the commentator establishes the Atom, the Single Soul as the Matter in its rectified and developed form. Further, this Atom will be termed the 'Substance'' in the Vedānta Darśana when it will go beyond the sphere of the intellect.

2. These five appearances of the elements are but the four Steps and the Purposefulness of the Energies. (*Y.S.* II. 19).

महिमा महान्भवति । प्राप्तिरङ्गुल्यग्रेणापि स्पृशति चन्द्रमसम् । प्राकाम्यमिच्छानभिघातः । भूमावुन्मज्जति निमज्जति यथोदके। वशित्वं भूतभौतिकेषु वशीभवत्यवश्यश्चान्येषाम्। ईशित्वं तेषां प्रभवाप्ययव्यूहानामीष्टे ।

There the Attenuation (*Aṇimā*) means that (the body) becomes an atom. The Lightness (*Laghimā*) means that (the body) becomes light. The Enlargement (*Mahimā*) means that (the body) becomes large. The attainment (*Prāpti*) means that he touches the moon even by the tip of his finger. The "Irresistibility" (*Prākāmya*) means the unrestrained will-power by which he sinks into the earth and gets up just as in water. The Mastery (*Vaśitva*) means that he becomes possessed of control over all the elements and the elemental powers and is not subject to the control of others. The Creative power (*Īśitva*) means that creation, destruction and aggregation all depend upon his will.

यत्रकामावसायित्वं सत्यसङ्कल्पता यथा सङ्कल्पस्तथा भूतप्रकृतीनामवस्थानम् । न च शक्तोऽपि पदार्थविपर्यासं करोति । कस्मात्? अन्यस्य यत्रकामावसायिनः पूर्वसिद्धस्य तथाभूतेषु सङ्कल्पादिति ।

The Settlement-at-Will (*yatra-kāmāvasāyitva*) means the perfection of will-power. As he wills, so becomes the position of the elemental powers. Although he is able, yet he does not cause any upset of the objects. Why? Because his will coincides with that of the other "Pūrva Siddha" (Original perfect Entity) who is the possessor of the perfection of "Settlement-at will".[1] These are the eight powers.

एतान्यष्टावैश्वर्याणि । कायसम्पद्वक्ष्यमाणा तद्धर्मानभिघातश्च पृथ्वी मूर्त्या न निरुणद्धि योगिनः शरीरादिक्रियां शिलामप्यनुविशतीति । नापः स्निग्धाः क्लेदयन्ति । नाग्निरुष्णो दहति । न वायुः प्रणामी वहत्यनावरणात्मकेऽप्याकाशे भवत्यावृतकायः सिद्धानामप्यदृश्यो भवति ॥ ४४ ॥

The perfection of the body is to be described. "Also the non-resistance of its (of the body) characteristics" means that the earth does not resist the working of the Yogi's body by its hardnesss; he can pass even through a stone. The sticky water does not wet him. The hot fire does not burn him. The air in motion does not carry him. His body becomes concealed even within the coverless ether and he becomes invisible even to the Siddhas (perfect beings).

रूपलावण्यबलवज्रसंहननत्वानि कायसम्पत् ॥ ४५ ॥

Beauty, Charm, Strength and Adamantine Hardness are the bodily perfections—45

रूपलावण्यबलवज्रसंहननत्वानि कायसम्पत् । दर्शनीयः कान्तिमानतिशयबलो वज्रसंहननश्चेति ॥ ४५ ॥

His body becomes amiable, charmful, excessively strong and hard like the adamant.

ग्रहणस्वरूपास्मितान्वयार्थवत्त्वसंयमादिन्द्रियजयः ॥ ४६ ॥

From the Saṁyama upon action, real nature, egoism, correlation and purposefulness, (comes) the mastery over the senses—46

ग्रहणस्वरूपास्मितान्वयार्थवत्त्वसंयमादिन्द्रियजयः। सामान्यविशेषात्मा शब्दादिर्विषयः । तेष्विन्द्रियाणां वृत्तिर्ग्रहणम् । न च तत्सामान्यमात्रग्रहणाकारं कथमनालोचितः स विषयविशेष इन्द्रियेण मनसा वानुव्यवसीयेतेति ?

Sound, etc., possessed of the generic and the specific nature, are the objects. The operation of the senses in them is the receiving action. Further, this operation is not the form of receiving the generic nature only. If that specific property were not considered, then how would it be determined by the senses and by the mind?

स्वरूपं पुनः प्रकाशात्मनो बुद्धिसत्त्वस्य सामान्यविशेषयोरयुतसिद्धावयवभेदानुगतः समूहो द्रव्यमिन्द्रियम् ।

Further, the real nature is the sense or the matter which is the collection followed by the difference of the inseparable-accomplished-body of both the

1. This *Pūrva-Siddha* is the Active Creator, *Īśvara* (*Eka-jīva*) of the Vedānta-Darśana. (*Y.S.* IV-4).

generic and the specific nature of the luminous Intellective Essence.

तेषां तृतीयं रूपमस्मिता लक्षणोऽहङ्कारः तस्य सामान्य इन्द्रियाणि विशेषाः ।

Their (of the senses) third appearance is the (Pure) Egoism. Its feature in the form of Ego is its generic appearance and the senses are the specific.

चतुर्थं रूपं व्यवसायात्मकाः प्रकाशक्रियास्थितिशीला गुणा येषामिन्द्रियाणि साहङ्काराणि परिणामः ।

The fourth appearance is the determinative Energies possessed of illumination, activity and inertia; the senses together with Egoism, are their effect.

पञ्चमं रूपं गुणेषु यदनुगतं पुरुषार्थवत्त्वमिति ।

The fifth appearance is the same Purposefulness of the Puruṣa's interest as is inherent in the Energies.

पञ्चस्वेवैतेष्विन्द्रियरूपेषु यथाक्रमं संयमस्तत्र तत्र जयं कृत्वा पञ्चस्वरूपजयादिन्द्रियजयः प्रादुर्भवति योगिनः ॥ ४६ ॥

The Saṁyama should be applied successively to all these five forms of the senses. By conquering those respective appearances[1] and from the conquest of these five manifestations, the mastery over the senses is born to the Yogi.

ततो मनोजवित्वं विकरणभावः प्रधानजयश्च ॥ ४७ ॥

Thence (come) the mind-like-velocity, the uninstrumental-state and also the control over the Pradhāna—47

ततो मनोजवित्वं विकरणभावः प्रधानजयश्च । कायस्यानुत्तमो गतिलाभो मनोजवित्वम् । विदेहानामिन्द्रियाणामभिप्रेतकालदेशविषयापेक्षो वृत्तिलाभो विकरणभावः । सर्वप्रकृतिविकारवशित्वं प्रधानजय इत्येतास्तिस्रः सिद्धयो मधुप्रतीका उच्यन्ते । एताश्च करणपञ्चकस्वरूपजयादधिगम्यन्ते ॥ ४७ ॥

The attainment of the highest speed of the body is the mind-like-velocity. The acquisition of functions of the senses, having no connection with the body regarding the sphere of desirable time and space, is the uninstrumental state. The mastery over the modification of all the Intensive Causes is the conquest over the Pradhāna (the Principal Cause). These three perfections are called Madhupratīkas. Further, these are attained by the mastery over the real nature of the five senses.

सत्त्वपुरुषान्यताख्यातिमात्रस्य सर्वभावाधिष्ठातृत्वं सर्वज्ञातृत्वं च ॥ ४८ ॥

The Yogi, possessed of the pure revelation of the distinction between the Essence and the Puruṣa, attains the Controllership of all states and also Omniscience—48

सत्त्वपुरुषान्यताख्यातिमात्रस्य सर्वभावाधिष्ठातृत्वं सर्वज्ञातृत्वं च । निर्धूतरजस्तमोमलस्य बुद्धिसत्त्वस्य परे वैशारद्ये परस्यां वशीकारसंज्ञायां वर्तमानस्य सत्त्वपुरुषान्यताख्यातिमात्ररूपप्रतिष्ठस्य सर्वभावाधिष्ठातृत्वम् । सर्वात्मानो गुणा व्यवसायव्यवसेयात्मकाः स्वामिनं क्षेत्रज्ञं प्रत्यशेषदृश्यात्मत्वेनोपस्थिता इत्यर्थः ।

On the highest transparency of the Intellective-Essence freed from the dirt of the active and the Inert Energies, the Yogi, who is present in the highest consciousness of control and is established in the manifestation of the pure revelation of the distinction between the Essence and the Puruṣa, attains the Controllership of all states. The meaning is that the all-formative Energies, which are of the nature of cause and effect, become present before the Lord, the Knower of the Field[2] with the personality of the whole Perceivable.

सर्वज्ञातृत्वं सर्वात्मनां गुणानां शान्तोदिताव्यपदेश्यधर्मत्वेन व्यवस्थितानामक्रमोपारूढं विवेकजं ज्ञानमित्यर्थः । इत्येषा विशोका नाम सिद्धिर्यां प्राप्य योगी सर्वज्ञः क्षीणक्लेशबन्धनो वशी विहरति ॥ ४८ ॥

Omniscience is the Intellect-born knowledge independent of succession with regard to the all-formative Energies which are essablished with the function of the past, the present and the unpredicable-

---

1. These five appearances of the senses should be understood as the four Steps and the Purposefulness of the Energies. (*Y.S.* II-19).

2. The term "Knower of the Field" has been fully explained in the thirteenth chapter of the *Gītā*

characteristics; this is the meaning. This perfection is indeed known as the "Sorrowless", by obtaining which the Yogi, being omniscient and freed from the bondage of *affliction*, moves as a Controller.

तद्वैराग्यादपि दोषबीजक्षये कैवल्यम् ।। ४९ ।।

On the destruction of the evil seeds, due to the non-attachment to that even, (comes) Absoluteness —49

तद्वैराग्यादपि दोषबीजक्षये कैवल्यम् । यदास्यैवं भवति क्लेशकर्मक्षये सत्त्वस्यायं विवेकप्रत्ययो धर्मः सत्त्वं च हेयपक्षे न्यस्तं पुरुषश्चापरिणामी शुद्धोऽन्यः सत्त्वादित्येवमस्य ततो विरज्यमानस्य यानि दोषबीजानि दग्धशालिबीजकल्पान्यप्रसवसमर्थानि तानि सह मनसा प्रत्यस्तं गच्छन्ति । तेषु प्रलीनेषु पुरुषः पुनरिदं तापत्रयं न भुङ्क्ते । तदेतेषां गुणानां मनसि कर्मक्लेशविपाकस्वरूपेणाभिव्यक्तानां चरितार्थानामप्रतिप्रसवे पुरुषस्यात्यन्तिको गुणवियोगः कैवल्यं तदा स्वरूपप्रतिष्ठा चितिशक्तिरेव पुरुष इति ।। ४९ ।।

When it so happens to the Yogi that on the destruction of *affliction* and action, this distinguishing cognitive characteristic of the Essence and also the Essence (itself) are placed on the side of the Avoidable, and also the Puruṣa is realised to be unchanging, pure and different from the Essence, then to him who is unattached to that (Intellective vision) the evil seeds become incapable of germination like the parched up paddy-seeds and go to destruction along with the mind.

On their destruction, the Puruṣa no more suffers from the three-fold pain. Then on the absence of germination of the Energies which, being manifested in the mind with the nature of action; *affliction* and fruition, have discharged their duties; this complete separation of the Puruṣa from the Energies is the Absoluteness. Then the Puruṣa is only the Self Established Con-Science-power.[1]

स्थान्युपनिमन्त्रणे सङ्गस्मयाकरणं पुनरनिष्टप्रसङ्गात् ।। ५० ।।

On the invitation of the Residential chiefs, non-adoption of association and pride due to the possibility of connection with the evil again-—50

स्थान्युपनिमंत्रणे सङ्गस्मयाकरणं पुनरनिष्टप्रसङ्गात् । चत्वारः खल्वमी योगिनः प्रथमकल्पिको मधुभूमिकः प्रज्ञाज्योतिरतिक्रान्तभावनीयश्चेति । तत्राभ्यासी प्रवृत्तमात्रज्योतिः प्रथमः । ऋतम्भरप्रज्ञो द्वितीयः । भूतेन्द्रियजयी तृतीयः, सर्वेषु भावितेषु भावनीयेषु कृतरक्षाबन्धः कृतकर्तव्यः साधनादिमान् । चतुर्थस्त्वतिक्रान्तभावनीयस्तस्य चित्तप्रतिसर्ग एकोऽर्थः सप्तविधा अस्य प्रान्तभूमिप्रज्ञाः ।

These are, indeed, the four Yogis: (1) the Prathama-kalpika. (2) the Madhubhūmika, (3) the Prajñā jyoti and (4) the Atikrānta-bhāvanīya. There the Yogi, given to the practice and possessed of the light just manifested, is the first. The second is he who is possessed of the "Intellective-Vision full of Truth". The conqueror of the elements and the senses is the third who is ever watchful for the preservation of all that have been produced and are to be produced, and who has done his duties and is persevering in the practice of means, etc. The fourth however is the Atikrānta-bhāvanīya; the dissolution of the mind is his only aim. His Intellective-Vision with final ground is sevenfold (*Y. S.* II-27).

तत्र मधुमतीं भूमिं साक्षात्कुर्वतो ब्राह्मणस्य स्थानिनो देवाः सत्त्वविशुद्धिमनुपश्यन्तः स्थानैरुपनिमन्त्रयन्ते—भो! इहास्यतामिह रम्यतां कमनीयोऽयं भोगः कमनीयेयं कन्या रसायनमिदं जरामृत्युं बाधते वैहायसमिदं यानममी कल्पद्रुमाः पुण्या मन्दाकिनी सिद्धा महर्षय उत्तमा अनुकूला अप्सरसो दिव्ये श्रोत्रचक्षुषी वज्रोपमः कायः स्वगुणैस्सर्वमिदमुपार्जितमायुष्मता प्रतिपद्यतामिदमक्षयमजरममरं स्थानं देवानां प्रियमिति ।

There, the Residential-chiefs, i.e., the gods, on seeing the purity of life of the Brāhmaṇa who has been seeing the Madhumatī stage, invite him from all the places :—"O, sit here, be comfort-

1. In the Vedānta-Darśana, this Con-Science-Power will be termed "Self-expressive-Principle" and will be considered as the Attribute of the Substance termed "Pure Con-Science".

able, this enjoyment is delightful, this girl is attractive, this elixir resists old age and death. This vehicle moves through the air, these trees fulfil all desires, here is the sacred river Mandākinī, here are the perfect ones, the great seers, the beautiful obedient nymphs, the divine power of hearing and seeing, the adamantine body, all this has been earned through your own labour by you, the long-lived. Enjoy this indestructible, undecaying and imperishable position dear to the gods."

एवमभिधीयमानः सङ्गदोषान्भावयेत्—घोरेषु संसाराङ्गारेषु पच्यमानेन मया जननमरणान्धकारे विपरिवर्तमानेन कथंचिदासादितः क्लेशतिमिर-विनाशी योगप्रदीपस्तस्य चैते तृष्णायोनयो विषय-वायवः प्रतिपक्षाः। स खल्वहं लब्धालोकः कथमनया विषयमृगतृष्णया वञ्चितस्तस्यैव पुनः प्रदीप्तस्य संसाराग्नेरात्मानमिन्धनीकुर्यामिति। स्वस्ति वः स्वप्नोपमेभ्यः कृपणजनप्रार्थनीयेभ्यो विषयेभ्य इत्येवं निश्चितमतिः समाधिं भावयेत्।

The Yogi, being thus addressed, should contemplate upon the defects of the association :—"Being burnt up with the horrible fire of the world and being turned about into the darkness of birth and death, somehow I have secured the light of Yoga which is the destroyer of the darkness of *affliction*. Further, these winds of sense-objects, having their origin in desire, are its opponents. How indeed can I, after obtaining the light, be deceived by this mirage of sense-objects? How can I again make myself the fuel of that same blazing fire of the world? Adieu, ye visionary sense-objects! You are suitable to be begged by the foolish one." Thus the resolute Yogi should produce the Spiritual Absorption.

सङ्गमकृत्वा स्मयमपि न कुर्यादेवमहं देवानामपि प्रार्थनीय इति। स्मयादयं सुस्थितमन्यतया मृत्युना केशेषु गृहीतमिवात्मानं न भावयिष्यति। तथा चास्य छिद्रान्तरप्रेक्षी नित्यं यत्नोपचर्यः प्रमादो लब्धविवरः क्लेशानुत्तम्भयिष्यति ततः। पुनरनिष्ट-प्रसङ्गः। एवमस्य सङ्गस्मयावकुर्वतो भावितोऽर्थो दृढीभविष्यति भावनीयश्चार्थोऽभिमुखीभविष्यतीति ॥ ५० ॥

By not coming into the association, he should not assume any pride even :—"Oh! I am such that I am entreated by the gods even." If he assumes the false idea of happiness from pride, he will never understand himself to be caught by the hair by Death. Similarly, the inadvertence, ever heedful for a hole and full of effort, after getting its way, will uphold the afflictions. Thence, there is the possibility of connection with evil again. Thus the produced virtue of the Yogi who does not give himself up to the association and pride, will become firm and the producible virtue will be nearing.

क्षणतत्क्रमयोः संयमाद्विवेकजं ज्ञानम् ॥ ५१ ॥

From the Saṁyama upon the moment and its succession, (comes) the Intellect-born-Knowledge—51

क्षणतत्क्रमयोः संयमाद्विवेकजं ज्ञानम्। यथा अपकर्षपर्यन्तं द्रव्यं परमाणुरेवं परमापकर्षपर्यन्तः कालः क्षणो यावता वा समयेन चलितः परमाणुः पूर्वदेशं जह्यादुत्तरदेशमुपसम्पद्येत स कालः क्षणः तत्प्रवाहाविच्छेदस्तु क्रमः। क्षणतत्क्रमयोर्नास्ति वस्तुसमाहार इति। बुद्धिसमाहारो मुहूर्ताहोरात्रा-दयः। स खल्वयं कालो वस्तुशून्योऽपि बुद्धिनिर्माणः शब्दज्ञानानुपाती, लौकिकानां व्युत्थितदर्शनानां वस्तुस्वरूप इवावभासते।

As the Matter, reaching the limit of its diminution, is an atom, so the time reaching the extreme limit of its diminution is a moment. Or that much of time by which an atom in motion gives up its previous position and reaches the next place, is the moment. The uninterruption of the flow thereof is however the succession. The moment and its succession have no aggregation as a substance; it is but an intellectual aggregation as the Muhūrta (48 minutes), the day, the night, etc. It is in fact this time, which, although devoid of reality, becomes an intellectual creation following the literal idea. To ordinary persons with the exhibitive vision, it appears to be the real nature of the Substance.

क्षणस्तु वस्तुपतितः क्रमावलम्बी। क्रमश्च क्षणानन्तर्यात्मा तं कालविदः काल इत्याचक्षते योगिनः।

The moment however, falling under the head of reality, is supported by succession. Further, the succession possesses the nature of intervention of the moments. The Yogis who are the knowers of time, call it by the name of time.

न च द्वौ क्षणौ सह भवतः । क्रमश्च न द्वयोः सहभुवोरसंभवात्पूर्वस्मादुत्तरस्य भाविनो यदानन्तर्यं क्षणस्य स क्रमस्तस्माद्वर्तमानः एवैकः क्षणो न पूर्वोत्तरक्षणाः सन्तीति तस्मान्नास्ति तत्समाहार: ।

Again, two moments can never coexist; also the succession cannot happen to two co-existent moments on account of its impossibility. The immediate proximity of the latter moment which happens just after the former, is the succession. Therefore, the present one is but the single moment. The former and the latter moments do not exist. Accordingly there is no aggregation of them.

ये तु भूतभाविनः क्षणास्ते परिणामान्विता व्याख्येयास्तेनैकेन क्षणेन कृत्स्नो लोकः परिणाममनुभवति तत्क्षणोपारूढाः खल्वमी सर्वे धर्मास्तयोः क्षणतत्क्रमयोः संयमात्तयोः साक्षात्करणं ततश्च विवेकजं ज्ञानं प्रादुर्भवति ॥ ५१ ॥

On the other hand, those moments which happened and are to happen should be described as connected with the change. The whole world undergoes the change by that single moment; all the characteristics are in fact installed on that single moment. From the Saṁyama upon the moment and its succession, the direct vision of them appears; thence also the Intellect-born-Knowledge manifests.

जातिलक्षणदेशैरन्यतानवच्छेदात् तुल्ययोस्ततः प्रतिपत्तिः ॥ ५२ ॥

Thence comes the perception of two similar things when they are indistinguishable owing to the absence of separation of their difference by means of species, feature and position—52

तस्य विषयविशेष उपक्षिप्यते । जातिलक्षण-देशैरन्यतानवच्छेदात्तुल्ययोस्ततः प्रतिपत्तिः । तुल्ययोर्देशलक्षणसारूप्ये जातिभेदोऽन्यतायां हेतुः । गौरियं वडवेयमिति ।

The distinct sphere of that (Intellect-born-knowledge) is being described :— Thence comes the perception of two similar things when they are indistinguishable owing to the absence of separation of their difference by means of species, feature and position. In the similarity of position and feature of two similar things, the difference of species is the cause of their differentiation : this is a cow, this is a mare and so on.

तुल्यदेशजातीयत्वे लक्षणमन्यत्वकरं कालाक्षी गौः स्वस्तिमती गौरिति । द्वयोरामलकयोर्जातिलक्षण-सारूप्याद् देशभेदोऽन्यत्वकर इदं पूर्वमिदमुत्तरमिति ।

In the similarity of equal position and species, the feature causes their distinction : the cow with black eyes and the cow having white spot on head. On account of the conformity of species and feature of two emblic fruits, the difference of position is the cause of their distinction :—"It is the former, it is the latter."

यदा तु पूर्वमामलकमन्यव्यग्रस्य ज्ञातुरुत्तरे देश उपावर्तते तदा तुल्यदेशत्वे पूर्वमेतदुत्तरमेतदिति प्रविभागानुपपत्तिः । असन्दिग्धेन च तत्त्वज्ञानेन भवितव्यमित्यत इदमुक्तम्—ततः प्रतिपत्तिर्विवेकज-ज्ञानादिति । कथं ? पूर्वामलकसहक्षणदेश उत्तरा-मलकसहक्षणाद् देशाद्भिन्नः ।

When however the former emblic fruit of a knower whose attention is engaged elsewhere, is placed in the latter position, then from the similarity of positions, there comes the failure of their differentiation such as 'it is the former, it is the latter.' Further, it becomes possible only by means of the indubitable knowledge of reality. Hence it is said:— "thence comes the perception," i.e., from the Intellect-born-Knowledge. How ? The position of the moment, correlated with the former emblic fruit, is different from the position of the moment correlated with the latter emblic.

ते चामलके स्वदेशक्षणानुभवभिन्ने । अन्यदेश क्षणानुभवस्तु तयोरन्यत्वे हेतुरिति । एतेन दृष्टान्तेन परमाणोस्तुल्यजातिलक्षणदेशस्य पूर्वपरमाणुदेश-सहक्षणसाक्षात्करणादुत्तरस्य परमाणोस्तद् देशा-तद्देशानुपपत्तावुत्तरस्य तद्देशानुभवो भिन्नः सहक्षण-भेदात्तयोरीश्वरस्य योगिनोऽन्यत्वप्रत्ययो भवतीति ।

Further, these two emblic fruits are distinguished by the perception of the moments of their respective positions. The perception of the moment of different position becomes indeed the cause of their differentiation. By this example, with reference to the atoms possessed of similar species, feature and position, the perception of that position of the latter (atom) is different (from that of the former atom) due to the difference of the correlated moments on the ascertainment of the respective position of the latter atom from the direct observation of the moment correlated with the position of the former atom. This cognition of differentiation comes to the Yogi who has mastery over these two.

अपरे तु वर्णयन्ति—येऽन्त्या विशेषास्तेऽन्यताप्रत्ययं कुर्वन्तीति । तत्रापि देशलक्षणभेदो मूर्तिव्यवधिजातिभेदश्चान्यत्वे हेतुः । क्षणभेदस्तु योगिबुद्धिगम्य एवेत्यत उक्तं मूर्तिव्यवधिजातिभेदाभावान्नास्ति मूलपृथक्त्वमिति वार्षगण्यः ॥ ५२ ॥

Others, however, describe that those that are the last peculiarities (the Specific Step of the Energies), cause the cognition of differentiation[1]. Even there the difference of position and feature and also the difference of form, intervening space and species are the cause for the differentiation. The difference of moment, however, can be grasped only by the Yogi's intellect. Hence, it is said by Vārṣagaṇya (a great Seer) that on the absence of the difference of form, intervening space and species, there is no difference in the Root[2].

तारकं सर्वविषयं सर्वथाविषयमक्रमं चेति विवेकजज्ञानम् ॥ ५३ ॥

The intellect-born-knowledge is the rescuer, has the sphere of all objects, has the sphere of all conditions and also has no succession—53

तारकं सर्वविषयं सर्वथाविषयमक्रमं चेति विवेकजज्ञानम् । तारकमिति स्वप्रतिभोत्थमनौपदेशिकमित्यर्थः ।

The rescuer means that it comes out of one's own genius, and is not born of instruction[3].

सर्वविषयत्वान्नास्य किंचिदविषयीभूतमित्यर्थः ।

"Has the sphere of all objects" means that it has nothing left which is not within its sphere.

सर्वथाविषयमतीतानागतप्रत्युत्पन्नं सर्वं पर्यायैः सर्वथा जानातीत्यर्थः ।

"Has the sphere of all conditions" means that it knows all whether the past, the not-yet-come and the present with all systems and with all conditions.

अक्रममित्येकक्षणोपारूढं सर्वं सर्वथा गृह्णातीत्यर्थः ।

"Has no succession" means that it takes all to be installed on the single moment in all respects.

एतद्विवेकजं ज्ञानं परिपूर्णमस्यैवांशो योगप्रदीपो मधुमतीं भूमिमुपादाय यावदस्य परिसमाप्तिरिति ॥ ५३ ॥

This Intellect-born-Knowledge is a complete whole; the Yoga-light, beginning from the Madhumatī stage up to its last limit, is only a part of this.

सत्त्वपुरुषयोः शुद्धिसाम्ये कैवल्यम् ॥ ५४ ॥

On the coincidence of purity of both the Essence and the Puruṣa, (comes) Absoluteness—54

प्राप्तविवेकजज्ञानस्याप्राप्तविवेकजज्ञानस्य वा सत्त्वपुरुषयोः शुद्धिसाम्ये कैवल्यमिति । यदा निर्धूतरजस्तमोमलं बुद्धिसत्त्वं पुरुषस्यान्यताप्रतीतिमात्राधिकारं दग्धक्लेशबीजं भवति तदा पुरुषस्य

1. This is the Viśeṣa of the Vaiśeṣika. The commentator does not refute this theory, but after accepting it as a beginning step, he shows the higher one. It must be admitted that the Sāṅkhya-Yoga is proceeding towards perfection by taking its stand upon Nyāya-Vaiśeṣikas.

2. Here on the authority of Vārṣagaṇya, the Commentator establishes the Ultimate Reality as the Single Whole.

3. From the commentary on the term "Tārakam" (rescuer), it is clear that Emancipation cannot be attained by blindly following the examples and precepts of others. But it should be achieved by personal effort, indomitable perseverance and constant application to the practice of Yoga.

शुद्धिसारूप्यमिवापन्नं भवति । तदा पुरुषस्योपचरितभोगाभावः शुद्धिस्तस्यामवस्थायां कैवल्यं भवति । ईश्वरस्यानीश्वरस्य वा विवेकजज्ञानभागिन इतरस्य वा । नहि दग्धक्लेशबीजस्य ज्ञाने पुनरपेक्षा काचिदस्ति सत्त्वशुद्धिद्वारेणैतत्समाधिजमैश्वर्यं ज्ञानं चोपक्रान्तं परमार्थतस्तु ज्ञानाददर्शनं निवर्तते ।

With reference to the Yogi whether possessed of the Intellect-born-Knowledge or not possessed of the Intellect-born-Knowledge, Absoluteness comes from the coincidence of purity of both the Essence and the Puruṣa. When the Intellective-Essence, being freed from the dirt of the active and the inert Energies and being possessed of the only duty of the cognition of distinction of the Puruṣa, gets the seed of *afflictions* burnt up, then it seems to have obtained the conformity of the Puruṣa's purity. At that time, the absence of Experience represented to him is the purity of the Puruṣa. In that state, Absoluteness comes to the Yogi whether powerful or not powerful, or (in other words) whether he be the possessor of the Intellect-born-Knowledge or not, because the Yogī whose seed of *afflictions* has been burnt up, has no further dependence upon Knowledge. The power and the knowledge born of Spiritual-Absorption have been dealt with in accordance with the purity of the Intellective-Essence. However in reality, Non-Observation disappears with the appearance of Knowledge[1].

तस्मिन्निवृत्ते न सन्त्युत्तरे क्लेशाः क्लेशाभावात्कर्मविपाकाभावश्चरिताधिकाराश्चैतस्यामवस्थायां गुणा न पुरुषस्य दृश्यत्वेन पुनरुपतिष्ठन्ते तत्पुरुषस्य कैवल्यं तदा पुरुषः स्वरूपमात्रज्योतिरमलः केवली भवति ॥ ५४ ॥

On its cessation, there can be no further *afflictions*. From the absence of the *afflictions* comes the absence of action and fruition. In that state, the Energies with their duties finished, no more appear before the Puruṣa as the Perceivable; this is the Absoluteness of the Puruṣa. At that time, the Puruṣa, being pure and shining with the only light of his own manifestation, becomes Absolute.

इति श्रीपातञ्जलभाष्ये सांख्यप्रवचने विभूतिपादस्तृतीयः समाप्तः ॥३॥

---

1. This Knowledge is neither the knowledge of books nor of the words of mouth, but it is the Observation known as the Intellective Revelation which has been described in II. 23. Here it is clear from the aphorism and the commentary that Absoluteness comes from Oneness or Coincidence of the Intellective Essence with the Puruṣa.

Here ends the Third Chapter known as the Subject of the Accomplishments with regard to the Science of Yoga composed by Patañjali in the Excellent Teaching of the Sāṅkhya.

CHAPTER IV

THE SUBJECT OF ABSOLUTENESS

जन्मौषधिमन्त्रतपःसमाधिजाः सिद्धयः ॥ १ ॥

The Accomplishments are born by means of Birth, Herbs, Incantations, Penance and Spiritual Absorption.—1.

जन्मौषधिमन्त्रतपःसमाधिजाः सिद्धयः । देहान्तरिता जन्मसिद्धिः ओषधीभिरसुरभवनेषु रसायनेनेत्येवमादिः । मन्त्रैराकाशगमनमणिमादिसिद्धिः । तपसा सङ्कल्पसिद्धिः । कामरूपी यत्र तत्र कामग इत्येवमादिः, समाधिजाः सिद्धयो व्याख्याताः ॥ १ ॥

The accomplishment by means of birth[1] is inherent in the body. In the houses of the Asuras, elixir, etc., are made up by herbs. By incantations the accomplishments of the passage through the sky, attainment of particle-form (Aṇimā), etc., are obtained. The accomplishment of will-power is achieved by penance; he takes any shape at will and is able to act upon that as he pleases, etc. The accomplishments born of Spiritual Absorption have been described (in the Third Chapter).

जात्यन्तरपरिणामः प्रकृत्यापूरात् ॥ २ ॥

The change into different life-states takes place on account of the current of the Intensive Cause. —2.

तत्र कायेन्द्रियाणामन्यजातिपरिणतानां जात्यन्तरपरिणामः प्रकृत्यापूरात् । पूर्वपरिणामापाये उत्तरपरिणामोपजनस्तेषामपूर्वावयवानुप्रवेशाद्भवति । कायेन्द्रियप्रकृतयश्च स्वं स्वं विकारमनुगृह्णन्त्यापूरेण धर्मादिनिमित्तमपेक्षमाणा इति ॥ २ ॥

There, with reference to the bodies and the senses transformed into another life-state, the change of different life-states takes place on account of 'the current of the Intensive Cause.'[2] On the Cessation of the former change, takes place the appearance of the latter owing to the coming in of their (of the bodies, etc.,) constituent parts which did not exist before. The Intensive Causes of the bodies and the senses favour their respective modifications by the current dependent upon the Exciting Cause as virtue, etc.

निमित्तमप्रयोजकं प्रकृतीनां वरणभेदस्तु ततः क्षेत्रिकवत् ॥ ३ ॥

The Exciting Cause is not the founder of the Intensive Causes; simply the separation of the covering comes there-from as by the farmer.—3

निमित्तमप्रयोजकं प्रकृतीनां वरणभेदस्तु ततः क्षेत्रिकवत् । नहि धर्मादिनिमित्तं तत्प्रयोजकं भवति प्रकृतीनाम् । न कार्येण कारणं प्रवर्त्यंत इति। कथं तर्हि? वरणभेदस्तु ततः क्षेत्रिकवत् । यथा क्षेत्रिकः केदारादपां पूर्णात्केदारान्तरं विप्लावयिषुः समं निम्नं निम्नतरं वा नापः पाणिनापकर्षंत्यावरणं त्वासां भिनत्ति तस्मिन्भिन्ने स्वयमेवापः केदारान्तर-

1. It should be understood here that whatever a man inherits by his birth is called the Accomplishment by Birth (*Janma-Siddhi*). It is not produced by his own effort in his present life.

2. Here the Intensive Causes refer to the function of the Energies. And the Exciting Cause is the Action performed by a man.

माप्लावयन्ति तथा धर्मः प्रकृतीनामावरणमधर्मं भिनत्ति तस्मिन्भिन्ने स्वयमेव प्रकृतयः स्वं स्वं विकारमाप्लावयन्ति ।

The Exciting Cause such as virtue, etc., can never be the founder of those Intensive Causes[1]. The cause is never generated by the effect. How then ? Simply the separation of the covering comes therefrom as by the farmer. Just as a farmer, willing to overflow a different plot of land either of equal or low or lower level with water from a well-filled land, does not draw the water with his own hand but cuts its resistence and when that (resistence) is cut off, the water itself overflows that different plot of land, similarly, virtue separates vice which is the covering of the Intensive Causes. When it is separated, then the Intensive Causes themselves flow over their respective modifications.

यथा वा स एव क्षेत्रिकस्तस्मिन्नेव केदारे न प्रभवत्यौदकान्भौमान्वा रसान्धान्यमूलान्यनुप्रवेशयितुम् । किं तर्हि? मुद्गगवेधुकश्यामाकादींस्ततोऽपकर्षति । अपकृष्टेषु तेषु स्वयमेव रसधान्यमूलान्यनुप्रविशन्ति । तथा धर्मो निवृत्तिमात्रे कारणमधर्मस्य शुद्ध्यशुद्ध्योरत्यन्तविरोधात् न तु प्रकृतिप्रवृत्तौ धर्मो हेतुर्भवतीति । अत्र नन्दीश्वरादय उदाहार्याः ।

Or as the same farmer is not able to transfer the watery and the earthly juices into the roots of the paddy plants in the same plot of land, what he does is that he weeds out the Mudga, Gavedhuka, Śyāmāka, etc., therefrom and when they are pulled away, the juices themselves enter into the roots of the paddy plants. Similarly virtue is the cause only for the cessation of vice on account of the extreme contradiction in purity and impurity. Virtue can never be the cause for the rise of the Intensive Causes. Here Nandīś-vara and others are the illustrations.

विपर्ययेणाप्यधर्मो धर्मं बाधते । ततश्चाशुद्धिपरिणाम इति । तत्रापि नहुषाजगरादय उदाहार्या इति ॥ ३ ॥

Vice also contradicts virtue by perversive cognition; therefrom comes impurity as the result. Even there Nahuṣa as a serpent and others are the illustrations.

निर्माणचित्तान्यस्मितामात्रात् ॥ ४ ॥

The created minds proceed from the Pure Egoism.—4

यदा तु योगी बहून्कायान्निर्मिमीते तदा किमेकमनस्कास्ते भवन्त्यथानेकमनस्काः? निर्माणचित्तान्यस्मितामात्रात् ।

When however the Yogi[2] creates many bodies, are they one-minded or many-minded? The created minds proceed from the Pure Egoism.

अस्मितामात्रं चित्तं कारणमुपादाय निर्माणचित्तानि करोति ततः सचित्तानि भवन्तीति ॥ ४ ॥

The Pure Egoism[3], taking up the mind as a cause, makes the created minds; therefrom the bodies become possessed of minds.

प्रवृत्तिभेदे प्रयोजकं चित्तमेकमनेकेषाम् ॥ ५ ॥

On the difference of rise, the Single Mind is the founder of the many,—5

प्रवृत्तिभेदे प्रयोजकं चित्तमेकमनेकेषाम् । बहूनां चित्तानां कथमेकचित्ताभिप्रायपुरःसरा प्रवृत्तिरिति? सर्वचित्तानां प्रयोजकं चित्तमेकं निर्मिमीते ततः प्रवृत्तिभेदः ॥ ५ ॥

How does the rise of many minds take place after taking, in front, the purpose of the single mind ? The Founder[4] of all minds creates the Single Mind; therefrom comes the difference of rise.

---

1. It is to be understood here that owing to the beginninglessness of the Substance, its Power is also beginningless. Accordingly the Intensive Causes which ensue from the Power are natural and without any beginning; they are not produced by the Exciting Cause as virtue or vice which is dependent upon Human Action. They simply being united with the varieties of the Exciting Cause, take the form of the Intensive Force for the fruition of the vehicle-of-action.

2. Here the Yogi is the Active Creator known as the Intensive Force.

3. This Pure-Egoism is the *Ekajīva* (*Īśvara*) of the Vedānta Darśana in the form of the Pure Traceable Step of the Pradhāna and is the Creator of the world.

4. Here the 'Founder' refers to the Con-Science-Power (*Brahmā*), and the Single Mind to the single Soul or the 'Consciousness' in the terminology. Here the commentator leaves the subject over to the Vedānta Darśanta. The full explanation of this can only be had therein.

तत्र ध्यानजमनाशयम् ॥ ६ ॥

There the meditation-born (mind) is devoid of the vehicle—6

तत्र ध्यानजमनाशयम् । पञ्चविधं निर्माणचित्तं जन्मौषधिमन्त्रतपःसमाधिजाः सिद्धय इति । तत्र यदेव ध्यानजं चित्तं तदेवानाशयं तस्यैव नास्त्याशयो रागादिप्रवृत्तिः । नातः पुण्यपापाभिसम्बन्धः क्षीणक्लेशत्वाद्योगिन इति ॥ ६ ॥

The created mind is of five descriptions (as each mind rises with the aim of accomplishment and it has been said before that) the Accomplishments are born by means of birth, herbs, incantations, penance and Spiritual-Absorption. There that which is the meditation-born mind, is alone devoid of the vehicle. It alone has no vehicle which is the manifestation of attachment, etc. Therefore the Yogi has no connection with virtue and vice on account of the destruction of his afflictions[1].

कर्माशुक्लाकृष्णं योगिनस्त्रिविधमितरेषाम् ॥ ७ ॥

The action of the Yogi is neither white nor black; that of the others is three-fold—7

इतरेषां तु विद्यते कर्माशयो यतः—कर्माशुक्लाकृष्णं योगिनस्त्रिविधमितरेषाम् चतुष्पात्खल्वियं कर्मजातिः । कृष्णा शुक्लकृष्णा शुक्लाऽशुक्लाकृष्णा चेति ।

Relating to others however, the vehicle of action exists; because the action of the Yogi is neither white nor black; that of the others is three-fold. The class of action has in fact four steps: the black, the white-black, the white and the neither-white-nor-black.

तत्र कृष्णा दुरात्मनाम् । शुक्लकृष्णा बहिः साधनसाध्या । तत्र परपीडानुग्रहद्वारेणैव कर्माशयप्रचयः ।

There the black (prohibited Action is of the sinful ones. The white-black is accomplished by the external means (Ritual Actions). So there, the formation of the vehicle of action is caused by means of injury and kindness to others.

शुक्ला तपःस्वाध्यायध्यानवताम् । सा हि केवले मनस्यायत्तत्वाद् बहिः साधनानधीना न परान्पीडयित्वा भवति ।

The white is of those that are given to penance, study and meditation; because it is not dependent upon the external means on account of its dependence upon the mind alone. So it does not appear by causing injury to others.

अशुक्लाकृष्णा संन्यासिनां क्षीणक्लेशानां चरमदेहानामिति । तत्राशुक्लं योगिन एव फलसंन्यासादकृष्णं चानुपादानात् । इतरेषां तु भूतानां पूर्वमेव त्रिविधमिति ॥ ७ ॥

The neither-white-nor-black is of the renouncers whose afflictions have been destroyed and who have got their last bodies. There the Yogi alone has neither white action due to the renouncement of fruit, nor has he black one on account of withdrawing the organs of senses from the outer world. The others, however, have three-fold action only as described above.

ततस्तद्विपाकानुगुणानामेवाभिव्यक्तिर्वासनानाम् ॥ ८ ॥

Therefrom comes the manifestation of the habitual residua suitable to their fruition alone—8

ततस्तद्विपाकानुगुणानामेवाभिव्यक्तिर्वासनानाम् । तत इति त्रिविधात्कर्मणस्तद्विपाकानुगुणानामेवेति—यज्जातीयस्य कर्मणो यो विपाकस्तस्यानुगुणा या वासनाः कर्मविपाकमनुशेरते । तासामेवाभिव्यक्तिः । नहि दैवं कर्म विपच्यमानं नारकतिर्यङ्मनुष्यवासनाभिव्यक्तिनिमित्तं संभवति । किंतु दैवानुगुणा एवास्य वासना व्यज्यन्ते ।

---

1. The accomplishment born of Spiritual Absorption alone can produce Oneness with the Creator termed "Single Soul" (*Ekajiva*); so the skilful Yogi has no separate will-power. Accordingly he has no attachment and aversion which are the real character of the vehicle, the cause of rebirth.

It is clear from the commentary that the created minds are subject to changes but not the Creative Mind, the Pure Egoism which is always in the unchanging position (*kūṭastha*) even though it is the relative cause.

"Therefrom" means from those three kinds of action. "Suitable to their fruition alone" means that only that relative residua which are suitable to that fruition of actions of the respective class, follow the fruition of action. (So) the manifestation of those residua alone takes place, because the action fructifying the state of a god can never be the exciting cause for the manifestation of the residua of the hellish, the animal and the human states; but simply the residua competent to the divine state are roused.

नारकतिर्यङ्मनुष्येषु चैवं समानश्चर्चः ॥ ८ ॥

Similarly, the same consideration should be applied to the hellish, the animal and the human states.

जातिदेशकालव्यवहितानामप्यानन्तर्यं स्मृतिसंस्कारयोरेकरूपत्वात् ॥ ९ ॥

There is the interposition of them (of the residua), even though separated by life state, space and time, on account of the similar forms of the memories (प्रारब्ध) and the habitual potencies (संस्कार).—9

जातिदेशकालव्यवहितानामप्यानन्तर्यं स्मृतिसंस्कारयोरेकरूपत्वात् । वृषदंशविपाकोदयः स्वव्यञ्जकाञ्जनाभिव्यक्तः । स यदि जातिशतेन वा दूरदेशतया वा कल्पशतेन वा व्यवहितः पुनश्च स्वव्यञ्जकाञ्जन एवोदियाद्द्रागित्येवं पूर्वानुभूतवृषदंशविपाकाभिसंस्कृता वासना उपादाय व्यज्येत कस्मात् ? यतो व्यवहितानामप्यासां सदृशं कर्माभिव्यञ्जकं निमित्तीभूतमित्यानन्तर्यमेव । कुतश्च? स्मृतिसंस्कारयोरेकरूपत्वात् ।

The rise of the fruition of a cat is manifested by the colour of its own manifestative cause. If it be separated by hundred life-states or by hundred distant intervals or by hundred kalpas (periodical dissolution), it, being only possessed of the colour of its own manifestative cause, thus again gets excited very quickly after taking up the residua thoroughly formed by the fruition of the feline state experienced previously. Why ? Because even though separated, they have the similar manifestative action becoming the exciting cause; this is verily the interposition. What more ? (The other cause is) on account of the similar forms of the memories and the habitual potencies.

यथानुभवास्तथा संस्काराः ते च कर्मवासनारूपाः । यथा च वासनास्तथा स्मृतिरिति । जातिदेशकालव्यवहितेभ्यः संस्कारेभ्यः स्मृतिः, स्मृतेश्च पुनः संस्कारा इत्येवमेते स्मृतिसंस्काराः कर्माशयवृत्तिलाभवशाद् व्यज्यन्ते । अतश्च व्यवहितानामपि निमित्तनैमित्तिकभावानुच्छेदादानन्तर्यमेव सिद्धमिति । वासनाः संस्कारा आशया इत्यर्थः ॥ ९ ॥

As are the experiences (actions), so are the habitual potencies. Further, the latter are of the forms of the residua of actions. And also as is the residue so is the memory. The memory comes from the habitual potencies separated by life-state, space and time; again from the memory come the habitual potencies. Thus the memory and the habitual potencies are roused by the strength of the operative function of the vehicle-of-action. Also for this reason, it is established that even though they are separated, there is indeed the interposition (of those actions) on account of the non-extinction of the relation of cause and effect[1]. The meaning is that the residua are the habitual potencies and the vehicles.

तासामनादित्वं चाशिषो नित्यत्वात् ॥ १० ॥

They have also the state of being beginningless, due to the eternity of the benediction (love of life).—10

तासामनादित्वं चाशिषो नित्यत्वात् । तासां वासनानामाशिषो नित्यत्वादनादित्वम् । येयमात्माशीर्मा न भूवं भूयासमिति सर्वस्य दृश्यते सा न स्वाभाविकी । कस्मात्? जातमात्रस्याननुभूतमरणधर्मकस्य द्वेषो दुःखानुस्मृतिनिमित्तो मरणत्रासः कथं भवेत?

1. By this it is clear that the relation of cause and effect is the same as the vehicle-of-action with seed-power. So long as the cause (**the vehicle**) exists, it must produce the effect in the form of rebirth. Here the terms "habitual potencies" signify the actions done in the present life (*Kriyamāṇa*). 'Memories" denotes the actions of the regulated fruition (*Prārabdha*). And the term "residua" indicates the actions stored up in the vehicle (*Sañcita Karma*).

They, i.e., the residua are beginningless on account of the eternity of the benediction (love of life). The self-benediction : "May I not cease to exist, may I ever live" which is to be seen in all, is not natural. Why ? How can the aversion, the fear of death caused by the remembrance of pain, come to a just-born being who has not experienced mortality ?

न च स्वाभाविकं वस्तु निमित्तमुपादत्ते । तस्मादनादिवासनानुविद्धमिदं चित्तं निमित्तवशात्काश्चिदेव वासनाः प्रतिलभ्य पुरुषस्य भोगायोपावर्तत इति ।

Further, a natural thing never takes up any exciting cause. Therefore, this mind intermixed with the beginningless residua, after obtaining only certain residua by virtue of the exciting cause, evolves for the experience of the Puruṣa.

घटप्रासादप्रदीपकल्पं संकोचविकासि चित्तं शरीरपरिमाणाकारमात्रमित्यपरे प्रतिपन्नाः, तथा चान्तराभावः संसारश्च युक्त इति ।

Others believe that the mind, having the power of contraction and expansion like the light of a lamp placed in a pot or in a palace, is possessed of the form only of the dimension of the body; so there is also the absence of interposition and the continuity (of the mind with the successive bodies) is proper[1].

वृत्तिरेवास्य विभुनश्चित्तस्य संकोचविकासिनीत्याचार्यः । तच्च धर्मादिनिमित्तापेक्षम् । निमित्तं च द्विविधम् । बाह्यमाध्यात्मिकं च । शरीरादिसाधनापेक्षं बाह्यं स्तुतिदानाभिवादनादि, चित्तमात्राधीनं श्रद्धाद्याध्यात्मिकम् । तथाचोक्तम्—ये चैते मैत्र्यादयो ध्यायिनां विहारास्ते बाह्यसाधननिरनुग्रहात्मानः प्रकृष्टं धर्ममभिनिर्वर्तयन्ति, तयोर्मानसं बलीयः । कथं? ज्ञानवैराग्ये केनातिशय्येते ? दण्डकारण्यं च चित्तबलव्यतिरेकेण शारीरेण कर्मणा शून्यं कः कर्तुमुत्सहेत, समुद्रमगस्त्यवद्वा पिबेत् ॥१०॥

The Perfect Vedic Teacher says that simply the operation of this constant mind is possessed of contraction and expansion. Further, it is dependent upon the exciting cause such as virtue, etc. Also the exciting cause is two-fold: the Material and the Spiritual. What is dependent upon the body, etc.[2] as instruments, is material such as prayer, charity, salutation, etc., and what is dependent upon the mind alone, is Spiritual such as faith (vehement aspiration), etc. Accordingly it has also been said "those which are friendship, etc., are the amusements of the meditators; they, possessing the nature independent of the material instruments, accomplish the highest virtue." Of these two, the mental (Spiritual Exciting Cause) is powerful. How ? By what can knowledge and desirelessness be excelled ? Who can determine to empty the Daṇḍaka forest by bodily action without the mental force, or can drink the ocean like Agastya?

हेतुफलाश्रयालम्बनैः संगृहीतत्वादेषामभावे तदभावः ॥ ११ ॥

---

1. Some people think that as the light of a lamp takes the form of a thing either large or small in which it is placed, so also the mind is of the dimension of the body whether large or small. Accordingly they hold that it is in continuous flow without any interposition of rebirth, i.e., the mind goes from one body to another simply by the transformation of the father as a son. They say that the son is nothing but a part of the mind together with the body of his father.

The commentator solves this question by establishing that the mind by itself does not expand or contract; simply the operation of that constant mind contracts and expands like the light of a lamp. Again the lamp by itself neither contracts nor expands; simply its light becomes as such according to the dimension of the room in which it is placed. Similarly, the mind expands when it is dependent upon virtue, and contracts when dependent upon vice. This question has been fully solved in the Ābhāsa-vāda (the theory of reflection) of the Vedānta Darśana.

2. The Material Exciting cause is the Karma Yoga (Yoga of Action) of the Gītā; and the Spiritual Exciting Cause is termed *Buddhi Yoga Jñāna Yoga, Jñāna Yajña, Bhakti Yoga* in the Gītā. It has already been stated in the ninth aphorism of the first chapter that the lower form of Jñāna (knowledge) is the function of the intellect in both its exhibitive and inhabitive habits, and is also the same as Bhakti; because they both signify the spiritual action. The higher form of Jñāna is the Substance known as the Con-Science pure and simple in the terminology. This subject will be fully discussed in the Gītā.

Friendship, etc., are the four-helping qualities for the embellishment of the mind. And faith (vehement aspiration), etc., are the five successive steps for the course of proceeding with the component parts of Yoga (*Y.S.* I-33 and 20 respectively).

On account of being held together by Cause, Motive, Basis and Support, they (the residua) cease on the absence of these—11

हेतुफलाश्रयालम्बनैः संगृहीतत्वादेषामभावे तदभावः । हेतुर्धर्मात्सुखमधर्माद् दुःखम् । सुखाद्रागो दुःखाद्द्वेषस्ततश्च प्रयत्नस्तेन मनसा वाचा कायेन वा परिस्पन्दमानः परमनुगृह्णात्युपहन्ति वा ततः पुनर्धर्माधर्मौ सुखदुःखे रागद्वेषाविति । प्रवृत्तमिदं षडरं संसारचक्रमस्य च प्रतिक्षणमावर्तमानस्याविद्या नेत्री मूलं सर्वक्लेशानामित्येष हेतुः ।

The Cause means that pleasure is born of virtue, and pain of vice. Attachment comes from pleasure, and aversion from pain; effort also comes therefrom. Thereby one, being moved either by mind or by speech or by body, favours or injures others; therefrom again come virtue and vice, pleasure and pain, attraction and aversion. Accordingly this six-spoked wheel of rebirth is set in motion[1] and the Non-Science, the root of all afflictions is the driver of this (wheel) turning every moment; this is the Cause.

फलं तु यमाश्रित्य यस्य प्रत्युत्पन्नता धर्मादेः । नह्यपूर्वोपजनः ।

The motive however is that, depending upon which, his virtue, etc., are regenerated. There can be no birth of a non-existing thing.[2]

मनस्तु साधिकारमाश्रयो वासनानाम् । नह्यवसिताधिकारे मनसि निराश्रया वासनाः स्थातुमुत्सहन्ते ।

The mind however, being invested with duty, is the Basis of the residua. The baseless residua can never incline to stay in the mind, the duty of which has been finished.

यदभिमुखीभूतं वस्तु यां वासनां व्यनक्ति तस्यास्तदालम्बनम् ।

That is the Support of that residua, being faced towards which, the Substance manifests some residua.[3]

एवं हेतुफलाश्रयालम्बनैरेतैः संगृहीताः सर्वा वासनाः । एषामभावे तत्संश्रयाणामपि वासनानामभावः ॥ ११ ॥

Thus all residua are held together by these:—cause, motive, basis and support. On the absence of these, there is also the absence of the residua maintained by them.

अतीतानागतं स्वरूपतोऽस्त्यध्वभेदाद्धर्माणाम् ॥ १२ ॥

The past and the not-yet-come exist in reality on account of the difference of paths of the characteristics—12

नास्त्यसतः सम्भवः । न चास्ति सतो विनाश इति द्रव्यत्वेन सम्भवन्त्यः कथं निवर्तिष्यन्ते वासना इति अतीतानागतं स्वरूपतोऽस्त्यध्वभेदाद्धर्माणाम् । भविष्यद्व्यक्तिकमनागतमनुभूतव्यक्तिकमतीतं स्वव्यापारोपारूढं वर्तमानं त्रयं चैतद्वस्तु ज्ञानस्य ज्ञेयम् ।

It is a rule that there is no manifestation of a non-existing thing and also there is no destruction of the existing one: how then can the residua which exist as qualification of the Matter[4], cease? The past and the not-yet-come exist in reality on account of the difference of paths of the characteristics. The-not-yet-come is that which has its manifestation in future; the past is that the manifestation of which has been experienced,

---

1. These six spokes are these pairs of opposites such as virtue and vice, pleasure and pain, attachment and aversion.

2. This Motive is the same as Purposefulness. There is nothing in the world without purpose; this is the idea.

3. The support is the vehicle. The Substance is the union of the three Energies termed "Pradhāna". (*Y.S.* Chap. II-18).

4. Here, the Matter to be understood as the 'Single Soul' (the Ultimate Atom) who is present with the manifested condition in the PurerTraceable-Step of the Energies, and is the Relative Cause of all the Created Beings. Similarly, the commentator has already concluded that this Ultimate Atom is the pure and simple form of Matter which has been maintained by the Nyāya-Vaiśeṣika in the specific step of the Energies (Y.S. III 44, 52). Further, this Single Soul will be considered to be the Substance in the *Brahma-Sūtra* which deals with the subject beyond the sphere of Action; because the Matter (द्रव्य) is called as such so long as it remains within the province of the intellect; but when the same Matter goes beyond the intellect, it is then called the Substance (वस्तु)

and the present is that which is installed on its own operation; this trio is the Substance—the cognizable of the Con-Science.

यदि चैतत्स्वरूपतो नाभविष्यन्नेदं निर्विषयं ज्ञानमुदपत्स्यत तस्मादतीतानागतं स्वरूपतोऽस्तीति। किंच भोगभागीयस्य वाऽपवर्गभागीयस्य वा कर्मणः फलमुत्पित्सु यदि निरूपाख्यमिति तदुद्देशेन तेन निमित्तेन कुशलानुष्ठानं न युज्येत। सतश्च फलस्य निमित्तं वर्तमानीकरणे समर्थं नापूर्वोपजनने सिद्धम्। निमित्तं नैमित्तिकस्य विशेषानुग्रहं कुरुते नापूर्वमुत्पादयतीति।

Further, if this trio had been non-existent in reality, this Con-Science, having no scope, would not have any rise. Hence, the past and the not-yet-come exist in reality. What more? If the Reality wishing to produce the fruit of either of the actions pertaining to Experience or Emancipation, could not be pointed out, then the performance of welfare with that aim by that exciting cause could not be possible. Further, the exciting cause is able to bring to the present state, the consequence of the Reality but it is not successful in bringing about the consequence of any non-existing thing. The exciting cause helps much in bringing the effect to a specific state but cannot produce anything anew.

धर्मी चानेकधर्मस्वभावः। तस्य चाध्वभेदेन धर्माः प्रत्यवस्थिताः। न च यथावर्तमानं व्यक्तिविशेषापन्नं द्रव्यतोऽस्त्येवमतीतमनागतं च। कथं तर्हि? स्वेनैव व्यंग्येन स्वरूपेणानागतमस्ति स्वेन चानुभूतव्यक्तिकेन स्वरूपेणातीतमिति। वर्तमानस्यैवाध्वनः स्वरूपव्यक्तिरिति। न सा भवत्यतीतानागतयोरध्वनोरेकस्य चाध्वनः समये द्वावध्वानौ धर्मिसमन्वागतौ भवत एवेति नाभूत्वा भावस्त्रयाणामध्वानामिति ॥ १२ ॥

The Characterized Substance is possessed of the nature of many Characteristics; its characteristics are also placed in opposition (to one another) owing to the difference of paths. Further, as the present has obtained specific manifestation as Matter, the past and the not-yet-come do not exist as such. How then? The not-yet come exists indeed by its own suggestive manifestation, the past exists by its own individual manifestation which has been experienced. The path of the present alone has its manifestation in individuality. It does not heappen in relation to the paths of the past and the not-yet-come. At the time of one path, the other two paths remain coincident with the Characterized Substance. Hence, the existence of these three paths is not non-existent.[1]

ते व्यक्तसूक्ष्मा गुणात्मानः ॥ १३ ॥

They are manifested and subtle, and are of the nature of the Energies—13

ते व्यक्तसूक्ष्मा गुणात्मानः। ते खल्वमी त्र्यध्वानो धर्मा वर्तमाना व्यक्तात्मानोऽतीतानागताः सूक्ष्मात्मानः षडविशेषरूपाः। सर्वमिदं गुणानां सन्निवेशविशेषमात्रमिति। परमार्थतो गुणात्मानस्तथा च शास्त्रानुशासनम्—"गुणानां परमं रूपं न दृष्टिपथमृच्छति। यत्तु दृष्टिपथं प्राप्तं तन्मायेव सुतुच्छकमिति" ॥ १३ ॥

They are, in fact, the characteristics possessed of the three paths. The present ones are possessed of the manifested nature and the past ones and the not-yet-come are possessed of the subtle nature, i. e., the six unspecific appearances (Y. S. II-19). All this is but the special aggregation of the Energies. In reality they are of the nature of the Energies. Similar is also the final teaching of the Authoritative Science:—"The highest form of the Energies does not come within the range of sight; that, however, which comes within the range is but the most insignificant Illusion."

परिणामैकत्वाद्वस्तुतत्त्वम् ॥ १४ ॥

The reality of the Substance comes from the unity of the changes—14

1. From this aphorism, the commentator begins to refute the theory of Nihilism. The meaning is that the Substance in itself always remains unchanged; simply its characteristicts undergo manifestations and cessations. Thus the transmigration of soul has emphatically been established here by the commentator.

यदा तु सर्वे गुणाः कथमेकः शब्द एकमिन्द्रियमिति ? परिणामैकत्वाद्वस्तुतत्त्वम् । प्रख्याक्रियास्थितिशीलानां गुणानां ग्रहणात्मकानां करणभावेनैकः परिणामः श्रोत्रमिन्द्रियम् । ग्राह्यात्मकानां शब्दतन्मात्रभावेनैकः परिणामः शब्दो विषय इति । शब्दादीनां मूर्तिसमानजातीयानामेकः परिणामः पृथिवीपरमाणुस्तन्मात्रावयवस्तेषां चैकः परिणामः पृथिवी गौर्वृक्षः पर्वत इत्येवमादिर्भूतान्तरेष्वपि स्नेहौष्ण्यप्रणामित्वावकाशदानान्युपादाय सामान्यमेकविकारारम्भः समाधेयः ।

When however all are the Energies, how then does a single change become the sound and a single change the sense? The reality of the Substance comes from the unity of the changes. A single change of the Energies possessed of illumination, activity and inertia as an instrumental appearance of (their) receiving nature, is the auditory sense: and a single change as a purely audible subtile appearance of (their) receivable nature is the object sound. A single change of sound, etc., which are of the same class in form, is the atom of earth or the body of the subtile rudiments. Further, a single change of those atoms is the earth, the cow, the tree, the mountain and so on. Even in the case of other elements, a single action of modification pertaining to viscosity, heat, motivity and vacancy should equally be understood.

नास्त्यर्थो विज्ञानविसहचरः । अस्ति तु ज्ञानमर्थविसहचरं स्वप्नादौ कल्पितमित्यनया दिशा ये वस्तुस्वरूपमपह्नुवते—ज्ञानपरिकल्पनामात्रं वस्तु ।

"There is no truth which is not co-existent with conception, but there is the conception which is not co-existent with any truth as fancied in dream,"—from this point of view, some people conceal the real character of the Substance by saying that the Substance is but the fabrication of the conception[1].

स्वप्नविषयोपमं तु न परमार्थतोऽस्तीति ये आहुस्ते तथेति । प्रत्युपस्थितमिदं स्वमाहात्म्येन वस्तु । कथमप्रमाणात्मकेन विकल्पज्ञानबलेन वस्तुस्वरूपमुत्सृज्य तदेवापलपन्तः श्रद्धेयवचनाः स्युः? ॥ १४ ॥

They, who say that this (Substance) is mere visionary and does not exist in reality, are visionaries themselves. The Substance is present by its own power. How can their teachings be believed who conceal the real character of the Substance by refuting it on the strength of the false fictitious knowledge ?

वस्तुसाम्ये चित्तभेदात्तयोर्विभक्तः पन्थाः ॥ १५ ॥

On account of the difference of the mind (in regard to many puruṣas) about the identity of the Substance, the way of these two is different—15.

कुतश्चैतदन्याय्यम्? वस्तुसाम्ये चित्तभेदात्तयोर्विभक्तः पन्थाः । बहुचित्तालम्बनीभूतमेकं वस्तु साधारणं तत्खलु नैकचित्तपरिकल्पितं नाप्यनेकचित्तपरिकल्पितं किंतु स्वप्रतिष्ठम् । कथम्? वस्तुसाम्ये चित्तभेदात् । धर्मापेक्षं चित्तस्य वस्तुसाम्येऽपि सुखज्ञानं भवत्यधर्मापेक्षं तत एव दुःखज्ञानमविद्यापेक्षं तत एव मूढज्ञानं सम्यग्दर्शनापेक्षं तत एव माध्यस्थ्यज्ञानमिति । कस्य तच्चित्तेन परिकल्पितम्?

For what other reason is it improper? On account of the difference of the minds about the identity of the Substance, the way of these two is different. The Single Substance, being the support of many minds is common (to all). It is, in fact neither projected by one mind nor projected by many minds but is established in itself. How ? On account of the difference of the minds about the identity of the Substance. Even in the identity of the Substance, comes the pleasurable feeling of the mind when dependent upon virtue; from the same comes the painful feeling being dependent upon vice; from the same comes the stupid imagination depending upon Non-Science; and depending upon the Integral Vision, from the same comes the knowledge of neutrality. By whose mind is that (Substance) projected ?

न चान्यचित्तकल्पितेनार्थेनान्यस्य चित्तोपरागो युक्तस्तस्माद्वस्तुज्ञानयोर्ग्राह्यग्रहणभेदभिन्नयोर्विभक्तः पन्थाः । नानयोः सङ्करगन्धोऽप्यस्तीति

1. This is the theory of the "Momentary Conception" put forward by the opponents. Now the commentator refutes this theory by proper reasonings in the following.

Further, it is not proper that the mind of one should be coloured by the object imagined by the mind of another. Therefore, the way of both the Substance and the conception separated by the difference of the receivable and the receiving characters, is different. There is not even the touch of mixture between these two.

साङ्ख्यपक्षे वस्तु पुनस्त्रिगुणं चलं च गुणवृत्तमिति। धर्मादिनिमित्तापेक्षं चित्तैरभिसम्बध्यते निमित्तानुरूपस्य च प्रत्ययस्योत्पद्यमानस्य तेन तेनात्मना हेतुर्भवति।

According to the Sāṅkhya-theory, the Substance however is possessed of three Energies; and also the function of the Energies is ever changeful. The Substance depending upon virtue, etc., as an exciting cause is related to the minds; further, it becomes the source of the notions which are being produced in accordance with the exciting cause, and (it) partakes of their respective nature (in the form of the intensive force).

केचिदाहुः ज्ञानसहभूरेवार्थो भोग्यत्वात्सुखादिवदिति। त एतया द्वारा साधारणत्वं बाधमानाः पूर्वोत्तरक्षणेषु वस्तुस्वरूपमेवापह्नवते ॥ १५ ॥

Some people say that the truth is coexistent with the conception on account of being enjoyable like pleasure, etc. By this reasoning, they refuse its generic nature and conceal the very reality of the Substance in the former and in the latter moments.

न चैकचित्ततन्त्रं चेद्वस्तु तत्प्रमाणकं तदा किं स्यात् ॥ १६ ॥

Further, if the Substance were not linked to one mind (in regard to one Puruṣa), what would be its cognition then?—16.

न चैकचित्ततन्त्रं चेद्वस्तु तत्प्रमाणकं तदा किं स्यात्? एकचित्ततन्त्रं चेद्वस्तु स्यात्तदा चित्ते व्यग्रे निरुद्धे वा स्वरूपमेव तेनापरामृष्टमन्यस्याविषयीभूतमप्रमाणकमगृहीतस्य भावकं केनचित्तदानीं किं न स्यात्? सम्बध्यमानं वा पुनश्चित्तेन कुत उत्पद्येत? ये चास्यानुपस्थिता भागास्ते चास्य न स्युरेवं नास्ति पृष्ठमित्युदरमपि न गृह्येत। तस्मात्स्वतन्त्रोऽर्थः सर्वपुरुषसाधारणः स्वतन्त्राणि च चित्तानि प्रतिपुरुषं प्रवर्तन्ते तयोः सम्बन्धादुपलब्धिः पुरुषस्य भोग इति ॥ १६ ॥

If the Substance is linked to one mind, then in the case of the mind whether distracted (conscious) or restrained (unconscious), the Reality is certainly untouched thereby and is not made to come in the sphere of any other mind. It (the Reality) is beyond the cognition i.e., beyond the feeling of acceptance by any one else. Does it not exist then? And, being related to the mind again in the inhibitive cognition, whence does it take its rise? Further, if its absent parts do not exist, then in this way, where there is no back, the front also cannot be taken. Therefore the Objective Reality is independent and is common to all Puruṣas; the minds are also independent and are engaged to every Puruṣa. On account of the connection of these two, comes the acknowledgment which is the Experience of the Puruṣa.

तदुपरागापेक्षित्वाच्चित्तस्य वस्तु ज्ञाताज्ञातम् ॥ १७ ॥

On account of the dependence of the mind upon the colour thereof (of the Objective Reality) the Substance remains cognized and uncognized—17.

तदुपरागापेक्षित्वाच्चित्तस्य वस्तु ज्ञाताज्ञातम्। अयस्कान्तमणिकल्पा विषयाः अयः सधर्मकं चित्तमभिसम्बध्योपरञ्जयन्ति। येन च विषयेणोपरक्तं चित्तं स विषयो ज्ञातस्ततोऽन्यः पुरुषोऽज्ञातः। वस्तुनो ज्ञाताज्ञातस्वरूपत्वात्परिणामि चित्तम् ॥ १७ ॥

The objects, just like a load-stone, simply by close connection colour the mind which is of similar characteristics to iron. Further, the Object, by which the mind is coloured, becomes cognized. What is other than that, is the (Subject) Puruṣa who remains uncognized. The mind is changeful on account of its having the cognized and the uncognized characters of the Substance[1].

सदा ज्ञाताश्चित्तवृत्तयस्तत्प्रभोः पुरुषस्यापरिणामित्वात् ॥ १८ ॥

The operations of the mind are always known to its Lord on account of the changelessness of the Puruṣa—18.

यस्य तु तदेव चित्तं विषयस्तस्य सदा ज्ञाताश्चित्तवृत्तयस्तत्प्रभोः पुरुषस्यापरिणामित्वात् । यदि चित्तवत्प्रभुरपि पुरुषः परिणमेत्ततस्तद्विषयाश्चित्तवृत्तयः शब्दादिविषयवज्ज्ञाताज्ञाताः स्युः । सदा ज्ञातृत्वं तु मनसस्तत्प्रभोः पुरुषस्यापरिणामित्वमनुमापयति ॥ १८ ॥

In regard to Him (the Lord), however, whose sphere is this mind alone, the operations of the mind are always known to its Lord on account of the unchangeability of the Puruṣa. If the Puruṣa, the Lord, also changes like the mind, then the mental operations regarding those (changes) would be known and unknown like the object sound, etc., but the constant knowership of the mind proves the unchangeability of the Puruṣa, the Lord of that (mind).

न तत्स्वाभासं दृश्यत्वात् ॥ १९ ॥

This (mind) is not self-illuminating, on account of its perceptibility—19

स्यादाशङ्का चित्तमेव स्वाभासं विषयाभासं च वैनाशिकानां चित्तात्मवादिनां च भविष्यतीत्यग्निवत्—न तत्स्वाभासं दृश्यत्वात् । यथेतराणीन्द्रियाणि शब्दादयश्च दृश्यत्वान्न स्वाभासानि तथा मनोऽपि प्रत्येतव्यम् ।

Here a doubt is raised by the Vaināśikas[2] and also by those who believe the mind to be the Soul[3] that the mind alone is self-illuminating and also the illuminator of the object, like fire. This is not self-illuminating on account of its perceptibility. As the other senses and the objects sound, etc., are not self-illuminating on account of perceptibility, so also the mind is to be understood.

न चाग्निरत्र दृष्टान्तः । न ह्यग्निरात्मस्वरूपमप्रकाशं प्रकाशयति । प्रकाशश्चायं प्रकाश्यप्रकाशकसंयोगे दृष्टो न च स्वरूपमात्रेऽस्ति संयोगः । किंच स्वाभासं चित्तमित्यग्राह्यमेव कस्यचिदिति शब्दार्थः । तद्यथा स्वात्मप्रतिष्ठमाकाशमित्यप्रतिष्ठमेवेत्यर्थः ।

Further, fire cannot be the example here, because fire does nor illuminate any of its form which is dark. Moreover this illumination is found in the conjunction of the illuminable and the illuminator; also the conjunction of anything cannot take place with its own pure nature. What more ? The "self-illuminating mind" means "not receivable by any one else", this is the meaning of the words. Similarly if it is said that "the ether (*Ākāśa*) is self-supporting", the meaning is that "it is supportless only."

स्वबुद्धिप्रचारप्रतिसंवेदनात्सत्त्वानां प्रवृत्तिर्दृश्यते । क्रुद्धोऽहं भीतोऽहममुत्र मे रागोऽमुत्र मे क्रोध इत्येतत्स्वबुद्धेरग्रहणेन युक्तमिति ॥ १९ ॥

The manifestation of all beings is seen in the reflex-knowledge of the movement of their own intellect such as I am angry, I am afraid, here is my attachment, there is my anger, etc. All this is proper by not taking one's own intellect (as Self)

एकसमये चोभयानवधारणम् ॥ २० ॥

Also, the absence of ascertainment of both at one and the same time—20

एकसमये चोभयानवधारणम् । न चैकस्मिन्क्षणे स्वपररूपावधारणं युक्तं क्षणिकवादिनो यद्भवनं सैव क्रिया तदेव च कारकमित्यभ्युपगमः ॥ २० ॥

---

1. As the *Yoga-Sūtra* deals with the sphere of Action, the commentator describes here the twofold division of the Substance (the Existing Reality). Its material aspect is the Pradhāna which is the front of the Substance and is cognized by the mind; and the Spiritual Aspect is the Puruṣa who remains uncognized for being the back side of the Substance. In the Vedānta Darśana, this Puruṣa will be considered to be the Substance (*Brahma*) and the Pradhāna as its Power termed the 'Self-expressive Principle (*Māyā*).

2. The Vaināśikas are the believers in the theory of Momentary Conception.

3. The Cittātma-vādins believe the mind to be the Soul. They are also called the Nihilists.

Also at a single moment, the ascertainment of one's own nature and that of the Other is not proper. The conception of the supporter of the momentary existence is that the existence itself is the action and the same also is likewise the agent.

चित्तान्तरदृश्ये बुद्धिबुद्धेरतिप्रसङ्गः स्मृतिसङ्करश्च ॥ २१ ॥

In the case of different minds, (come) the unwarrantable stretch of the intellect after intellect and also the confusion of memories —21

स्यान्मतिः स्वरसनिरुद्धं चित्तं चित्तान्तरेण समनन्तरेण गृह्यत इति—चित्तान्तरदृश्ये बुद्धिबुद्धेरतिप्रसङ्गः स्मृतिसङ्करश्च । अथ चित्तं चेच्चित्तान्तरेण गृह्येत बुद्धिबुद्धिः केन गृह्यते साप्यन्यया साप्यन्ययेत्यतिप्रसङ्गः स्मृतिसङ्करश्च । यावन्तो बुद्धिबुद्धीनामनुभवास्तावत्यः स्मृतयः प्राप्नुवन्ति तत्सङ्कराच्चैकस्मृत्यनवधारणं च स्यादित्येवं बुद्धिप्रतिसंवेदिनं पुरुषमपलपद्भिर्वैनाशिकैः सर्वमेवाकुलीकृतम् ।

There is a view that the mind, being restrained in its own habit, is taken by another mind next to it : In the case of different minds, (come) the unwarrantable stretch of the intellect after intellect and also the confusion of the memories. Now if the mind be taken by another mind, then by whom is intellect after intellect taken? This also (is taken) by another intellect and that also by another; so comes the unwarrantable stretch of intellect after intellect and also the confusion of memories. As many are the cognitions of intellect after intellect, so many are the memories. Further, on account of this confusion, there will also be the absence of ascertainment of one memory. Thus all is indeed confused by the Vaināśikas who do away with the Puruṣa, the reflective knower of the intellect.

ते तु भोक्तृस्वरूपं यत्र क्वचन कल्पयन्तो न न्यायेन सङ्गच्छन्ते । केचित्तु सत्त्वमात्रमपि परिकल्प्यास्ति स सत्त्वो य एतान्पञ्चस्कन्धान्निक्षिप्यान्यांश्च प्रतिसन्दधातीत्युक्त्वा तत एव पुनस्तप्यन्ति ।

On the other hand, they are not logical wherever they imagine the character of the Enjoyer. Some people again, even after projecting the pure existence, say that there is an existing reality which gives up the five Skandhas[1] (the varieties of mundane consciousness) and takes up others. After saying so, they again get further-more pain.

तथा स्कन्धानां महन्निर्वेदाय विरागायानुत्पादाय प्रशान्तये गुरोरन्तिके ब्रह्मचर्यं चरिष्यामीत्युक्त्वा सत्त्वस्य पुनः सत्त्वमेवापह्नवते । साङ्ख्ययोगादयस्तु प्रवादाः स्वशब्देन पुरुषमेव स्वामिनं चित्तस्य भोक्तारमुपयन्तीति ॥ २१ ॥

Similarly "I shall observe the vow of continence near the teacher for the complete disparagement, non-attachment, non-productiveness and also for the peacefulness of the Skandhas[1]". after saying thus of Being again they do away with that very Being. The theories of the Sāṅkhya-Yoga and others[2] however conclude by the word "Sva" (Self) the Puruṣa only, the Lord or the Enjoyer of the mind.

चितेरप्रतिसङ्क्रमायास्तदाकारापत्तौ स्वबुद्धिसंवेदनम् ॥ २२ ॥

The immutable Con-science has the perception of its own intellect through its transformation into the form of the latter—22

कथम्? चितेरप्रतिसङ्क्रमायास्तदाकारापत्तौ स्वबुद्धिसंवेदनम् । अपरिणामिनी हि भोक्तृशक्तिरप्रतिसङ्क्रमा च परिणामिन्यर्थे प्रतिसङ्क्रान्तेव तद्वृत्तिमनुपतति । तस्याश्च प्राप्तचैतन्योपग्रहस्वरूपाया बुद्धिवृत्तेरनुकारमात्रतया बुद्धिवृत्त्यविशिष्टा हि ज्ञानवृत्तिराख्यायते । तथा चोक्तम्, न पातालं न च विवरं गिरीणां नैवान्धकारं कुक्षयो नोदधीनां गुहा यस्यां निहितं ब्रह्म शाश्वतं बुद्धिवृत्तिमविशिष्टां कवयो वेदयन्त इति ॥ २२ ॥

How? The immutable Con-Science has the perception of its own intellect

1. The Skandhas are five in number : *Vijñāna* (apprehension), *Vedanā* (conception), *Saṁjñā* (resolution), *Rūpa* (formation) and *Saṁskāra* (Habituation). These are the five varieties of mundane consciousness.

2. Here the term "others', denotes the Nyāya, the Vaiśeṣika and the Sāṅkhya which precede the Yoga-Sūtra.

through its transformation into the form of the latter. The unchanging power of the Enjoyer is indeed immutable, but regarding the changing object (intellect), it (the power of the Enjoyer) follows the operation thereof[1] as if transformed into that (intellect). The operation,—which, in fact, being unqualified by the intellectual function, belongs to the pure imitation of the activity of the intellect that has received the favourite form of the Consciousness"[2]—is called the operation of the Con-Science. Similarly it has also been said "Neither the nether world, nor a hole, nor the dark recess of a mountain, nor the wombs of the great oceans, is the cave where is placed Brahma, the Eternal. The Sages point out to the Absolute Intellective Function (in which Brahma is placed)."

द्रष्टृदृश्योपरक्तं चित्तं सर्वार्थम् ॥ २३ ॥

The mind, being coloured by the Perceiver and the Perceivable, is omniobjective—23

अतश्चैतदुपगम्यते—द्रष्टृदृश्योपरक्तं चित्तं सर्वार्थम्। मनो हि मन्तव्येनार्थेनोपरक्तं तत्स्वयं विषयत्वाद्विषयिणा पुरुषेणात्मीयया वृत्त्याभिसम्बद्धम्। तदेतच्चित्तमेव द्रष्टृदृश्योपरक्तं विषयविषयिनिर्भासं चेतनाचेतनस्वरूपापन्नं विषयात्मकमप्यविषयात्मकमिवाचेतनं चेतनमिव स्फटिकमणिकल्पं सर्वार्थमित्युच्यते।

Hence it is also understood that the mind, being coloured by the perceiver and the perceivable, is omni-objective, because the mind becomes coloured by the thinkable object. On account of its objectivity, the mind itself is related to the function which is made His own by the Subjective Puruṣa, the Lord. It is that very mind which, being coloured by the perceiver and the perceivable, appearing as the subject and the object respectively, being transformed into the conscious and the unconscious characters, although being of the objective nature yet appearing as of the subjective nature, although unconscious yet appearing as conscious like a crystal, is said to be omni-objective.

तदनेन चित्तसारूप्येण भ्रान्ताः केचित्तदेव चेतनमित्याहुः। अपरे चित्तमात्रमेवेदं सर्वम्—नास्ति खल्वयं गवादिर्घटादिश्च सकारणो लोक इति। अनुकम्पनीयास्ते। कस्मादस्ति हि तेषां भ्रान्तिबीजं सर्वरूपाकारनिर्भासं चित्तमिति।

Some persons, being confused by this unification of the mind, say that it by itself is conscious. Others say that all this is the mind alone, and that in reality there is no world with its Cause such as the cow etc., the pot, etc. They are pitiable. Why? Because they have a mind which is the seed of misunderstanding and which appears in the shape of all truths.

समाधिप्रज्ञायां प्रज्ञेयोऽर्थः प्रतिबिम्बीभूतस्तस्यालम्बनीभूतत्वादन्यः। स चेदर्थश्चित्तमात्रं स्यात् कथं प्रज्ञयैव प्रज्ञारूपमवधार्येत? तस्मात्प्रतिबिम्बीभूतोऽर्थः प्रज्ञायां येनावधार्यते स पुरुष इति। एवं ग्रहीतृग्रहणग्राह्यस्वरूपचित्तभेदात् त्रयमप्येतज्जातितः प्रविभजन्ते ते सम्यग्दर्शिनस्तैरधिगतः पुरुषः ॥२३॥

In the Spiritual-Absorbent-Cognition the Cognizable Truth gets reflected. It having the nature of being grasped by that (mind), is the Other. If that Truth were the mind itself, how then could the form of cognition be ascertained by cognition itself? Therefore He, by whom the Truth reflected in the Spiritual-Absorbent Cognition is determined, is the Puruṣa. Thus on account of the change of the mind about the manifestations of the Receiver, Receiving Instrument and the Receivable Object, they who divide also the three-fold transformation of the mind[3] by this classification (of the Spiritual-Absorbent-Cognition), are the true seers. The Puruṣa is attained by them.

1. This refers to the exhibitive operation of the intellect.
2. This refers to the inhibitive operation of the Intellect.
3. The Spiritual Absorbent-Cognition regarding the receivable object is the Gross and the Subtle manifestations; that regarding the receiving instrument is the Instrumental and that about the receiver is the Subjective one. By this, it is fully clear that there can be no real Knowledge at all where there is no such successive change of the Spiritual-Absorbent-Cognition by these four successive steps. The Puruṣa or the Existing Reality can never be attained to simply by the knowledge of books. This is the idea here.

तदसङ्ख्येयवासनाभिश्चित्तमपि परार्थं संहत्यकारित्वात् ।। २४ ।।

Variegated by those innumerable residua, the mind is also possessed of the interests of the Other on account of its action by combination—24

कुतश्चैतत्? तदसङ्ख्येयवासनाभिश्चित्तमपि परार्थं संहत्यकारित्वात् । तदेतच्चित्तमसङ्ख्येयाभिर्वासनाभिरेव चित्रीकृतमपि परार्थं परस्य भोगापवर्गार्थम् । न स्वार्थं संहत्यकारित्वात् । गृहवत्संहत्यकारिणा चित्तेन न स्वार्थेन भवितव्यं न सुखं चित्तं सुखार्थं न ज्ञानं ज्ञानार्थमुभयमप्येतत्परार्थम् ।

Why is it so (what is the further reason for the mind being omni-objective)? Variegated by those innumerable residua the mind is also possessed of the interests of the Other on account of its action by combination. That is this mind which, being variegated by the innumerable residua, possessed of the interests of the Other, i.e., the interests of Experience and Emancipation of the Other. It has no interest of its own on account of the action by combination. The mind, acting in combination like a house, is not to happen for its own sake. The Pleasurable Thought is not for the sake of pleasure nor the Knowledge for the sake of knowledge; but they both are the interests of the Other.

यश्च भोगेनापवर्गेण चार्थेनार्थवादपुरुषः स एव परो न परः सामान्यमात्रम् । यत्तु किंचित्परं सामान्यमात्रं स्वरूपेणोदाहरेद्वैनाशिकस्तत्सर्वं संहत्यकारित्वात्परार्थमेव स्यात् । यस्त्वसौ परो विशेषः स न संहत्यकारी पुरुष इति ।। २४ ।।

Further, the Puruṣa who is marked out by the interests, i.e., by Experience and Emancipation, is verily the Other; He is not an individual of a common class. On the contrary, whatever other individual of a common class with its natural character is described by the Vaināśikas, is indeed possessed of the interests of the Other on account of its action by combination. He, however, who is the Other, the Distinct and does not act in combination, is the Puruṣa.

विशेषदर्शिन आत्मभावभावनाविनिवृत्तिः ।। २५ ।।

The cessation of the investigation of self-existence comes to the seer of the Distinct Truth—25

विशेषदर्शिन आत्मभावभावनाविनिवृत्तिः । यथा प्रावृषि तृणांकुरस्योद्भेदेन तद्बीजसत्तानुमीयते तथा मोक्षमार्गश्रवणेन यस्य रोमहर्षाश्रुपातौ दृश्येते तत्राप्यस्ति विशेषदर्शनबीजमपवर्गभागीयं कर्माभिनिर्वर्तितमित्यनुमीयते तस्यात्मभावभावना स्वाभाविकी प्रवर्तते यस्याभावादिदमुक्तं स्वभावं मुक्त्वा दोषाद्येषां पूर्वपक्षे रुचिर्भवत्यरुचिश्च निर्णये भवति ।

As the existence of the seed of grass is inferred by the germination of its sprout in the rainy season, so it is inferred that in him whose bristling of hair and the flow of tears are seen on hearing the path of Emancipation[1], there is also the seed of observing the Distinct Truth, i.e., the (stored up) action tending to Emancipation has begun its fruition. His investigation of self-existence naturally flows[2]; owing to the absence of that (seed), after leaving off this said tendency by defect their desire comes to the opposite side and the hatred for the complete ascertainment appears.

तत्रात्मभावभावना कोऽहमासं कथमहमासं किंस्विदिदं कथंस्विदिदं के वा भविष्यामः कथं भविष्याम इति । सा तु विशेषदर्शिनो निवर्तते । कुतः ? चित्तस्यैवैष विचित्रपरिणामः । पुरुषस्त्वसत्यामविद्यायां शुद्धश्चित्तधर्मैरपरामृष्ट इति । ततोऽस्यात्मभावभावना कुशलस्य विनिवर्तत इति ।। २५ ।।

There the investigation of self-existence is as follows: "Who was I? How was I? What is it? How is it? What shall we become? How shall we become?" This, however, ceases in the seer of the Distinct Truth. Wherefore? This is but a strange modification of the mind[3]. The Puruṣa however, on the

1. This is the first stage named the distressed condition of the Yogi who is the performer of good actions.

2. In this second stage, he becomes a seeker after the Truth.

3. This is the third stage in which he directs his effort to the proper means of Emancipation and passes over the successive steps of the Spiritual Absorption.

absence of the Non-Science, is pure and untouched by the characteristics of the mind[1]. For this reason the investigation of this adept (Yogi) about self-existence ceases.

तदा विवेकनिम्नं कैवल्यप्राग्भारं चित्तम् ॥ २६ ॥

Then the mind becomes inclined towards the Intellective Distinguishing Power, and has the load of Absoluteness in front—26

तदा विवेकनिम्नं कैवल्यप्राग्भारं चित्तम् । तदानीं यदस्य चित्तं विषयप्राग्भारमज्ञाननिम्नमासीत्तदस्यान्यथा भवति कैवल्यप्राग्भारं विवेकजज्ञाननिम्नमिति ॥ २६ ॥

His mind which had, before this, the load of sense-objects in front and was inclined towards ignorance, becomes otherwise at this time, i.e., the mind acquires the load of Absoluteness in front and becomes inclined towards the Intellect-born-knowledge.

तच्छिद्रेषु प्रत्ययान्तराणि संस्कारेभ्यः ॥ २७ ॥

Within those intervals, other notions come from the habitual potencies—27.

तच्छिद्रेषु प्रत्ययान्तराणि संस्कारेभ्यः । प्रत्ययविवेकनिम्नस्य सत्त्वपुरुषान्यताख्यातिमात्रप्रवाहारोहिणश्चित्तस्य तच्छिद्रेषु प्रत्ययान्तराण्यस्मीति वा ममेति वा जानामीति वा । कुतः ? क्षीयमाणबीजेभ्यः पूर्वसंस्कारेभ्य इति ॥ २७ ॥

Within those intervals of the mind which is inclined towards the Intellective Distinguishing Power of cognition and is elevated on the only flow of the revelation of the distinction between the Essence and the Puruṣa, come other notions such as 'I am', 'it is mine', 'I know' and so on. Whence? From the previous habitual potencies whose seed power is being destroyed.

हानमेषां क्लेशवदुक्तम् ॥ २८ ॥

The Avoidance of these has been prescribed like that of the afflictions—28.

हानमेषां क्लेशवदुक्तम् । यथा क्लेशा दग्धबीजभावा न प्ररोहसमर्था भवन्ति तथा ज्ञानाग्निना दग्धबीजभावः पूर्वसंस्कारो न प्रत्ययप्रसूर्भवति । ज्ञानसंस्कारास्तु चित्ताधिकारसमाप्तिमनुशेरत इति न चिन्त्यन्ते ॥ २८ ॥

As the afflictions, having reached the state of the burnt-up-seed, are not capable of germination, similarly the previous habitual potency, on attaining to the state of the burnt-up-seed by the fire of Knowledge (Observation), does not give birth to notions. But the habitual potencies of Knowledge stay upto the end of the duty of the mind; so they are not to be considered.

प्रसङ्ख्यानेऽप्यकुसीदस्य सर्वथा विवेकख्यातेर्धर्ममेघः समाधि. ॥ २९ ॥

The Spiritual Absorption known as the Cloud-of-Virtue comes to him who, being possessed of the Intellective Revelation in all respects, is not professional even on the full payment—29

प्रसङ्ख्यानेऽप्यकुसीदस्य सर्वथा विवेकख्यातेर्धर्ममेघः समाधिः । यदायं ब्राह्मणः प्रसङ्ख्यानेऽप्यकुसीदस्ततोऽपि न किंचित्प्रार्थयते तत्रापि विरक्तस्य सर्वथा विवेकख्यातिरेव भवतीति संस्कारबीजक्षयान्नास्य प्रत्ययान्तराण्युत्पद्यन्ते तदास्य धर्ममेघो नाम समाधिर्भवति ॥ २९ ॥

When this Brāhmaṇa is not professional even on the full payment, i.e., does not beg anything even of that (Intellective Revelation) he being unattached with that also, possesses the Intellective Revelation in all respects. And on account of the destruction of the seed of the habitual potencies, his other notions are not produced, then the Spiritual Absorption known as the Cloud of Virtue comes to him.

ततः क्लेशकर्मनिवृत्तिः ॥ ३० ॥

Thence the cessation of the afflictions and actions—30

ततः क्लेशकर्मनिवृत्तिः । तल्लाभादविद्यादयः क्लेशाः समूलकाषं कषिता भवन्ति । कुशलाकुशलाश्च

1. This is the fourth stage where he regains his sound state of existence, i.e., becomes adept after realising the Existing Reality (B.G. VII-16).

कर्माशयाः समूलघातं हता भवन्ति । क्लेशकर्मनिवृत्तौ जीवन्नेव विद्वान्विमुक्तो भवति । कस्मात्? यस्माद्विपर्ययो भवस्य कारणम् । नहि क्षीणक्लेशविपर्ययः कश्चित्केनचित्क्वचिज्जातो दृश्यत इति ॥ ३० ॥

On account of its attainment, the afflictions such as Non-Science, etc., become scraped along with their roots. The good and the bad vehicle-of-actions are destroyed along with their roots. On the cessation of the afflictions and actions the wise (Yogi) although living, becomes fully free. Why ? Because the perversive cognition is the cause of rebirth. A person whose afflictions and perversive cognitions have been destroyed, is not seen to be born by anybody anywhere.

तदा सर्वावरणमलापेतस्य ज्ञानस्यानन्त्याज्ज्ञेयमल्पम् ॥ ३१ ॥

Then on account of the infinity of the Knowledge which has been freed from all covering impurities, the knowable becomes little—31

तदा सर्वावरणमलापेतस्य ज्ञानस्यानन्त्याज्ज्ञेयमल्पम् । सर्वैः क्लेशकर्मावरणैर्विमुक्तस्य ज्ञानस्यानन्त्यं भवति । तमसाभिभूतमावृतमनन्तं ज्ञानसत्त्वं क्वचिदेव रजसा प्रवर्तितमुद्घाटितं ग्रहणसमर्थं भवति ।

Infinity comes to the knowledge which has been freed from all coverings of the afflictions and actions. The infinite Essence of Knowledge, being covered, i.e., being overpowered by the Inert Energy, rarely becomes excited, i. e., opened up by the Active Energy and becomes capable of taking up (this infinity).

तत्र यदा सर्वैरावरणमलैरपगतं भवति तदा भवत्यस्यानन्त्यम् । ज्ञानस्यानन्त्याज्ज्ञेयमल्पं सम्पद्यते यथाकाशे खद्योतः । यत्रेदमुक्तम्—अन्धो मणिमविध्यत्तमनङ्गुलिरावयत् । अग्रीवस्तं प्रत्यमुञ्चत्तमजिह्वोऽभ्यपूजयदिति ॥ ३१ ॥

There when it (the Essence) becomes free from all covering-impurities, Infinity comes to it. From this infinity of the Knowledge, the knowlable is made little as a fire-fly in the sky. Here it has been said:—"The blind pierced the pearl, the fingerless threaded it, the neckless wore it and the tongueless praised it"[1].

ततः कृतार्थानां परिणामक्रमसमाप्तिर्गुणानाम् ॥ ३२ ॥

Thence the termination of the succession of change comes to the Energies which have fulfilled the interests—32

ततः कृतार्थानां परिणामक्रमसमाप्तिर्गुणानाम् । तस्य धर्ममेघस्योदयात्कृतार्थानां गुणानां परिणामक्रमः परिसमाप्यते । नहि कृतभोगापवर्गाः परिसमाप्तक्रमाः क्षणमप्यवस्थातुमुत्सहन्ते ॥ ३२ ॥

On account of the rise of that Cloud-of-Virtue, the succession in the change of the Energies whose interests are fulfilled, comes to an end; because they (the Energies) which have performed Experience and Emancipation and whose succession has come to an end, cannot dare to stay even for a moment.

क्षणप्रतियोगी परिणामापरान्तनिर्ग्राह्यः क्रमः ॥ ३३ ॥

The succession related to the moments is determined by the cessation of the change—33

अथ कोऽयं क्रमो नामेति ? क्षणप्रतियोगी परिणामापरान्तनिर्ग्राह्यः क्रमः । क्षणानन्तर्यात्मा परिणामस्यापरान्तेनावसनेन गृह्यते क्रमः । नह्यननुभूतक्रमक्षणान्नवस्य पुराणता वस्त्रस्यान्ते भवति ।

Now what is indeed this succession ? The succession related to the moments is determined by the cessation of the change. The succession, being possessed of the nature of intervention of the moments, is taken in by the cessation, i.e., by the end of the change; because without experiencing the moment of succession, the oldness of a new piece of cloth can never come in at the end.

नित्येषु च क्रमो दृष्टः । द्वयी चेयं नित्यता कूटस्थनित्यता परिणामिनित्यता च । तत्र कूटस्थनित्यता पुरुषस्य । परिणामिनित्यता गुणानाम् ।

1. It signifies that this Intellective Revelation is indefinable (*Anirvacanīya*). Further, this Indefinable Cognition is the basis of the Vedānta Darśana.

यस्मिन्परिणम्यमाने तत्त्वं न विहन्यते तन्नित्यम् । उभयस्य च तत्त्वानभिघातान्नित्यत्वम् ।

The succession is also seen in regard to the Eternal (Substance). This eternity is two-fold,—the unchanging eternity (*Kūṭastha-Nityatā*) and the changeful eternity (*Pariṇāmi-nityatā*). There the unchanging eternity belongs to the Puruṣa, and the changeful eternity belongs to the Energies. That is eternal in which, even though it is changed, the truth is not destroyed. Further, the eternity belongs to these both on account of their indestructible truth.

तत्र गुणधर्मेषु बुद्धयादिषु परिणामापरान्तनिर्ग्राह्यः क्रमो लब्धपर्यवसानो नित्येषु धर्मिषु गुणेष्वलब्धपर्यवसानः । कूटस्थनित्येषु स्वरूपमात्रप्रतिष्ठेषु मुक्तपुरुषेषु स्वरूपास्तिता क्रमेणैवानुभूयत इति । तत्राप्यलब्धपर्यवसानः शब्दपृष्ठेन अस्तिक्रियामुपादाय कल्प्यत इति ।

There within the intellect, etc., shining with the characteristics of the Energies, the succession determined by the cessation of the change has obtained termination. And in regard to the eternal Characterized Object (known as the Energies), it is the unobtained-termination. In regard to the Unchanging Eternal, i.e., in the case of the emancipated Puruṣas[1] who are purely self-established, the existence of their selves is perceived only by succession. So even there the unobtained-termination is imagined by taking up the verb "Exists" in accordance with the arrangement of the words.

अथास्य संसारस्य स्थित्या गत्या च गुणेषु वर्तमानस्यास्ति क्रमसमाप्तिर्न वेति । अवचनीयमेतत् । कथम्? अस्ति प्रश्न एकान्तवचनीयः सर्वो जातो मरिष्यति मृत्वा जनिष्यत इति । ओं भो इत्यथ सर्वो जातो मरिष्यतीति मृत्वा जनिष्यति इति? विभज्य वचनीयमेतत्प्रत्युदितख्यातिः क्षीणतृष्णः कुशलो न जनिष्यत इतरस्तु जनिष्यते ।

Now is there or is there not a cessation to the succession of this Universe present in the Energies with rest or with motion? It cannot be answered. How? There is a question which can be answered with exclusive aim—"all that is born will die and after dying will be born again." If the question be thus—"Oh! is it so that all creatures will die and after dying will be born again?" It can be answered by division. The adept who is possessed of the appearance of the (Intellective) Revelation and whose desires have been destroyed, will not be born but the rest will be born again.

तथा मनुष्यजातिः श्रेयसी न वा श्रेयसीत्येवं परिपृष्टे विभज्य वचनीयः प्रश्नः पशूनधिकृत्य श्रेयसी देवानृषींश्चाधिकृत्य नेति ।

Similarly whether mankind is great or not? Being thus interrogated, the question can be answered by division. Mankind is superior in comparison to the beasts but not so when compared to the gods and the perfect seers (Ṛṣis)

अयं त्ववचनीयः प्रश्नः संसारोऽयमन्तवानथानन्त इति । कुशलस्यास्ति संसारक्रमपरिसमाप्तिर्नेतरस्येति । अन्यतरावधारणे दोषस्तस्माद्व्याकरणीय एवायं प्रश्न इति ।। ३३ ।।

Again this question "whether this universe has an end or not" cannot be answered. An adept has the cessation of the evolutionary change, the rest have not. There is defect in any other ascertainment. Therefore this question must be explained by division only.

पुरुषार्थशून्यानां गुणानां प्रतिप्रसवः कैवल्यं स्वरूपप्रतिष्ठा वा चितिशक्तिरिति ।। ३४ ।।

The disappearance of the Energies devoid of the Puruṣa's interests is Absoluteness, or the Con-Science-Power is self-established. —34

गुणाधिकारक्रमपरिसमाप्तौ कैवल्यमुक्तं तत्स्वरूपमवधार्यते — पुरुषार्थशून्यानां गुणानां प्रतिप्रसवः कैवल्यं स्वरूपप्रतिष्ठा वा चितिशक्तिरिति । कृतभोगापवर्गाणां पुरुषार्थशून्यानां यः प्रतिप्रसवः कार्यकारणात्मकानां गुणानां तत्कैवल्यम् । स्वरूपप्रतिष्ठा पुनर्बुद्धिसत्त्वानभिसम्बन्धात्पुरुषस्य चितिशक्तिरेव केवला तस्याः सदा तथैवावस्थानं कैवल्यमिति ।। ३४ ।।

1. For the manifoldness of the Puruṣa, see note on II. 22.

It has been said that Absoluteness comes at the cessation of succession in the duties of the Energies. Now its character is being ascertained. The disappearance of the Energies devoid of the Puruṣa's interests is Absoluteness or the Con-Science-Power is self-established. That which is the disappearance of the Energies that have the functions of cause and effect and that are devoid of the Puruṣa's interests after performing Experience and Emancipation, is Absoluteness. Again self-establishment means that only the Con-Science-Power of the Puruṣa[1] becomes Absolute on account of the absence of close connection with the intellective Essence; its (of the Con-Science-Power) existence in the same condition for all time is Absoluteness.

1. In this Science, the commentator speaks of bondage and freedom only with regard to the Con-Science-Power but not to the Puruṣa himself who will be termed "Brahma" or the "Substance" in the Vedānta-Darśana. By this it is clear that this Science of Yoga-Sūtra deals with the Sphere of Action which exists in the Power alone but not in the pure and simple Substance. Further the Brahma-Sūtra begins with the aim of ascertaining the true character of the Simple Substance beyond Action by taking the result of this Science as the stepping ground for attaining to that end.

Here ends the Fourth Chapter known as the subject of Absolute Freedom with regard to the Science of Yoga composed by Patañjali in the Excellent Teaching of the Sāṅkhya.

APPENDIX

On the suggestion of some of my friends about the foot-note on Y.S.1.9, pertaining to the meaning of ज्ञानयोग and भक्तियोग, I wish to hold out an explanation of these terms by pointing out their appropriate applications in our Authoritative Scriptures. The people in general erroneously think of the term भक्ति as an emotional love towards God, which ensues from irrationalism and from the exhaustion of mental force by means of pushing and shoving, rolling and tumbling, springing and jumping, crying and shouting and weeping and bursting in praise of their sectarial gods. They labour under the impression that the term *Bhakti śāstra* signifies a philosophy of love which has no concern with the *Six Texts* of the Indian System of Philosophy, but it is quite distinct and separate from all of them and even from the Vedic Authority. They hold that *Bhakti* (devotion) is the easiest path for becoming a lover of God by leaving off all the Scriptural Obligations pertaining to the Social and Religious Observances and even by forsaking all the moral obligations of humanity. They stick to their own principles by following the dictates of their free will without paying any heed to the rational and reasonable conclusions of any Authority. By taking *Bhakti* as female, many of them being male in form and shape, wear the female dress and ornaments, and mix themselves up with the females by leaving off the moral characters of the males for becoming a beloved to their created lord. Thus, we find that the people hold the idea of Bhakti as irrationalism and inactivity of the mind caused by the compression and suppression of the mental force. But, in reality, the root *Bhaj* signifies "to serve" which explicitly shows a special form of Action to be performed by an energetic mind.

On the Authority of the Vyāsa Commentary on Aph. No. 10 of the fourth chapter of the Yoga Sūtra, we can say that though the root *Bhaj* is used in the sense of "service", yet it cannot mean any material service to God but signifies the service rendered by the mind alone, because we find everywhere in the *Bhagavadgītā* that the root *yaj* has been used in the sense of Material Action and *Bhaj* in the Spiritual Service termed *Jñānayoga* signifying the last three component parts of Yoga, namely Concentration (धारणा), Meditation (ध्यान) and Spiritual Absorption (समाधि). This subject has been fully dealt with in the explanation of the *Bhagvadgītā*. Accordingly there is no room for us to hold any idea of variation and contradiction with regard to the said terms which appear to be different in shape and form but hold out the one and the same truth by showing up the Spiritual Action to be accomplished by the help of the mind alone.

In fact, our Perfect Seers have classified the whole Course of Action (*Yoga*) in three divisions with regard to the attainment of the Supreme Spirit. The Dharma-Sūtra shows the first portion of the Course called Material Sacrifices which are to be performed with the help of the body for the acquirement of Enjoyment; the fulfilment of which renders a *yogī* fit for having recourse to Spiritual Sacrifice in the grade of *Great Vow* (संन्यास) by producing Non-attachment towards the worldly objects. So the Dharma-Sūtra deals with the Spirit of Connotation (शब्द ब्रह्म) pertaining to the Science of Material Action. Then the Sāṅkhya Yoga shows the next portion of the Course called Spiritual sacrifice (ज्ञानयज्ञ or भक्तियोग) which is accomplished with the help of the mind alone for having a direct communion with the Creator. This Communion cuts off the bonds of actions and afflictions by showing forth Emancipation. It is for this reason that the root *dṛś* (to see), signifying the "Intellective Vision", has been used in the verses of the *Bhagavadgītā* which deal with the visible result of the Spiritual Sacrifice in the sphere of the Cognitive Spiritual Absorption. So the Yoga

Sūtra deals with the Spirit of Meditation (ध्येयब्रह्म) pertaining to the Science of Spiritual Action. At last the *Brahma-Sūtra* shows the last portion of the Course by exhibiting the true character of Final Emancipation and does not prescribe any kind of Action to be performed but lays down the Highest Non-attachment as the only means for achieving this end which is nothing but the Cessation of all activities by going beyond the Sphere of Action. So the Brahma-Sūtra deals with the Spirit of Realisation (ज्ञेयब्रह्म) pertaining to the Supreme Perfection of the Human Soul. Only for this reason we find that the root *Vid* (to realise) or 'jñā' (to know) has been used in the verses of the *Gītā* which are meant for dealing with the subject-matter of the Brahma-Sūtra. Hence, it is evident that the term *Bhaktiśāstra* cannot mean any seventh philosophy contrary to or different from the System of Philosophy referred to in the Terminology, but signifies the Science of Spiritual Sacrifice by holding out the Starting and the Finishing Ends of the *Great Vow* (संन्यास).